A Who's Who of
Glamorgan
County Cricket Club
1888-1991

A Who's Who of
Glamorgan
County Cricket Club
1888-1991

Andrew Hignell

BREEDON
BOOKS

First published in Great Britain by
The Breedon Books Publishing Company Limited
44 Friar Gate, Derby DE1 1DA
1992

ISBN 1 873 626 02 9

Printed and bound in Great Britain by Bath Press, Bath and London.

Contents

Foreword by Wilfred Wooller 7

Preface...9

A Brief History of Glamorgan CCC 10

Glamorgan Cricketers A-Z.............................36

Career Records 229

Acknowledgements

THIS book would not have been possible without the invaluable help and guidance from the following individuals: Dr John Alban, Tim Auty, Philip Bailey, Mervyn Baker, Edward Bevan, Ernie Billings, John Billot, Chris Brain, Robert Brooke, Jack Burrell, Phil Clift, Brian Croudy, Gareth Davies, Morton Davies, Philip Defriez, Byron Denning, A.Leslie Evans, Howard Evans, Mike Fatkin, Mike Glenn, Gwyn Gratton, Bob Harragan, Ron Harries, Ernie Harris, Les Hatton, Michael Hill, Lawrence Hourahane, John Vivian Hughes, David Irving, David James, John Jenkins, Bryn Jones, Eddie Lawrence, Gordon Lewis, Brian Lile, Bill Meale, Bob Mole, Hugh Morgan, Bryn Owen, Frank Peach, Duncan Pierce, Jim Pleass, the late Dai Samuel, Geoffrey Saulez, Don Shepherd, David Smith, Mike Spurrier, Hugh Thomas, Philip Thorn, Peter Wilks, Graham Williams, Stewart Williams, Wilfred Wooller and Peter Wynne-Thomas, together with the officials librarians and archivists of the following establishments: Otago University; the New Zealand Law Society; the New Zealand Family History Society; Durban Library; Plymouth Library; Trinity Hall, Cambridge; Church House; Magdalene College, Cambridge; British Medical Association; Merton College, Oxford; Clifton College; Jesus College, Cambridge; Haileybury School; Eton College; Denstone College; the Welsh Folk Museum; Christ's College, Christchurch; Dyfed County Record Office; Winchester College; Edinburgh University; Somerset County Records Office; Oriel College, Oxford; St John's School, Leatherhead; Repton School; Wycliffe College; Harrow School; Cheltenham College; Radley College; Malvern College; Bedford School; Charterhouse School and Glamorgan County Record Office.

The photographs are from the archives of Glamorgan CCC and the private collections of the author, Ron Harries, David James, Gwyn Gratton, David Smith and Bob Harragan.

Foreword

CRICKET was slow to reach Wales. It spread from the South of England in the early nineteenth century, a cultured thread that was closely interwoven with the economic development — particularly in the South — and the growing ideals of the landed gentry who had done much to fashion the great game.

Various clubs, like Cardiff, Maesteg and Swansea, were formed, often by the courtesy of the large landowners, and, by 1888, Glamorgan County Cricket Club came into being and so on to Minor Counties cricket.

Glamorgan entered first-class cricket in 1921 and their first few years in the Championship were ones of immaturity, inexperience and near-disaster which lasted until 1930, when M.J.L.Turnbull was entrenched as captain and secretary. Method and sanity then prevailed until the outbreak of war in 1939, although things were always tight.

After the war, I took over the mantle of Maurice Turnbull, who was killed in action, and Glamorgan CCC moved into a new era of affluence, power and success.

In 1948, to the surprise of the cricket world, Glamorgan, who had hitherto been virtually confined to the bottom half of the table, won the County Championship. The county now had a considerable influence at Lord's and further strengthened its reputation when Tony Lewis captained an unbeaten Championship-winning team in 1969. He later captained England on a successful tour of India.

Glamorgan have always had the habit of producing the unexpected. They defeated the Australians on two successive tours, twice beat the West Indians, New Zealanders, Indians and Pakistanis, and once the South Africans. It is one of the best county records against the tourists.

Games against the tourists always have the flavour of a minor Test Match and, particularly when Welsh success is near, they are laced with some real rugby fervour.

A number of Welsh players have represented England. Maurice Turnbull was the first, in 1929-30, and the Usk all-rounder 'Allan' Watkins had an excellent run in the Test team after the war. Jeff Jones, who was capped in 1964, was the only genuine Welsh fast bowler until Greg Thomas came along in 1986. Also, let us not forget Cyril Walters of Worcestershire, for he, too, was a Welshman and began his career with Glamorgan.

For Glamorgan, guile rather than speed was always the great strength until the Pitches Committee interfered with playing surfaces around the country. Johnny Clay, for instance, was a fine off-spin bowler, and was 50 when he played a part in Glamorgan's first Championship title win. Len Muncer came to Wales from Middlesex and we turned him into a regular off-spin bowler. Muncer, of course, profited from the Welsh fielding, acknowledged to be the best in the land in that great year of 1948. The leg-trap of Watkins, Clift, Dyson and Wooller caught flies and we won several matches due to our great fielding.

We set a pattern of leg-side fielders to the medium-fast bowlers which quickly caught on with the other counties. We also started the practice of the wicketkeeper, Haydn Davies, standing back to the slower bowlers. Don Shepherd, for example, benefited from this and he was surely the finest England-qualified bowler never to play for his country. What a godsend he would have been to the present England side.

The theory, at first somewhat criticised by the purists, was simply that the wicketkeeper standing back could catch thick edges on either side of the wicket and this saved a fielder who could be used elsewhere. All of this was profitable on aggregate, taking into account the occasional stumping chance that went begging. It was some years, however, before this was vindicated by Test wicketkeepers putting Glamorgan theory into practice.

Following a period in the late 1970s and much of the 1980s, Glamorgan cricket lost its way. This happens to most counties at some time or another. It is more often than not due to poor administration and in Glamorgan's case, nine captains in 13 years resulted in a return to the bottom end of the County Championship table. In short, it was a dismal period.

A reshuffling of the Committee and the appointment of Tony Lewis, a much experienced former captain, cricket writer, commentator and adminstrator, as chairman has led to a revival of fortunes.

It was a pleasure to watch one of the best county opening pairs, Alan Butcher and Hugh Morris, score over 2,000 runs each as they set a record seasonal county partnership in 1990 and they continued the good work in 1991; to see Matthew Maynard in an aggressive assault on any belligerent attack; and to watch the young Robert Croft plying his skills in the Welsh hope of becoming another of the fine off-spinners in Glamorgan's history.

If the Gods are so inclined, then the future signs are propitious, and whether it be success at the very top or not, it is certain that the only county to represent Wales will continue to give us much pleasure.

Wilfred Wooller

8

Preface

This book contains the biographical and statistical details of everyone who has played in the following games for Glamorgan since the club's formation in 1888. This includes:
(a) all first-class matches 1921-1991.
(b) all limited over games 1963-1991.
(c) minor county matches and major friendlies 1897-1920.
(d) all friendlies and inter-county games 1889-1896.
(e) trial games 1891-1907.

Glamorgan played a number of friendlies between 1902 and 1920 against club teams or scratch elevens, but these have been excluded, together with the first-class matches played by South Wales (1894-1912), Wales (1923-1930) and the friendlies staged by the Gentlemen of Glamorgan (1904-1920).

All the statistics refer to performances for Glamorgan, unless stated otherwise, and are correct to the end of the 1991 English season.

The following abbreviations are also used in the text:
BB — Best bowling
HS — Highest score
LB — Leg-break bowler (leg-spinner)
LF — Left-arm fast bowler
LHB — Left-handed batsman
LM — Left-arm medium pace bowler
OB — Off-break bowler (off spinner)
RFM — Right-arm fast-medium bowler
RHB — Right-handed batsman
RM — Right-arm medium pace bowler
SLA — Slow left-arm bowler
*not out.

A Brief History of Glamorgan CCC

GLAMORGAN CCC was formed at a meeting on 6 July 1888 at the Angel Hotel, Cardiff, but there are records of earlier Glamorgan sides and county matches well before this date. The first cricket match on record in South Wales was held in 1783 at Cwmgwili near Carmarthen. A cricket club was in existence in Swansea in 1785, and by the early 19th century a number of other sides had emerged in the expanding commercial centres and flourishing market towns of South Wales. During the 1820s a side was formed at Raglan called the Monmouthshire Cricket Club and until the 1840s they staged regular matches with teams from Breconshire and neighbouring parts of England. However, the Club's membership was restricted to gentlemen and consequently they were not a truly representative county eleven.

By the middle of the century a number of other county elevens and representative sides were established. In 1859 Captain Homfray of Newport formed a team called the South Wales Cricket Club which staged fixtures against the leading clubs in the West Country and the London area. In all, 90 matches were held by the club until 1886, when it was disbanded. Several of their leading players also took part in the early 'county' matches. The first of these was held on 5 and 6 August 1861 when a Glamorgan XI was assembled by J.T.D.Llewelyn, the squire of Penllergaer, to play Carmarthenshire. He invited players from Swansea, Cardiff and his own Cadoxton club of Neath, so although it was the first team to carry the name of the county, it once again was not a representative county team in the modern sense.

Llewelyn also helped organize special exhibition matches, such as the match in July 1868 between the Gentlemen of Swansea and the Australian Aborigines. The success of these grand matches and 'county' matches led Llewelyn to call a meeting at The Castle Hotel, Neath on 13 March 1869 to form a proper club to represent the county. The gathering was well attended and enough money was raised to allow Llewelyn to arrange fixtures with Monmouthshire, Breconshire and Radnorshire. Consequently, the 1870s saw a regular series of inter-county fixtures involving Llewelyn's Glamorgan side, but it still remained a gentleman's club with a limited and rather exclusive membership. These factors, plus its limited

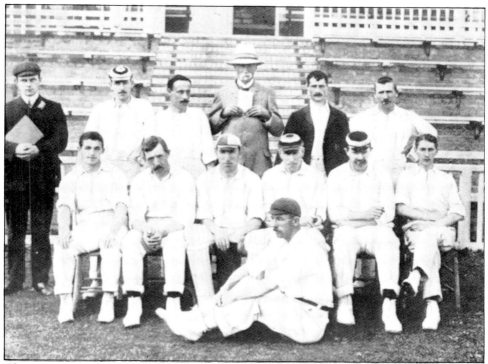

Glamorgan pictured before a match against Surrey in 1904. Standing, left to right (players only): A.Nash, H.Creber, S.H.Rees, W.J.Bancroft. Seated: T.A.L.Whittington, H.E.Morgan, W.H.Brain, J.H.Brain, W.Russell, H.B.Letcher. On ground: E.R.Sweet-Escott.

resources meant that this early organization was never going to develop into a substantial county club.

In 1879 the officials of the South Wales Cricket Club inaugurated the South Wales Cricket Challenge Cup, and together with the flood of English-born and educated migrants into the booming industrial region, it helped to raise the standard of cricket during the 1860s, whilst the Cup added an extra competitive thrust which the inter-club friendlies failed to provide. The success of the Cup and the improved standard of play, plus the growing pool of players, meant the time was finally right for the creation of a proper county club, so after approaches from representatives of the Cardiff and Swansea clubs, Llewelyn called a meeting at The Angel Hotel in Cardiff in 1888 at which the present Glamorgan CCC came into being.

A committee was formed, including several of the leading figures from the now defunct South Wales CC, and fixtures were arranged with the MCC, Surrey Club & Ground, and Warwickshire for 1889. The latter were Glamorgan's first opponents on 21 and 22 June at Cardiff Arms Park, but the

Welsh side found Warwickshire much too strong and lost by eight wickets. However, it was a start and saw players coming together from many clubs, and a month later at The Oval Glamorgan recorded their first win, defeating Surrey by six wickets. This win boosted Llewelyn's belief that the cricketers of Glamorgan, both amateur and professional, could compete with English sides, and during the 1890s Glamorgan's fixture list was expanded to include two-day friendlies with neighbouring English counties, plus an annual London tour.

The captain from 1891 was J.H.Brain, the former Gloucestershire batsman and Oxford blue, and he agreed with Llewelyn that Glamorgan would only make further progress if they took part in a higher standard of play. Brain's goal was entering the minor county championship and through his influence they were admitted to the competition in 1897. Much to his delight, they finished in second place in their first season, and then in 1900 went one stage further by becoming joint champions with Durham after winning nine of their 11 games. The teams playing resources were swelled as South Wales continued to attract a steady flow of well-to-do and public school educated migrants who were keen to play cricket as a means of relaxing and escaping from the hustle and bustle of industry and commerce. This ensured that Glamorgan maintained their position as one of the top minor counties, and they finished runners-up in 1907, 1908, 1909 and 1913.

Their leading batsman at the time was Norman Riches of Cardiff, and in 1911 he underlined his claim as the top batsman outside the first-class game by becoming the first minor county batsman to aggregate over 1,000 runs in a season. He was ably supported by Welsh rugby international Billy Bancroft, bowlers Sam Lowe, 'Jack' Nash and Harry Creber, wicketkeeper William Brain, and a wide number of well-travelled amateurs with public school backgrounds who had made the occasional appearance for an English county.

In 1913 there was talk of the county championship being extended to include some of the more successful minor county teams. Llewelyn and his supporters had long held dreams of Glamorgan taking part in first-class games, and a campaign began for the county's elevation. Fund-raising games were staged and fixtures held with touring sides, but hopes were dashed by the outbreak of war and with the cessation of cricket, many of the Glamorgan amateurs went off to war believing that their pipe dreams of rubbing shoulders with the first-class counties would never come true.

However, their dreams eventually became a reality in 1921

The last Glamorgan 1st XI to play in the Minor Counties Championship. Standing, left to right: J.L.G.Thomas, Dr T.F.Reason, J.W.J.Hinwood, W.E.Bates, D.J.Reason. Seated: J.R.Tait, N.V.H.Riches, T.A.L.Whittington, J.Nash, H.Arundale. On ground: T.R.Morgan.

but only after a lot of hard talking and lobbying by Tom Whittington, a solicitor from Neath. For many his success came too late and when the side entered the first-class ranks, they were too long in the tooth and well past their best. Even so, there was a pool of young talent and experienced professionals, and during 1920 Whittington travelled the length and breadth of England persuading officials of other county teams that Glamorgan were suitably equipped on and off the field to join the county championship. The requirements were home and away fixtures with a minimum of eight first-class counties, and after a lot of canvassing, Whittington acquired the necessary support and the MCC duly elevated Glamorgan to the championship for 1921.

The Welsh side had a fairy-tale start to their first-class career as they defeated Sussex in their inaugural match. 'Jock' Tait made 96 and Edgar Cooper took eight wickets as Sussex slipped to a 23-run defeat in front of an ecstatic Arms Park crowd. But the dream soon turned into a nightmare as Glamorgan tasted the other side of life in the county championship. They won only one other game and ended up at the bottom of the table with 14 defeats from their 19 games. Their chief

Australia take the field at Swansea on Bank Holiday Monday, 1921.

problem was that the amateurs still batted with the cavalier attitude of the minor county days, and coupled with their business requirements, a settled team never emerged. There were a lot of grey whiskers around, and it was not surprising that Wisden's correspondant summed up the 1921 season by stating that 'it is clear that to hold their own in first-class company Glamorgan must find young talent and not depend so much on middle-aged men'.

Several young players were drafted in from other counties including Jack Mercer, a seam bowler from Sussex and Frank Ryan, a left-arm spinner who had played for Hampshire, whilst trials were given to a host of other professionals. In an attempt to preserve the Welsh indentity, the county also secured the services in the 1920s of home-bred youngsters including bowlers Trevor Arnott and Johnnie Clay, and batsmen Cyril Walters, Dai Davies and Maurice Turnbull. They gradually found their feet in the county game and in 1923 even managed to defeat the West Indies at Cardiff. This was Glamorgan's first-ever victory over a touring team, and the 43-run win was due to Arnott taking eight wickets and Mercer five.

In 1924 Clay took over the captaincy and converted from bowling pace to spin. Under his astute leadership the side continued their steady improvement and in 1926 finished in a commendable 8th place. But there was a financial cost to this success, as the hiring of outside professionals and moderate

Glamorgan in 1932. Standing, left to right: T.Every, A.R.Howard, W.E.Jones, D.E.Davies, R.G.Duckfield, G.Lavis, A.H.Dyson. Seated: J.Mercer, J.C.Clay, M.J.L.Turnbull, V.G.J.Jenkins, D.Davies.

attendances, meant that the club's balance sheet was rarely in profit. Only one victory was recorded in 1927, plus a further two the following season, whilst in 1929 they lost 19 games and finished up at the bottom of the table once again. But at least the 1920s ended on a high note with the selection of Maurice Turnbull for the MCC winter tour, and in January 1930 he became Glamorgan's first-ever Test player as he made his England debut against New Zealand at Christchurch.

On his return, Turnbull took over the Glamorgan captaincy and together with Johnnie Clay helped transform the team from habitual losers into a competitive unit, and saw the club's finances improve so that there was a cash balance in hand. But it was not an easy route out of either the cricketing or financial red, and in 1931 several of the seasoned players such as Ryan, Bates, Bell and Hills were released to reduce the expense on professionals. It weakened the team for a while, but it also gave a greater chance to home-bred players such as Emrys Davies and Dick Duckfield, and with a greater Welsh identity, it also raised the interest of the general public. Matches were taken to venues such as Pontypridd, Cowbridge and

Glamorgan in 1938. Standing, left to right: H.G.Davies, T.L.Brierley, C.C.Smart, E.C.Jones, D.A.Davies, R.G.Duckfield. Front: A.H.Dyson, D.Davies, J.C.Clay, J.Mercer, D.E.Davies.

Llanelly, and a cricket Development Fund was started to help improve facilities.

Yet in the winter of 1932-3 the financial situation was still grim, and the Secretary and Treasurer resigned. Turnbull and Clay took over their duties, and enthusiastically launched a special Appeal to raise £5,500. Nevertheless, they realized the gravity of the situation and added a rider that donations would be returned if it was impossible to continue in first-class cricket. Fund raising events, dances and sweepstakes, were organized in almost every town and village in South Wales, and during the winter months, Clay and Turnbull were out almost every night raising funds for their beloved county side.

Fortunately, their efforts were not in vain, and enough cash was raised to carry on. The early matches at out grounds, such as Stradey Park, also swelled the coffers, and in 1934 a decision to amalgamate with Monmouthshire provided Glamorgan with both a pool of young talent from Gwent, and other lucrative venues at Newport and later Ebbw Vale.

Steadily, the playing performances improved with Turnbull, Mercer, Clay, Dyson, Smart, Brierley, Duckfield and the two Davies', Dai and Emrys, forming the nucleus of a useful team. In 1935 Emrys Davies became the first Glamorgan cricketer to achieve the double, whilst in 1936 Duckfield scored a record 280 at The Oval and Mercer took all ten Worcestershire wickets in an innings.

The perseverance of Clay and Turnbull was rewarded in 1937 by a rise up to seventh place as Glamorgan won 13 of their 30 matches. The attack was strengthend by the arrival of Austin Matthews from Northants, whilst Closs Jones emerged as the best young off-spinner in the country. Dyson and Emrys Davies also formed a reliable partnership as opening batsmen, whilst young Welsh players such as Wilf Wooller, Allan Watkins and Phil Clift were successfully blooded during the late 1930s. The match with Gloucestershire at Newport in 1939 highlighted the improvements Turnbull's side had achieved. Gloucestershire made a mammoth 505-5, and in the bad old days, the Welsh side would have wilted in the face of such a daunting score and Wally Hammond's majestic 302. But not Turnbull's side, for he had instilled a sense of purpose and an air of confidence during the 1930s, and the influential captain was delighted as Glamorgan replied with 577-4 with Emrys Davies scoring an unbeaten 287. It won the opener a place on the MCC winter tour, but events on a wider stage cruelly intervened to deprive Davies of an England cap, as World War Two meant an early end to the 1939 season.

Five years later they also robbed Glamorgan of their influential leader. By 1944 Maurice Turnbull was a Major in the Welsh Guards and was on active service in Normandy. As a player, he had always led from the front and typically he was not afraid to undertake reconnaissance whilst his company were on the attack. Tragically, he was killed by a sniper's bullet and his death stunned everyone connected with Glamorgan who were staging fund-raising matches to boost the war effort. The news came through during a match at the Arms Park, the scene of his first century and his many subsequent triumphs. The pavilion bell rang and a minute's silence was observed with players and public alike paying their respects to the man who more than anyone else had ensured the club's survival.

Clay was determined that his late friend's efforts would not be in vain, so together with Wilf Wooller, he ensured that when county cricket resumed in 1946, Glamorgan were able to continue where they had left off before the war. Sadly, the club had to operate on a shoe-string budget and were missing several of the old familiar faces, but there were talented young players, such as Gilbert Parkhouse and Willie Jones ready to fill their places, whilst some astute signings were made, such as Len Muncer from Middlesex to strengthen the playing staff. Clay took over the captaincy in 1946 and guided his side to sixth place in the championship. His wise leadership, drawing on his vast experience, was the linchpin of the team's success and he was wholeheartedly supported by the rest of his small squad, who guided Glamorgan to ten championship victories.

Wooller took over the captaincy from his mentor Clay in 1947, and built on this wonderful team spirit to steer Glamorgan to their first ever championship success in 1948. The season began well with wins over Essex, Worcestershire and Somerset, before Willie Jones hit two double centuries within a fortnight during June to set up further victories over Kent and Essex. The lead was whittled away during July before rain intervened in August to frustrate the team when they were in winning positions. Nevertheless, team morale remained high and Wooller's side entered the final month of the season knowing that they had to win two of their last three games to guarantee the title. A few eyebrows were raised when Wooller recalled the 50-year-old Clay for the Surrey match at the Arms Park, but it was a move which was to reap rewards beyond even the wildest hopes of Wooller as Surrey were defeated by an innings with the veteran returning match figures of 10-65.

Glamorgan travelled to play Hampshire at Bournemouth for the final match of the season, knowing that a victory would clinch the title. Clay was retained in the team, and after the batsman had rattled up 315, the spinner combined with Len Muncer to enforce the follow-on. Wickets continued to fall in the second innings, with the fielders, as they had throughout the season, taking some superb catches close to the wicket. The end came soon after lunch on the final day when Charlie Knott, the Hampshire number 11 was hit on the pads in front of the wicket by Clay. The umpire standing at Clay's end was Dai Davies, and with a smile on his face, the pre-war veteran said: "That's out and we've won the championship." Clay walked off with figures of 6-48, and the pavilion echoed with Welsh songs as the team and their loyal supporters toasted the club's first title.

There were high hopes for 1949 with talk of even retaining the championship, but Glamorgan's quartet of all-rounders,

Glamorgan in 1948, winners of the County Championship for the first time in the club's history. Standing, left to right: W.E.Jones, P.B.Clift, N.G.Hever, S.Trick, W.G.A.Parkhouse, J.T.Eaglestone, J.Pleass. Seated: H.Davies, J.C.Clay, W.Wooller, D.E.Davies, B.L.Muncer, A.Watkins.

Glamorgan in 1949. Standing, left to right: P.B.Clift, J.T.Eaglestone, W.G.A.Parkhouse, N.G.Hever, A.Watkins, J.E.Pleass. Seated: W.E.Jones, H.Davies, W.Wooller, E.Davies, B.L.Muncer.

Wooller, Watkins, Jones and Muncer, were all injured at various stages, and although Muncer took 100 wickets, they slipped back to the middle of the table. The only high spot was the emergence of Gilbert Parkhouse as a top-class number-three batsman. He continued his development in 1950, hitting a total of seven centuries and reaching 1,000 runs by mid-June. His outstanding form won him a place in the England side, followed by a tour to Australia and New Zealand during the winter. Without him, Glamorgan slipped back to 11th place, but they rose up to 5th in 1951 and also recorded a sensational victory over the touring South Africans. The architects of both of these achievements were the spinners Len Muncer and Jim McConnon. They shared 234 out of the 452 wickets taken in all of the matches, and turned the tables on the tourists at Swansea when they seemed to be coasting to victory. At tea they were 54-0, chasing 147 to win, but in the space of an hour, Muncer took 4-16 and McConnon 6-27 to bowl out the Springboks for 83 and set up a remarkable win.

The mid 1950s saw Glamorgan maintain their position in the middle of the table. Watkins, Willie Jones, McConnon and Muncer continued to perform with credit, whilst Wooller achieved the double in 1954. But injuries and a loss of form at crucial times all hindered progress, yet when they were firing on all cylinders, Wooller's team showed they were more than a match for other sides, as testified in 1952 by their first-ever victory at Lords as Middlesex were defeated by 131 runs. Off-the-field improvements were also made to the grounds at Cardiff and Swansea, whilst the construction of a purpose-built Indoor School at Neath considerably improved the coaching facilities. By 1954 some of the older faces such as Emrys Davies and Len Muncer were slipping into retirement, but there were a host of promising youngsters such as Jim Pressdee and Don Shepherd ready to take their places. The latter had begun his career as a fast-medium bowler, and took over 100 wickets during 1952. But in the mid 1950s he failed to hit the seam regularly and after advice from Wooller and wicketkeeper Haydn Davies, Shepherd experimented with off-cutters and changed style. For the next 17 seasons 'Shep' was amongst the finest spinners in the country, and in 1956, his first full season as a slow bowler, he took 168 wickerts for Glamorgan at a cost of only 14 and ended eight short of Clay's county record set back in 1937.

Despite this magical transformation, not everything went right for the club during the second half of the 1950s. Firstly,

Worth an appeal for lbw? For once, Wilf Wooller looks a shade apprehensive.

Don Shepherd bowling in the early days of his great career. The umpire is Dai Davies, who played for Glamorgan before Shepherd was born.

Glamorgan in 1954. Standing, left to right: J.E.Pleass, P.B.Clift, N.G.Hever, D.J.Shepherd, B.Hedges, W.E.Jones. Seated: L.B.Muncer, H.G.Davies, W.Wooller, D.E.Davies, W.G.A.Parkhouse.

they lost George Lavis in July 1956 when the highly rated coach tragically died after a short illness. Secondly, the quality of the Arms Park wicket began to deteriorate, and in 1957 the club started negotiations for a stadium of their own at Sophia Gardens. Wooller and Clay, now a Trustee of the club, had long dreamed of a Welsh Lord's where the county could have a base of their own, rather than renting the use of various grounds in South Wales and using a small office in the centre of Cardiff. Discussions reached a high level with Cardiff Corporation, but officials of Cardiff Athletic Club did not like the thought of a move from their ground at the Arms Park, and they persuaded the Mayor to use his casting vote to terminate the Sophia Gardens scheme.

It was a blow to Wooller who did not exactly see eye-to-eye with some of the county's committee. A certain amount of friction developed coincidentally at a time when Wooller was considering his playing future. During 1957 he told the committee he would stand down if a suitable replacement could be found. Further rows took place over his future role and Wooller was so aggrieved that he tendered his resignation with effect from the end of the 1958 season. Trials were given to various replacements, including Tolly Burnett who had not played county cricket for eight years, and scored only 71 runs

Glamorgan in 1958. Standing, left to right (players only): B.Hedges, J.B.Evans, L.N.Devereux, P.M.Walker, J.E.McConnon, J.S.Pressdee, D.J.Ward. Seated: D.J.Shepherd, H.G.Davies, W.Wooller, A.J.Watkins, W.G.A.Parkhouse.

in 11 innings. A number of other players retired as team morale dropped, and matters came to a head in October 1958 at the club's first-ever Special General Meeting. Many members felt that the committee had been acting unwisely to even think of dispensing with Wooller's services after all that he had done for the club. A vote was taken, and the pro-Wooller lobby won the day.

The 1959 AGM reinstated the all-rounder as captain, and after all the public debate and rumours flying around, the atmosphere within the club became much healthier and there was a return to form. The fine batting of Gilbert Parkhouse and the all-round performances of Peter Walker were two of the factors behind the rise back up to 6th place. Parkhouse amasssed a record 2,071 runs and won a long overdue place back in the England side, whilst Walker made 1,540 runs and held a record 64 catches. Once again, spinners McConnon and Shepherd made a major contribution with both taking over 100 wickets.

Glamorgan in 1962. Standing, left to right (players only): A.Harris, I.J.Jones, J.B.Evans, D.G.L.Evans, A.Jones, A.Rees, D.J.Ward. Seated: J.S.Pressdee, D.J.Shepherd, O.S.Wheatley, W.G.A.Parkhouse, A.R.Lewis, P.M.Walker.

There was a change of captaincy in 1961 when Wooller eventually retired after 18 years of loyal service to the club. His replacement was Ossie Wheatley, a 26-year-old fast bowling amateur from Warwickshire, and with the retirement also of McConnon and Watkins, he had at his disposal a young, and often inexperienced, side. His first few seasons in charge witnessed a rebuilding process, but fortunately several of the young Colts made encouraging progress. Alan Jones moved up to open with huge success, whilst Tony Lewis developed into a graceful strokemaker. David Evans also proved to be a sharp and competant 'keeper, but the one player to hit the headlines was left-armer Jeff Jones who emerged as a hostile fast bowler, and after claiming 58 wickets during the 1963 season, won a place in the England side.

Confirmation that Ossie Wheatley's side had turned the corner came in 1964 with a memorable win over the Australians at Swansea. Chasing a target of 268, the tourists faltered against the wily spin of Shepherd and Pressdee, who were supported

The Glamorgan team that defeated the Australians in 1964. Standing, left to right: J.Evans (masseur), A.Rees, EW..Jones, A.E.Cordle, W.D.Slade, G.Hughes, E.J.Lewis, A.Jones, Dr J.Parry. Seated: J.S.Pressdee, D.J.Shepherd, O.S.Wheatley, A.R.Lewis, P.M.Walker.

by some exceptional fielding by the young Welsh team. The batsmen were forced into making mistakes or hitting the ball in the air and both Alan Rees and Billy Slade took some wonderful catches. When Eifion Jones caught Neil Hawke, Glamorgan had won an enthralling game and the St Helen's ground echoed with celebrations of a historic 36-run victory.

The side went from strength to strength in 1965, and made a sustained bid in the title race before finishing in third place. Batting of the highest order from Jones and Lewis, plus fine bowling by Shepherd and Jeff Jones saw the Welsh club come close to repeating their success of 1948. Two remarkable bowling performances came against Leicestershire. Firstly, Shepherd returned the figures of 10-8-2-5 as the visitors were dismissed for 33 at Ebbw Vale, and a month later, Jones returned career-best figures of 13-9-11-8 as Leicestershire were routed for 40 on a damp and green Grace Road wicket. Such performances kept Jones in the England side, so in 1966 the county blooded West Indian Tony Cordle and Abergavenny's Malcolm Nash. But there was no replacement for experience as the team slipped back to 14th place, and also played for the last time at the Arms Park as the WRU developed a National Stadium.

In 1967 Glamorgan moved to Sophia Gardens for their east area games, and took the field under a new captain, as Tony Lewis continued the amateur tradition with Wheatley going into semi-retirement. The rebuilding continued with Majid Khan, the gifted Pakistan batsman being hired after a magnificent 147 before lunch at Swansea, and Bryan Davis of Trinidad also agreeing to join the club. But a major set-back occurred in June 1968 when Jeff Jones severely damaged shoulder and elbow ligaments, forcing him prematurely out of the game. So the rebuilding process continued with Eifion Jones taking over from David Evans and despite six sixes in an over from Gary Sobers, more opportunities for Malcolm Nash as an opening bowler.

The reward for this policy began in August 1968 as Glamorgan achieved a unique double over the Australians by winning for the second time in four years at St Helens. Acting captain Don Shepherd set the tourists a target of 365 on the final day, and once again accurate bowling, athletic fielding and patriotic support all combined to set up a nerve-tingling 79-run victory. It owed much to Shepherd's canny brain, and he was paid many plaudits by the ecstatic crowd who thronged in front of the pavilion. The compliments continued in 1969 as he helped Tony Lewis to guide Glamorgan to their second championship title.

The 1968 Australian win had hinted that Lewis' team were finally fulfilling their potential, and during 1969 they confirmed this belief by winning 11 games and losing none to become the first unbeaten champions since 1930. A settled team emerged under the captaincy of Tony Lewis, yet their initial win did not come until early June. Two victories over Sussex and a win against Worcestershire saw the side into second place behind Gloucestershire. The top two sides met at Cardiff in mid July, but some fine bowling by Nash, Cordle and Lawrence Williams sent Gloucestershire crashing to a demoralizing 208-run defeat. The gap was closed in August thanks to some fine batting, as Alan Jones and Majid added 132 in 77 minutes as Glamorgan beat Northamptonshire, and the talented Pakistani batted with amazing dexterity on a poor wicket at Cheltenham to see Gloucestershire lose by an innings.

The Welsh side went to the top of the table as Middlesex were beaten by three wickets at Swansea, and with a game in hand over Gloucestershire, Lewis' side realized that like

Glamorgan in 1969, County Champions for the second time. Standing, left to right: E.W.Jones, B.A.Davis, M.A.Nash, D.L.Williams, R.C.Davis, Majid Khan. Seated: A.E.Cordle, P.M.Walker, A.R.Lewis, D.J.Shepherd, A.Jones.

1948, a victory in two of the last three matches would clinch the title. An enormous crowd turned up at Swansea over the August Bank Holiday to see a nail-biting victory over Essex as Glamorgan won by one run off the final ball when Ossie Wheatley ran out John Lever. Majid then produced another magical innings against Worcestershire at Cardiff, making 156 out of Glamorgan's total of 265 on an unpredictable wicket. The visitors could only muster 183 and then Glamorgan's batsmen went for quick runs before Lewis challenged the visitors to make 255. Nash, Wheatley and the veteran Don Shepherd then steadily worked their way through the Worcestershire batting, and when Brian Brain was caught at slip, Glamorgan had won by 147 runs to become county champions once again.

Lewis' side went on a celebratory tour of the West Indies in 1969-70, their first ever overseas venture outside the UK, whilst Lewis led the MCC winter tour to the Far East, with the party including Alan Jones and Don Shepherd. Their winter exploits were beneficial as Glamorgan had another highly successful season in 1970, winning nine matches and finishing in second place after rain and a few injuires in the closing weeks of the season had prevented them from retaining the title. As congratulations were paid to Don Shepherd for finishing on top of the national averages, and Eifion Jones for creating a county record of 90 victims, few could have predicted the traumas which lay ahead for the Welsh county as they entered the most troubletorn decade in their history. Firstly, Bryan Davis returned to the West Indies, and then in 1971 Roger Davis came close to death after being hit on the head fielding at short leg. The year 1971 was not a happy 50th anniversary of first-class cricket for Glamorgan as the championship-winning unit started to break up. Several young players were tried out in 1972 as the side went through a championship season without a home win for the first time since 1922.

They had little success either in the rapidly expanding one-day competitions, but one ray of sunshine came in 1972-3 when Tony Lewis led the England side to India and Pakistan, and became Glamorgan's first Test captain. But his knee was increasingly troubling him and he stood down from the Glamorgan captaincy in 1973 with Majid being appointed in his place. The injury did not improve and sadly Lewis was forced into retirement in 1974. At the end of the 1973 season the club also released Roy Fredericks, their aggressive West Indian batsman, in the hope of securing a Test class fast bowler to strengthen the attack. But 1974 was another bleak season as the side ended in 16th place in the championship, and the club's officials made contact with a number of pace bowlers. Their eventual choice was Greg Armstrong, who was on the fringe of the West Indies side. But the Barbadian proved to be a huge disappointment, being plagued by run-up problems and producing a spate of no-balls. Nevertheless, the team rose up to ninth spot with Roger Davis, Majid and Alan Jones all having successful seasons. The finest display of the season came from the Pakistani at Wellingborough in the Sunday League against Northants as Majid raced to 75 in only 27 minutes, with five sixes and seven fours as Glamorgan made a competition-best 266-6.

Some of the young Welsh cricketers such as John Hopkins, Barry Lloyd, Gwyn Richards and Alan Lewis Jones made headway during the season, and there was a feeling that Glamorgan had turned the corner. But this proved to be wrong as 1976 became notable more for events off the field than out in the middle. The side finished bottom of the championship and in the first half of the season suffered a series of heavy

Glamorgan in 1977. Standing, left to right: D.A.Francis, B.J.Lloyd, M.J.Llewellyn, C.L.King, A.H.Wilkins, G.Richards. Seated: J.A.Hopkins, E.W.Jones, A.Jones, M.A.Nash, A.E.Cordle.

defeats. Armstrong was still hampered by no-balls, whilst a number of batsmen were out of form, including Majid himself. The committee wrote letters to six players at the end of June informing them of their concern about playing standards. There had been more than a little friction betweeen the committee-room and the dressing-room, and the letters to Roger Davis, Lawrence Williams and Len Hill proved to be the final straw and all three resigned from the staff.

This prompted a protest campaign by some members, and Cardiff and Swansea were buzzing with rumours and speculation about other departures and criticism of Majid's captaincy. As the team struggled, a feeling of resentment grew towards the laid-back Pakistani who found it difficult to communicate and relax with the young Welshmen. However, he was a proud man, and with criticism reaching a crescendo, he quit the county scene in mid season amidst public confusion and deep personal sadness.

A new and united team spirit was forged in 1977 under the captaincy of Alan Jones, and with Collis King replacing

Armstrong as the overseas player, the Welsh team rose like a phoenix out of the ashes of 1976 and reached the final of the Gillette Cup. It was even more remarkable given the Welsh county's poor record in limited-overs cricket, yet they became an effective and well balanced side, beating Worcestershire at Worcester, and then Surrey at Cardiff. Leicestershire were the opponents in the semi-final at St Helens, and after rain interference, Gwyn Richards and young left-armer Alan Wilkins bowled tightly to restrict the visitors, before Alan Jones and his partner John Hopkins put on 108 to see the Welsh side home.

On the day of the final, Lord's resembled Cardiff Arms Park as trains, coaches and cars galore headed for London in the hope of seeing Alan Jones' team overcome Middlesex. But luck was not on Glamorgan's side, as they were put in and found run scoring difficult over a damp outfield after overnight rain. Mike Llewellyn gave the innings a much needed lift, hitting his first three balls for 4, 6 and 4, before hoisting Emburey for a mighty six on to the top tier of the pavilion. But a score of 178 was always well within Middlesex's sights, and despite losing Mike Brearley off Nash's first ball, Clive Radley steered Middlesex to an easy five-wicket win.

The year 1978 proved to be yet another frustrating one as the side slipped back to 13th place and failed to make any impact in limited-overs games. The major weakness lay in the bowling, where for the first time, no one took over 50 wickets. Changes were needed for 1979 and the club caused a surprise by signing 37-year-old leg spinner Robin Hobbs who had retired from county cricket with Essex in 1975. It came as an even greater shock when it was announced that Hobbs would be taking over the captaincy from Alan Jones.

Not surprisingly, Hobbs found the task of returning to the first-class scene a formidable one, and ended up with a mere 22 wickets. Team success was also elusive as the side finished at the bottom of the championship without a win for the first ever time. Not surprisingly, there was criticism for signing a veteran spinner in the modern era of pace bowlers and one-day cricket, but the hard pressed officials refuted claims that they were out of touch by signing Pakistani Javed Miandad, West Indian pace bowler Ezra Moseley and both Norman Featherstone and Allan Jones from Middlesex. All were wise signings and in particular strengthened the Glamorgan attack now under the leadership of Malcolm Nash. The side rose up to 12th place in 1980 and won the Tilcon Trophy at the Harrogate Festival.

These overseas signings were crucial to the new phase of

Glamorgan in 1979. Standing, left to right: J.Derrick, M.Thornton, G.C.Holmes, J.Newman, A.J.Mack, N.J.Perry, M.N.Davies, D.A.Francis, A.L.Jones. Seated: R.C.Ontong, M.J.Llewellyn, P.D.Swart, R.N.S.Hobbs, A.E.Cordle, J.A.Hopkins, G.Richards.

team building in the early 1980s. Javed displayed his fine batting talents in 1981 with a record 2,083 runs with eight centuries, two of which were double-centuries, and his quick scoring abilities saw the side to some good one-day victories. A number of new Welsh faces also emerged, including batsman Hugh Morris and bowlers Steve Barwick and Greg Thomas, but just as the rebuilding programme seemed to be well on course, it was dealt a cruel blow when Moseley broke down with a severe back injury in August 1981, and at the end of the season, Featherstone, who had been tipped as a future captain, retired from county cricket.

With Pakistan touring England in 1982, uncapped off-spinner Barry Lloyd took over the captaincy when Javed left to join his countrymen. The absence of both the overseas stars was a huge blow and medical reports on Moseley's long-term fitness were far from encouraging. In mid-season, Winston Davis, a young West Indian quick bowler, was signed to replace Moseley, but he was also hampered by run-up problems, and took time to settle, so the net result was another poor season

Glamorgan in 1983. Standing, left to right: G.C.Holmes, A.H.Wilkins, W.W.Davis, R.C.Ontong, A.L.Jones. C.J.C.Rowe, D.A.Francis. Seated: E.W.Jones, B.J.Lloyd, M.W.W.Selvey, A.Jones, J.A.Hopkins.

with Glamorgan slipping back to 16th place. The rebuilding started all over again in 1983 as Mike Selvey moved from Middlesex to become the county's seventh leader in eight years. With both Javed and Davis available, he had a tricky choice over who should fill the overseas berth. Preference was given to the West Indian, and although he took 52 wickets, his run-up problem persisted and with the Glamorgan batting struggling, the selection of Davis ahead of the Pakistani annoyed a faction of the club's members. Their feelings of disillusionment were heightened as the club finished in 15th place in the championship and failed to make an impact in the one-day games.

A remedy was sought to the batting problems through the acquisition of Younis Ahmed in 1984, whilst John Steele was signed as a spinning partner for Rodney Ontong. But midway through the season Selvey retired with shoulder and knee problems, whilst Javed was also hampered by injury. Yet despite these injuries, and losing Davis to the West Indian tourists, Glamorgan had a more successful season under new leader Rodney Ontong. The Javed-Winston debate was settled with the Pakistani being hired for 1985. He responded with a century in the opening game of the new season and a brilliant partnership of 306 with Younis Ahmed against the Australians at Neath. Despite injuries later in the season to Miandad and John Steele, the emergence of Matthew Maynard with a magnificent century on his county debut, showed that the club were moving at long last in the right direction.

However, captain Ontong felt that the club still needed an overseas fast bowler to be able to compete with other county sides, and the now fully-fit Ezra Moseley was re-signed to form a fiery partnership with Greg Thomas who had won a place in the England side. Unfortunately, Javed did not like the prospect of sharing the overseas spot again and playing on a rota basis, so he failed to return in 1986 and when Moseley failed to regain form, a rookie Australian called Denis Hickey came in as a short-term replacement. The side made a poor start to the season forcing Ontong to resign the captaincy and 22-year-old Hugh Morris became the club's youngest ever captain with barely a full season of county cricket behind him.

It seemed like the 1970s all over again, but hopes were lifted as Ravi Shastri was signed for the overseas spot in 1987, whilst experienced opener Alan Butcher and talented wicketkeeper Colin Metson joined the club from Surrey and Middlesex respectively. Matthew Maynard blossomed into an attacking batsman during 1987 whilst Ontong and Shastri became Glamorgan's new spin twins, and at the end of the season, the Welsh county seemed to be on the verge of a new era of success after the ups and downs of the previous 20 years.

In 1988 the club celebrated their centenary by having their best season in the one-day competitions since 1977. They reached the quarter-finals of the NatWest Bank Trophy, the semi-finals of the Benson and Hedges Cup and ended up in sixth place of the Sunday League. Maynard and Shastri proved to be match winners with the bat, whilst Ontong, Barwick and all-rounder John Derrick bowled as steadily and tightly as any other attack in the country. However, the smiles of delight were temporarily erased in August when Barwick and Ontong were involved in a horrendous car crash, *en route* from Colchester to Wellingborough. Both escaped badly shaken, but for Ontong his damaged knee meant the end of his career.

There was good news when Barwick returned to fitness for 1989, and even better news when the club announced that

Glamorgan in 1988 – their centenary season. Back row, left to right: B.T.Denning (first XI scorer), P.D.North, M.Davies, M.J.Cann, S.Bastien, P.G.P.Roebuck, S.Monkhouse, P.A.Todd, T.Jones (physiotherapist), P.A.Cottey, G.N.Lewis (second XI scorer). Middle: S.Moorcroft, S.L.Watkin, M.L.Roberts, J.Derrick, R.J.Shastri, S.R.Barwick, M.P.Maynard, C.J.P.G.Van Zyl, C.P.Metzon. Front: G.C.Holmes, J.A.Hopkins, R.C.Ontong, P.G.Carling (chief executive), A.R.Lewis, H.Morris, A.Jones, A.R.Butcher, J.F.Steele, J.G.Thomas.

Viv Richards, the great West Indian batsman, had agreed to join the county to share the duties with Ravi Shastri. But no sooner had the champagne corks flown around than news came through that Richards was suffering from haemorrhoids and this painful illness prevented him from appearing for the Welsh side in 1989. Another blow came in mid-season when after a series of defeats and a loss of form, Hugh Morris stood down from the captaincy and handed over the reins to Alan Butcher. It proved to be a wise decision as Morris returned to form in 1990, and together with the now fully fit Viv Richards, confirmed that the Welsh side had turned the corner and helped them to sixth spot in the championship, their best position since 1970. Hugh Morris broke almost every batting record in the club with 2,276 runs and ten centuries, and together with Alan Butcher, who himself passed 2,000 runs, they became the most consistent pair of openers in the country.

The presence of 'King Viv' packed in the crowds and the West Indian passed on wise words of advice to the young players in Butcher's side, and his presence gave the side a new found belief. Matthew Maynard was one to benefit from

Richard's presence and in 1991 he reaped the rewards as Glamorgan maintained their place in the top half of the championship and won a place in the last eight of the NatWest Bank Trophy. Steve Watkin and Hugh Morris both graduated from the England 'A' team to full Test honours, but perhaps the most satisfying aspect of 1991 was the mature display of strokeplay by Matthew Maynard, and together with Hugh Morris, they seem poised to create a new set of Glamorgan records in the 1990s as the Welsh county enter a new and, hopefully, more successful era in their history.

ABEL, Thomas Ernest

RHB; OB.
Born: Kennington, 10 September 1890.
Died: Lambeth, 23 January 1937.
Glamorgan debut: 1922 v Oxford and Cambridge Universities at Cardiff Arms Park.
Career: 32 matches 1922-25; Surrey 1919-20 (12 matches).
HS for Glamorgan: 107 v Leicestershire at Swansea, 1924.
BB for Glamorgan: 3-42 v Surrey at Swansea, 1924.
Full first-class record: 1,045 runs (15.83); 1 century; 31 wickets (31.48); 19 catches.

Tom Abel was the son of Bobby Abel, the popular Surrey and England cricketer and the brother of Billy Abel who played for Surrey between 1909 and 1926. The forceful opening batsman moved to South Wales after failing to secure a regular place in the Surrey side and qualified for Glamorgan after playing for Port Talbot and Maesteg Town.

ALEXANDER, Hubert Griffiths

Batsman.
Born: Pontypridd, 9 September 1873.
Died: Gileston Manor, St Athan, 20 December 1954.
Education: Tavistock Grammar School, Devon.
Glamorgan debut: 1898 v Surrey II at The Oval.
Career: 4 matches in 1898.
HS for Glamorgan: 14* v Wiltshire at Cardiff Arms Park, 1898.

Alexander played his club cricket for Cardiff, Penarth and Dinas Powis and was also a leading golfer with the Royal Porthcawl club and married the daughter of John Duncan, a well known amateur golfer. Alexander was a talented rugby player with Newport, Penarth and the Barbarians and was a reserve for the Welsh side. By profession, he was an auctioneer and land agent and, after retiring from a position with the Bath and West Agricultural Society, he served on the governing body of The Church In Wales and was chairman of the Prince of Wales Orthopaedic Hospital.

ALLIN, Anthony William

RHB; SLA.
Born: Bideford, Devon, 20 April 1954.
Education: Belmont College, Barnstable.
Glamorgan debut: 1976 v Essex at Swansea.
Career: 13 matches in 1976.
HS for Glamorgan: 32 v Somerset at Weston-super-Mare, 1976.
BB for Glamorgan: 8-63 v Sussex at Sophia Gardens, Cardiff, 1976.

Allin was plucked from Minor County cricket into the first-class game and after taking 8-63 against Sussex was tipped as a contender for a place on England's winter tour to India. However, Allin did

not enjoy the life of a county cricketer and at the end of the season returned to his father's farm. He has subsequently been a regular in the Devon side and represented the Minor Counties.

ANDERSON, Reginald Mervyn Bulford

RHB; RFM.
Born: Brynhyfryd, Swansea, 25 April 1914.
Died: Uplands, Swansea, 12 August 1972.
Education: Manseltown Central School, Swansea.
Career: 1 match in 1946 against Hampshire at Swansea scoring 0 in his only innings and taking 0-60.

Reg Anderson played for Swansea, Llanelli and Morewoods and was one of the leading fast bowlers in the South Wales Leagues during the late 1930s. He first played for the county in their Minor County games in 1936, but his subsequent appearances for both the first and second elevens were restricted by his duties as a policeman in Swansea.

ANTHONY, Hamish Aubrey Gervaise
RHB; RFM.
Born: Walings Village, Antigua, 16 January 1971.
Education: Urlings School, Antigua.
Glamorgan debut: 1990 v Oxford University at Oxford.
Career: 6 matches in 1990; Leeward Islands 1989-90; West Indies 1991.
HS for Glamorgan: 39 v Lancashire at Colwyn Bay, 1990.
BB for Glamorgan: 3-95 v India at Swansea, 1990.
Full first-class record: 386 runs (41.29); 77 wickets (28.92) and 13 catches.

against the Australian tourists and was rewarded by selection on the West Indies tour to England. He came close to selection for the Test side, but ended up playing only in the games against the counties. His first appearance for Glamorgan came during their friendly with Trinidad on the Welsh county's tour in 1989-90 and whilst on Glamorgan's staff he was attached to the Abergavenny club. His career-best performances came in 1990-91 for the Leewards against Jamaica at Basseterre when he scored 82 and took 5-23.

ARKELL, Thomas Norman
Batsman.
Born: Ham, Somerset, 1864.
Died: West Parley, Dorset, 6 March 1951.
Glamorgan debut: 1898 v Cornwall at Penzance.
Career: 2 matches in 1898.
HS for Glamorgan: 8 v Cornwall at Penzance, 1898.

Arkell played for Cardiff and was a brewing associate of the Brain family.

ARMSTRONG, Gregory de Lisle
RHB; RFM.
Born: Bank Hall, Barbados, 11 May 1950.
Glamorgan debut: 1974 v Pakistan at Swansea.

Anthony is one of the up and coming fast bowlers in the West Indies. He made his debut for the Leeward Islands in 1989-90 and won a place on the West Indies Youth tour to Zimbabwe. During 1990-91 he played for various representative elevens

Career: 30 matches 1974-76; Barbados 1973-74 to 1977-78 (10 matches).

HS for Glamorgan: 64 v Leicestershire at Swansea, 1976.

BB for Glamorgan: 6-91 v Warwickshire at Swansea, 1975.

Full first-class record: 642 runs (15.28); 91 wickets (35.15); 13 catches.

Greg Armstrong made his debut for Barbados in 1973 and joined the Welsh club the following summer. However, he was plagued by run-up and no-ball problems and failed to reproduce his West Indian form. In 1982-83 he was assistant manager of the 'rebel' West Indian team to South Africa. His career-best score was 93 for Barbados against the Combined Islands at Castries, St Lucia, in 1977-78.

ARNOTT, Trevor
RHB; RM.
Born: Radyr, 16 February 1902.
Died: Wilton, Ross-on-Wye, 2 February 1975.

Education: Monmouth School and Wycliffe College.

Glamorgan debut: 1921 v Northamptonshire at Northampton.

Career: 188 appearances 1921-30; Captain 1928; Wales 1924-30; MCC 1931.

HS for Glamorgan: 153 v Essex at Swansea, 1928.

BB for Glamorgan: 7-40 v West Indies at Cardiff Arms Park, 1923.

Full first-class record: 5,791 runs (17.03); 3 centuries; 408 wickets (33.11); 104 catches.

Trevor Arnott was a colourful amateur sportsman, playing cricket and rugby for Cardiff. He was a lively medium-pace bowler and an aggressive middle-order batsman. He became the first Glamorgan player to take a championship hat-trick, achieving the feat against Somerset at the Arms Park in 1926. His maiden century came in a whirlwind innings against Derbyshire at Swansea in 1924, which lasted only 75 minutes and Arnott reached three figures with a mighty six on to the roof of the rugby grandstand. He toured America with Incogniti in 1924, Jamaica with Tennyson's XI in 1927-28 and South America with Sir Julian Cahn's XI in 1929-30. He led the county in 1928 when his friend Johnnie Clay had to stand down from the captaincy owing to business and later in the season, Arnott played for both the Gentlemen against the Players and the South against the North. He retired from Glamorgan in 1930 and played for Monmouthshire until 1934. His final first-class match was for the MCC in 1931. Arnott was also a useful golfer and coached at Monmouth School before, and after, World War Two.

ARUNDALE, Harry
LHB; LM/SLA.
Glamorgan debut: 1914 v Monmouthshire at Newport.
Career: 2 matches; 1 appearance in 1914 and 1920.
HS for Glamorgan: 7 v Cheshire at Aigburgh, 1920.

BB for Glamorgan: 1-39 v Monmouthshire at Newport, 1914.

Harry Arundale played for Neath, Briton Ferry Town and Briton Ferry Steel and ran several pubs and clubs in the Neath and Briton Ferry area.

BAINTON, Henry George
RHB.
Born: Trowbridge, March 1885.
Career: 1 match in 1911 against Staffordshire at Stoke scoring 72* and 17.

Bainton was the professional with the Cardiff club in 1910 and 1911, before moving north and joining the Grange club in Edinburgh in 1914. He also played Minor County cricket for Monmouthshire.

BANCROFT, John
RHB; WK.
Born: Swansea, December 1879.
Died: Swansea, 7 January 1942.
Glamorgan debut: 1908 v Monmouthshire at Newport.
Career: 11 Minor County games 1908-10, plus 9 first-class matches in 1922.
HS for Glamorgan: 40 v Monmouthshire at Cardiff, 1909.

'Jack' Bancroft was the younger brother of Billy Bancroft and like his elder brother played rugby for Swansea and Wales. He won 18 Welsh caps as a full-back between 1908 and 1913. He was an outstanding wicketkeeper for the Swansea club and eventually made his first-class debut at the age of 43. He initially worked in a copper yard in Swansea before being a publican and running the York Hotel.

A famous Welsh cricketing family, from left to right: W.Bancroft (senior), W.Bancroft (junior), W.J.Bancroft and (on ground) J.Bancroft.

BANCROFT, William
RHB; RM.
Born: Bury St Edmunds, March 1848.
Died: Swansea, 26 April 1906.
Career: 1 match in 1891 against Devon at Swansea
but he did not bat or bowl.

William Bancroft was the father of Billy and Jack
Bancroft and was one of the leading professionals
in south Wales during the 1870s and 1880s. He lived
with his cricket-playing father in a cottage at the
St Helen's ground and acted as groundsman and
professional to the Swansea club, besides coaching
other clubs and the pupils of Swansea Grammar
School. He also coached at Rathway College,
Oxford, and was the professional with Settle,
Dunfermline and Merchiston Castle. Despite being
based in Northern England and Scotland, he regularly
appeared for the South Wales CC and Glamorganshire in the 1870s and early 1880s. Bancroft also
played for Glamorgan in the 1892 Trial match against
a Colts eleven at Swansea, scoring 0 and 11. His
son Billy Bancroft played alongside him in both of
his appearances for Glamorgan.

BANCROFT, William John
RHB; RM occ WK.
Born: Swansea, 2 March 1871.
Died: Swansea, 3 March 1959.
Education: St Helen's School.
Glamorgan debut: 1889 v Warwickshire at Cardiff
Arms Park.
Career: 230 matches 1889-1914; West of England 1910;
South Wales 1912.
HS for Glamorgan: 207 v Berkshire at Swansea, 1903.
BB for Glamorgan: 5-20 v Surrey II at Swansea, 1899.
Full first-class record: 38 runs (9.50); 3 catches.

Billy Bancroft was one of the leading sportsmen in
Wales during the late Victorian and Edwardian era.
The older son of William Bancroft, he followed in
the family footsteps by playing cricket and rugby
for Swansea. He won 33 caps for Wales between
1889 and 1900 and was widely renowned for his
kicking ability. He could drop and place kick with
unerring accuracy and as befits a county cricketer,
he had a safe pair of hands and was one of Wales'
finest full-backs. In 1895 he became Glamorgan's first
ever regular professional and in the early 20th century
acted as groundsman at St Helens. He made his first-
class debut in June 1910 for the West of England
against the East at Cardiff and also appeared for
South Wales against the South African tourists at
Swansea in June 1912. After retiring from county
cricket, he kept close links with the game by coaching
young players in the Swansea area, including Gilbert
Parkhouse.

BARLOW, Thomas Marriott
Batsman.
Born: Pendleton, Salford, December 1864.
Died: Chester, 27 January 1942.
Education: Heversham School, Manchester.
Glamorgan debut: 1894 v MCC at Cardiff Arms
Park.
Career: 11 matches 1894-97.
HS for Glamorgan: 75 v Herefordshire at Hereford,
1895.

Barlow played for Cardiff and the South Wales CC
and was invited to qualify for Gloucestershire by
W.G.Grace. He declined the invitation and instead
entered the legal profession. Barlow was also a
talented rugby player with Cardiff and won a Welsh
Cap as a full-back against Ireland in 1884, but his
career was ended by a knee injury the following
season. Barlow was a founder member of the
Glamorganshire Golf Club and Royal Porthcawl
club and became Welsh Amateur champion in 1900.
He was also treasurer of the Welsh Golfing Union
between 1899 and 1923 and was their secretary from
1926 until his death. He also served on Glamorgan's
committee between 1891 and 1908 and acted as
treasurer from 1893 until 1903.

BARRY, Jan

Batsman.
Born: Cape Town, 16 September 1875.
Education: Dulwich College.
Career: 1 match in 1900 against Wiltshire at Swansea scoring 24* in his only innings.
Barry played for Cardiff.

BARWICK, Stephen Royston

RHB; RM.
Born: Neath, 6 September 1960.
Education: Cwrt Sart Comprehensive and Dwr-y-Felin Comprehensive, Neath.
Glamorgan debut: 1981 v Oxford University.
Career: 150 matches 1981-; Cap 1987.
HS for Glamorgan: 30 v Hampshire at Bournemouth, 1988.
BB for Glamorgan: 8-42 v Worcestershire at Worcester, 1983.

Steve Barwick started playing club cricket for Briton Ferry Steel and was coached in his early days by Closs Jones. Barwick joined the staff in 1980 and made his debut as an accurate seam bowler in 1981. He took a career-best 8-42 at Worcester in 1983 and became a regular member of the Glamorgan side the following season. Barwick developed into a useful performer in one-day matches, but recently he has been handicapped by a knee injury and his quest for fitness has not been helped by being involved in a serious car crash in 1988. He appeared in only five games in 1990 and sporadically in 1991. Barwick has been increasingly experimenting with off-cutters and it is likely that he will bowl these more frequently in the future.

BASE, Simon John

RHB; RFM.
Born: Maidstone, 2 January 1960.

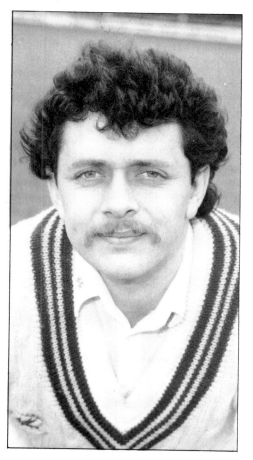

Education: Fish Hoek High School, Cape Town.
Glamorgan debut: 1986 v Gloucestershire at Bristol.
Career: 20 matches 1986-87; Derbyshire 1988 (53 matches, Cap 1990); Western Province 'B' 1981-84; Boland 1986-87 to 1988-89; Border 1989-90-.

HS for Glamorgan: 38 v Gloucestershire at Swansea, 1987.
BB for Glamorgan: 5-67 v Surrey at The Oval, 1987.
Full first-class record: 1,076 runs (12.23); 297 wickets (27.95) and 42 catches.

Simon Base joined Glamorgan in 1986 after being recommended to the county by Geoff Holmes who played alongside him in South African club cricket. However, Base failed to win a regular place in the Welsh side and in 1988 joined Derbyshire. However, the East Midlands county were fined £2,000 and Base was suspended from first-class cricket for ten weeks for a supposed breach of contract. He has played for Western Province, Boland and Border, but is England-born and toured Holland with the England 'A' team in 1989. His career-best performances were both achieved for Derbyshire against Yorkshire at Chesterfield 58 in 1990 and 7-60 in 1989. He has played club cricket for Harrogate.

BASTIEN, Steven
RHB; RM.
Born: Mile End, 13 March 1963.
Education: St Mary's Academy, Dominica; St

Bonaventure School, Forest Gate and Haringey College.
Glamorgan debut: 1988 v Leicestershire at Neath.
Career: 36 matches 1988-.
HS for Glamorgan: 36* v Warwickshire at Edgbaston, 1988.
BB for Glamorgan: 6-75 v Worcestershire at Worcester, 1990.

Bastien learnt his cricket in Dominica and then the Haringey College in London. He joined Glamorgan after trials with Essex, Surrey and Gloucestershire and took five wickets on his first-class debut. Bastien played occasionally in 1989, but won a regular place in the second half of the 1990 season when his swing bowling brought him 39 wickets. He was hindered by various ailments in 1991 and currently plays in the Three Counties League for Panteg.

BATES, William Ederick
RHB; SLA.
Born: Kirkheaton, Yorkshire, 5 March 1884.
Died: Belfast, 17 January 1957.
Glamorgan debut: 1914 v Northamptonshire at Swansea.
Career: 6 Minor County games 1914-20, plus 283 first-class matches 1921-31; Yorkshire 1907-13 (113 matches); Wales 1923-30.
HS for Glamorgan: 200* v Worcestershire at Kidderminster, 1927.

1,000 runs (7); 1,645 (44.45) 1927 best.
BB for Glamorgan: 8-93 v Essex at Leyton, 1928.
Full first-class record: 15,964 runs (24.40); 13 centuries; 230 wickets (37.70); 248 catches.
He was the son of William Bates, the Yorkshire

BATTY, Revd Arthur Montague

Batsman.
Born: Kensington, 11 July 1868.
Died: Hove, 26 December 1938.
Education: Haileybury and Oriel College, Oxford.
Career: 1 match against Gloucestershire at Cardiff Arms Park in 1891 scoring 0 and 9*.

'Ambo' Batty was in the Haileybury XI and represented his Oxford college, where he read Modern History. He was a sound batsman and a useful change bowler and whilst at Oriel became good friends with the Brains. In 1891 they invited Batty to play for Glamorgan against Gloucestershire. After leaving Oxford he entered Holy Orders and became curate of various parishes in Yorkshire and Durham, where he also played cricket. He moved back south and became Rector of West Hackney from 1911, until becoming Rector of Chingford in 1919. His final move took place in 1924 when he became Rector of Redgrave, a large country parish in Suffolk.

BAXTER, Herbert Wood

RHB.
Born: Stockport, June 1883.
Died: Stockport, 25 April 1962.
Glamorgan debut: 1920 v Carmarthenshire at Llanelli.
Career: 1 Minor County game in 1920 and 1 first-class appearance in 1921.
HS for Glamorgan: 56 v Carmarthenshire at Llanelli, 1920.

Baxter played for Swansea and was their captain in 1920. He also served on the Glamorgan committee in 1921.

BEASLEY, Sir Horace Owen Compton CBE

Batsman.
Born: Brentford, 2 July 1877.
Died: Putney, 1 January 1960.
Education: Westminster and Jesus College, Cambridge.
Glamorgan debut: 1899 v Cornwall at Truro.
Career: 3 matches in 1899.
HS for Glamorgan: 10 v Cornwall at Truro, 1899.

Sir Horace Beasley was the son of Amman Beasley, the general manager of the Taff Vale Railway, but he opted not to follow his father into the railway business and instead became a Barrister. He practised in South Wales on coming down from Cambridge and went on to serve as a High Court Judge in Burma and Madras in the inter-war period. He was also a Football Blue between 1896 and 1899, leading the Cambridge XI in 1898 and 1899, although he

batsman of the 1870s and 1880s. Bates joined Glamorgan after a brief career with Yorkshire between 1907 and 1913, where he played for Harrogate, Barnsley and Dewsbury. He qualified for the Welsh county by playing with Briton Ferry Steel and gained a regular place when Glamorgan entered the County Championship. He developed into a reliable and workmanlike opening batsman and formed a useful partnership with fellow Tyke Arnold Dyson. Ironically, they added 233 for the first wicket against Yorkshire at Sheffield in 1930. A measure of his popularity was that his Benefit in 1930 raised £602 and after retiring from Glamorgan he played Minor County cricket with Cheshire. Like his father, Bates was always elegantly dressed and acquired the nickname of 'The Marquis'. He also played football as a right-back for Bolton Wanderers and Leeds United and his son, Eddie Bates, played for, and managed, Southampton FC.

was unable to play in the 1899 Varsity match due to jaundice. He was knighted in 1930 and was later awarded a CBE for acting as president of the Pensions Appeal Tribunals between 1943 and 1958.

BELL, John Thompson

RHB.
Born: Batley, Yorkshire, 16 June 1895.
Died: Guiseley, Yorkshire, 14 August 1974.
Glamorgan debut: 1924 v South Africa at Cardiff Arms Park.
Career: 166 matches 1924-31; Yorkshire 1921-23 (116 matches); Wales 1924-30.

HS for Glamorgan: 225 v Worcestershire at Dudley, 1926.
1,000 runs (3); 1,551 (34.46) 1928 best.
BB for Glamorgan: 1-2 v Sussex at Hove, 1930.
Full first-class record: 8,390 runs (29.23); 12 centuries; 2 wickets (102.50); 63 catches.

Bell made his first-class debut in 1921, but failed to hold a regular place in the Yorkshire side and followed William Bates to South Wales to qualify for Glamorgan. He made his debut for his newly adopted county in 1924 and moved up to open the batting from 1926. His finest innings came that season when he registered a double century at Dudley, during which he and Trevor Arnott added 177 in only 70 minutes. He also scored 209 for Wales against the MCC in 1927. He retired in 1931 and rejoined Yeadon CC, for whom he had first played. Bell returned to county cricket after World War Two as an umpire and stood in games between 1948 and 1951.

BENNETT, Frank

Batsman.
Glamorgan debut: 1914 v Wiltshire at Cardiff Arms Park.
Career: 2 matches in 1914.
HS for Glamorgan: 14* v Wiltshire at Cardiff Arms Park, 1914.

Bennett was the professional with Llwynypia, Plymouth Lewis-Merthyr, Aberamman and Mountain Ash.

BESTWICK, William

RHB; RFM.
Born: Heanor, 24 February 1875.
Died: Nottingham, 2 May 1938.
Glamorgan debut: 1914 v Durham at Swansea.
Career: 4 matches 1914-20; Derbyshire 1898-1909, 1919-25 (321 matches).
HS for Glamorgan: 3* v Capt JHP Brain's XI at Cardiff Arms Park, 1920.
BB for Glamorgan: 6-44 v Durham at Swansea, 1914.
Full first-class record: 1,607 runs (4.71); 1,457 wickets (21.27); 89 catches.

Bestwick had a chequered and ill-tempered relationship with Derbyshire for whom he played from 1898 until he was released in 1909 for intemperance. He then played in the Lancashire Leagues, before joining Hill's Plymouth as their professional for 1912. The following season he played for Neath and remained in South Wales until 1919 when he rejoined Derbyshire. The following season he returned to Neath after another dispute with the county club and suggestions were made that Bestwick might join Glamorgan on a regular basis as the county were seeking first-class status. However, Bestwick returned north again and rejoined Derbyshire as player and assistant coach until retiring in 1925. During this time, he produced career-best bowling figures of 19-2-40-10, ironically against Glamorgan at the Arms Park in 1921. Even more remarkable was that Bestwick was aged 46 and bowled unchanged at fast-medium pace. He stood as an umpire in first-class cricket from 1926 until illness forced him to stand down in 1937.

BEVAN, John Maybery

Batsman.
Born: Llanelli, 12 September 1886.
Died: Swansea, 24 June 1970.
Education: Clifton College and Caius College, Cambridge.
Career: 1 match in 1920 against Monmouthshire at Ebbw Vale scoring 3 in his only innings.

He was the son of Isaiah Bevan, the captain of Llanelli between 1889 and 1896 and a member of the family who owned Briton Ferry Steelworks and Llanelli Steelworks. Bevan played for both Neath and Llanelli and also appeared in Minor County games for Carmarthenshire. Colonel Bevan served with the RAF in World War One and was awarded the Military Cross. He served on the Glamorgan committee from 1923 and was the club's chairman between 1940 and 1948, before becoming a trustee. He became managing director of Briton Ferry Steelworks and was president of Briton Ferry Steel from 1940 until 1961.

BIGGS, Cecil Frederick

Batsman.
Born: Kingston upon Thames, 22 May 1881.
Died: Southam, Banbury, 5 October 1944.
Glamorgan debut: 1906 v Monmouthshire at Newport.
Career: 2 matches in 1906.
HS for Glamorgan: 9 v Monmouthshire at Newport, 1906.

Cecil Biggs was one of the three Biggs brothers

who all played rugby for Cardiff. Cecil was a speedy centre and captained the Cardiff club in 1904-05. He was secretary of the Ocean Accident & Guarantee Corporation and served on the committee of Cardiff Athletic Club.

BIGGS, Selwyn Hanam

Batsman and medium pace bowler.
Born: Cardiff, June 1872.
Died: Weston-super-Mare, 12 January 1943.
Glamorgan debut: 1891 v MCC at Lord's.
Career: 30 matches between 1891 and 1900.
HS for Glamorgan: 47* v MCC at Cardiff Arms Park, 1891.
BB for Glamorgan: 8-48 v MCC at Cardiff Arms Park, 1896.

Selwyn Biggs captained Cardiff RFC and won 9 Welsh international caps between 1895 and 1900. He also played for the Barbarians, London Welsh, Bath, Somerset and Richmond and was a qualified solicitor. He was the brother of Cecil and Norman Biggs, and was badly gassed in World War One, causing him to become an invalid for the rest of his life.

BILLINGS, Edgar Arthur

RHB; WK.
Born: Swansea, 8 May 1880.
Died: Mumbles, 9 September 1952.
Glamorgan debut: 1911 v Wiltshire at Trowbridge.
Career: 17 matches 1911-14.
HS for Glamorgan: 62 v Carmarthenshire at Swansea, 1911.

Edgar Billings played cricket, rugby and water polo for Swansea. He captained Swansea in 1914 and 1919 and was a builder and architect by trade.

BINCH, David

All-rounder.
Born: Basford, June 1863.
Glamorgan debut: 1894 v Wiltshire at Swindon.
Career: 3 matches: 1 each in 1894, 1895 and 1900.
HS for Glamorgan: 16 v Herefordshire at Hereford, 1895.
BB for Glamorgan: 1-9 v Northamptonshire at Swansea, 1900.

Binch was the professional with Penarth and also held similar engagements with Lancaster and Calverton.

BLACKMORE, David

RHB.
Born: Swansea, March 1910.
Died: Swansea, 16 June 1988.
Glamorgan debut: 1 match in 1934 against

Somerset at Swansea scoring 34 in his only innings.
Blackmore played for Swansea and also appeared
for the West of England against Glamorgan in their
wartime friendly in 1944.

BOON, Ronald Winston
RHB; RM.
Born: Barry, 11 June 1909.
Education: Barry Boys School, Trinity College,
Carmarthen and Dunfermline College of PE.
Glamorgan debut: 1931 v Gloucestershire at
Cheltenham.
Career: 11 matches in 1931 and 1932.
HS for Glamorgan: 33 v Surrey at The Oval, 1932.

Ronnie Boon won 12 Welsh rugby caps as a winger
between 1929 and 1932 and played for the
Barbarians, Cardiff, London Welsh, Ayr, Dunfermline and New Brighton. He was also an outstanding
athlete and was Welsh sprint champion over 200
yards in 1929. After retiring, Boon became a PT
teacher in Dunfermline, Troon and Denbighshire,
before joining the HM Inspector of Schools and
serving as chairman of South Glamorgan Education
committee. He also acted as secretary of London
Welsh from 1961 until 1969, and was president of
Barry RFC in 1971. He was awarded an honorary
fellowship of Trinity College in July 1990.

BOWEN, Elvyn
LHB; SLA.
Born: Llanelli, September 1907.
Died: Gorseinon, 24 August 1965.
Glamorgan debut: 1928 v Lancashire at Swansea.
Career: 3 matches 1928-33.
HS for Glamorgan: 22 v Lancashire at Swansea,
1928.

Elvyn Bowen played for Gowerton and was also
a centre for Swansea RFC.

BOWEN, George Einon
RHB; RFM.
Born: Swansea, 1863.
Died: Porthcawl, 13 January 1919.
Education: Arnold College, Swansea.
Glamorgan debut: 1891 v MCC at Swansea.
Career: 3 matches in 1891 and 1892.
HS for Glamorgan: 17 v Monmouthshire at Cardiff
Arms Park, 1891.

Bowen won two caps for Wales and played rugby
for Morriston, Swansea and Llanelli, before joining
the committee of the WRU. He played cricket for
Morriston and Swansea and was also a member
of the Ashburnham and Porthcawl Golf Club. He
worked at the New Dock chemical works in Llanelli
and later the Ashburnham Tinplate Works in Burry
Port and was mayor of Kidwelly.

BRAIN, Joseph Hugh
RHB; RM occ WK.
Born: Kingswood, Bristol, 11 September 1863.
Died: Bonvilston, 26 June 1914.
Education: Clifton College and Oriel College,
Oxford.
Glamorgan debut: 1891 v Gloucestershire at Cardiff.
Career: 145 matches 1891-1908; Captain 1891-1908;
Secretary 1893-1908; Oxford University 1884-87
(Blue all four years); Gloucestershire 1883-89 (68
matches).
HS for Glamorgan: 144 v MCC at Lord's, 1896.
BB for Glamorgan: 6-62 v V.T.Hill's XI at Cardiff
Arms Park, 1895.
Full first-class record: 3,393 runs (19.50); 3
centuries; 8 wickets (38.25); 83 catches and 4
stumpings.

Brain was in the Clifton XI between 1881 and 1883,
before going up to Oxford where he won four Blues
and led the XI in 1887. As a Freshman, he was
in the Oxford side which defeated the 1884
Australian tourists and later that summer scored
108 against the tourists for Gloucestershire. He
played for them between 1883 and 1889 and was
rated as one of the finest young batsmen in the
West Country. His move across the Severn followed
his promotion in 1890 within the Brain family's
brewery business which included the Old Brewery
in the centre of Cardiff. Brain made his Glamorgan
debut in 1891 and during the next decade transformed the Welsh team both on and off the field.

In particular, it was through his initiative that they joined the Minor County championship in 1897. He served on the committee in 1892 until ill health forced him to stand down in 1913. He played club cricket for Clifton, Fairwater and Cardiff, who he captained between 1892 and 1901. J.H.Brain was widely regarded as one of the finest captains ever to lead Glamorgan and he tragically died after a short illness in 1914 before the fruits of his labour saw Glamorgan elevated to the first-class ranks.

BRAIN, John Henry Patrick

RHB; WK.
Born: Cardiff, 17 March, 1896.
Died: Dinas Powis, 11 December 1945.
Education: Winchester.
Glamorgan debut: 1920 v Carmarthenshire at Llanelli.
Career: 4 Minor County matches in 1920, plus 6 first-class games 1921-28; Combined Oxford and Cambridge XI 1922.
HS for Glamorgan: 42 v Carmarthenshire at Llanelli, 1920.
Full first-class record: 86 runs (8.60); 4 catches and 1 stumping.

He was the son of W.H.Brain and older brother of M.B.Brain. He played for Cardiff and the South Wales Hunts and served on the Glamorgan committee between 1922 and 1925. He also owned several successful racehorses and had his own wandering 11 of friends and acquaintances who played an annual series of fixtures against the top club sides in South Wales.

BRAIN, Michael Benjamin

RHB; WK.
Born: Cardiff, 13 April 1910.
Died: Trellech, Monmouthshire, 24 August 1971.
Education: Repton.
Glamorgan debut: One match in 1930 against Oxford University at Oxford scoring 9 and 0.

Michael Brain was in the Repton XI in 1928 and 1929 and like his older brother J.H.P.Brain, played for Cardiff and the South Wales Hunts. He appeared for Glamorgan II in Minor County games between 1935 and 1947. He served as chairman of Brains Brewery from 1955 until his death in 1971.

BRAIN, William Henry

RHB; WK.
Born: Clifton, 21 July 1870.
Died: Dinas Powis, 20 December 1934.

Education: Clifton College and Oriel College, Oxford.
Glamorgan debut: 1891 v Gloucestershire at Bristol.
Career: 105 matches 1891-1908; Oxford University 1891-93 (Blue all three years); Gloucestershire, 1893 (7 matches).
HS for Glamorgan: 113 v Monmouthshire at Newport, 1897.
Full first-class record: 458 runs (11.45); 39 catches and 22 stumpings.

William Brain was in the Clifton XI between 1887 and 1889 and then he followed in his brother Joseph's footsteps by winning a Blue at Oxford between 1891 and 1893. William Brain also played in the Gloucestershire XI, where he achieved the unique distinction of a hat-trick of stumpings against Somerset in 1893. Brain played regularly for the Welsh county from 1895 onwards and appeared in club cricket for Cardiff. He also won a Soccer Blue as a goalkeeper whilst at Oxford and served on the Glamorgan committee between 1901 and 1908. He was the father of J.H.P. and M.B.Brain and took great delight in the fact that his sons played first-class cricket for the family's adopted county. William Brain acted as chairman of Brains Brewery from 1914 until his death in 1954.

BRIERLEY, Thomas Leslie

RHB; WK.
Born: Southampton, 15 June 1910.
Died: Canada, 7 January 1989.
Glamorgan debut: 1931 v Nottinghamshire at Swansea.

Every, Brierley, Preece (with scythe) and Duckfield.

Career: 181 matches 1931-39; Lancashire, 1946-48 (46 matches, Cap 1946); Canada 1951-54.
HS for Glamorgan: 116 v Lancashire at Old Trafford, 1938.
1,000 runs (1); 1,183 (23.67) 1938 best.
Full first-class record: 6,244 runs (18.97); 4 centuries; 215 catches and 91 stumpings.

Brierley joined Glamorgan as a specialist batsman but won a regular place in the side from 1934 as a wicketkeeper when Trevor Every retired after going blind. He kept his place behind the stumps until Haydn Davies emerged in the late 1930s. Brierley joined Lancashire after World War Two and helped coach at Old Trafford before emigrating to Canada at the end of the 1948 season. He coached at Vancouver and taught economics at Shawnigan Lake School and became one of the leading cricket administrators in the Vancouver area. He made his debut for Canada in 1951 and toured England with the Canadian tourists in 1954. He coincidentally equalled his career-best score of 116 for Lancashire against Glamorgan at Liverpool in 1947.

BURNETT, Anthony Compton (later COMPTON-BURNETT)
RHB.
Born: Chipstead, Surrey, 26 October 1923.
Education: Lancing and Pembroke College, Cambridge.
Glamorgan debut: 1958 v New Zealand at Swansea.
Career: 8 matches in 1958; Cambridge University 1949-50 (Blue 1949).

HS for Glamorgan: 17 v Leicestershire at Loughborough, 1958.
Full first-class record: 790 runs (23.23); 20 catches.

'Tolly' Burnett won a Blue in 1949, during which he scored a career-best 79* against Middlesex at Fenners. For the next eight years Burnett played for Sussex II and the MCC whilst on holiday from teaching science at Eton. In 1958 the Glamorgan committee approached Burnett about taking over the captaincy from Wilf Wooller. It was a highly contentious decision and after a disappointing trial during August, Burnett decided to remain at Eton. His son, R.J.Compton-Burnett, won a Blue in 1981.

BURTON

All-rounder.
Glamorgan debut: 1891 v Gloucestershire at Cardiff Arms Park.
Career: 3 matches in 1891.
HS for Glamorgan: 13 v MCC at Lord's, 1891.
BB for Glamorgan: 5-63 v MCC at Lord's, 1891.

Burton was on the MCC groundstaff in 1889 and 1890, during which he appeared for the MCC against Glamorgan. He subsequently moved to South Wales to become the professional and groundsman with Bridgend in 1891 and 1892. He also played in the 1891 Trial match at Cardiff against a Colts XI scoring 9* and returning match figures of 8-36.

BUSH, Percy Frank

RHB.
Born: Cardiff, 23 June 1879.
Died: Cardiff, 19 May 1955.
Education: University College, Cardiff.
Glamorgan debut: 1900 v Wiltshire at Swansea.
Career: 4 matches 1900-03.
HS for Glamorgan: 5 v Wiltshire at Swansea 1900 and v Surrey at The Oval, 1903.
BB for Glamorgan: 1-16 v Monmouthshire at Newport, 1900.

Percy Bush was the leading fly half in Welsh rugby at the turn of the century. The Cardiff and London Welsh player won eight Welsh caps between 1905 and 1910 and toured Australia with a British team in 1904. He taught in Cardiff and served on the committee of Cardiff Athletic Club and after retiring from rugby, Bush emigrated to France to become the British Consul in Nantes and played rugby for Stade Nantes.

BUTCHER, Alan Raymond

LHB; LM/SLA.
Born: Croydon, 7 January 1954.
Education: Heath Clark Grammar School.
Career: 108 matches 1987-; Cap 1987; Captain 1989-; Surrey 1972-86 (283 matches, Benefit 1985, Cap 1975); England (1 Cap in 1979); MCC.
HS for Glamorgan: 171* v Warwickshire at Edgbaston, 1989.
1,000 runs (5); 2,116 (58.78) 1990 best.
BB for Glamorgan: 3-35 v Middlesex at Sophia Gardens, Cardiff, 1987.
Full first-class record: 22,543 runs (36.48); 46 centuries; 141 wickets (38.53); 183 catches.

Alan Butcher first played for Beckenham before emigrating with his parents to Australia where he played for Glenelg and South Australia U-15. He returned to the UK in the early 1970s and appeared for Surrey Young Cricketers. Butcher impressed as a left-arm seamer, appearing in two Sunday League matches at the end of 1971. He joined the Surrey staff in 1972 and in only his third first-class game took a career-best 6-48 against Hampshire at Guildford. Butcher steadily moved up the order from number eight in the mid-1970s and began opening with John Edrich in 1975. The following season he registered his maiden Championship century and his ability against fast bowling brought him appearances for the MCC against the West Indies at Lord's and a Test Trial in 1976.

His consistent batting eventually earned him an England cap in 1979 against India at The Oval. Butcher was very much on trial for the winter tour and despite scores of 14 and 20, he failed to win further Test recognition, although he was called up for a one-day international against Australia in 1980. Nevertheless, he remained one of the most regular openers in the country, playing for the MCC against the Champion County in 1980 and 1982, touring India with an Overseas XI in 1980-81 and Jamaica with an International XI in 1982-83. In 1980 he scored a career-best 216* against Cambridge University at Fenners, whilst in 1984 he scored a century in each innings at The Oval against Glamorgan, whom he joined in 1987 after leaving the Surrey staff.

'Butch' formed a sound opening pairing with

Hugh Morris and took over the Glamorgan captaincy midway through 1989 when his partner stood down. He proved to be a shrewd leader and continued to be a heavy run scorer, becoming the first English batsman to 1,000 runs in both 1989 and 1990. He passed 2,000 runs in a season for the first time in 1990 and his thoroughly professional efforts brought him the accolade of being one of Wisden's Cricketers of the Year. Alan's two younger brothers have also played county cricket — Ian appeared for Leicestershire and Gloucestershire, and Martin for Surrey — whilst his son Mark is on the Surrey staff. In 1991 Alan played against Mark in a Sunday League match at The Oval, making history as the first father and son to play against each other in county cricket.

BYASS, Geoffrey Robert Sidney

RHB.
Born: Port Talbot, 30 September 1895.
Died: Tilford, Surrey, 4 November 1976.
Education: Winchester.
Career: 1 match in 1920 against Carmarthenshire at Swansea scoring 21 and taking 1-38.

Sir Geoffrey Byass was the son of Sir Sidney and Lady Byass of Llandough Castle and was the managing director of the Margam and Mansel Tin Plate Works. He captained Bridgend and also played for the South Wales Hunts. He was mayor of Port Talbot and Aberavon in 1937-38 and married Marian Bruce, the sister of Lord Aberdare who played for Oxford University, Middlesex and Wales.

CADOGAN, John Philip

Batsman.
Born: Neath, March 1866.
Died: Cardiff, 29 June 1918.
Glamorgan debut: 1897 v Wiltshire at Swindon.
Career: 1 match in 1897 and 1900.
HS for Glamorgan: 39 v Monmouthshire at Cardiff Arms Park, 1900.

Cadogan played for Cathays and Cardiff and served on the Glamorgan committee between 1901 and 1914.

CAMERON, Alexander William Cumming

All-rounder.
Born: Scotland, 3 March 1866.
Died: Swansea, 14 March 1957.
Education: George Watson's College and Edinburgh University.
Glamorgan debut: 1900 v Wiltshire at Swansea.
Career: 18 matches 1900-13.
HS for Glamorgan: 39 v Wiltshire at Swindon, 1901.
BB for Glamorgan: 6-89 v Surrey II at Cardiff Arms Park, 1900.

Dr Alex Cameron won three Scottish rugby caps between 1887 and 1894, before moving to South Wales and sharing a practice in Swansea with Welsh international Teddy Morgan. He played for Swansea and served on the county committee between 1905 and 1920.

CANN, Michael James

LHB; OB.
Born: Cardiff, 4 July 1965.
Education: St Illtyds College, Cardiff and Swansea University.
Glamorgan debut: 1986 v Essex at Chelmsford.

Career: 36 matches 1986-91; Combined Universities 1986; Orange Free State 'B' 1989-90; Griqualand West 1990-91.
HS for Glamorgan: 109 v Somerset at Sophia Gardens, Cardiff, 1989.
BB for Glamorgan: 3-30 v Middlesex at Abergavenny, 1989.
Full first-class record: 1,608 runs (28.21); 3 centuries; 14 wickets (68.36) and 16 catches.

Michael Cann played for Welsh Schools before going to Swansea University to read biochemistry. He made his second eleven debut in 1983 and scored over 1,000 runs in second team games in 1984. Cann led the UAU in 1986 and 1987 and represented Combined Universities in the Benson & Hedges Cup in 1987. He made his championship debut in 1986 and appeared on a fairly regular basis in 1981 when he scored his maiden championship century, but he subsequently found opportunities rather limited. In 1989-90 he captained Orange Free State 'B' and scored a career-best 138 against Griqualand West on his debut. He has played club cricket for Gorseinon and Pontardulais and is currently captain of Cardiff. Cann was released from the staff at the end of the 1991 season.

CARLESS, Ernest Francis
RHB; occ WK.
Born: Barry, 9 September 1912.
Died: Barry, 26 September 1987.
Education: Cadoxton School.
Glamorgan debut: 1934 v Middlesex at Cardiff
Arms Park.
Career: 2 matches in 1934, plus 1 game in 1946.
HS for Glamorgan: 25 v Surrey at Cardiff Arms
Park, 1934.

Ernie Carless played cricket for Cardiff and Barry
and made his first-class debut in 1934. He played
for Glamorgan II in Minor County games from
1936 and also appeared in wartime friendlies
between 1943 and 1945. After the war he became
groundsman at Ninian Park, before joining
Plymouth Argyle and looking after Home Park.
He had earlier been an inside-forward with Cardiff
City. Whilst in the West Country, Carless played
Minor County cricket for Devon between 1947 and
1949. He returned to South Wales in the 1950s and
rejoined Barry for whom he continued to play until
he was in his 70s.

CARR, Harry Lascelles
RHB; WK.
Born: Lambeth, 8 October 1907.
Died: Marylebone, 18 August 1943.
Education: Clifton and Trinity Hall, Cambridge.
Career: 1 match in 1934 against Cambridge
University at Cardiff Arms Park scoring 6 in his
only innings.

Harry Carr was in the Clifton XI from 1924 until
1926 and made his first-class debut in 1931 for
Leveson-Gowers XI after coming down from
Cambridge. Carr was also a talented golfer and
billiards player and won Blues for both of these
games. He was a journalist with the *News of the
World,* working for his father Sir Emsley Carr. He
joined the RAF during World War Two and served
with the intelligence section before being struck
down by illness. His twin brother Walter Carr also
won a Golf Blue and was German Amateur golf
champion in 1932.

CARRINGTON, William George
Batsman.
Born: Herne Hill, 16 May 1880.
Career: 1 match in 1896 against Surrey II at The
Oval, scoring 10 in his only innings.

Carrington was a substitute from the Surrey
groundstaff who was drafted into the Glamorgan
side when they arrived at The Oval with only ten
fit players. Carrington also played for South
London Schools and Surrey Colts.

CARTWRIGHT, Thomas William
RHB; RM.
Born: Coventry, 22 July 1935.
Education: Foxford School, Coventry.
Glamorgan debut: 1977 v Derbyshire at Swansea.
Career: 7 matches in 1977; Warwickshire 1952-69
(353 matches, Cap 1958, Benefit 1968 £9,592);
Somerset 1970-76 (101 matches, Cap 1970, Testi-
monial 1975); England 1964-65 (5 Tests); Players
v Gentlemen, 1954.
HS for Glamorgan: 22* v Kent at Swansea, 1977.
BB for Glamorgan: 4-46 v Yorkshire at Sophia
Gardens, Cardiff, 1977.
Full first-class record: 13,710 runs (21.32); 7
centuries; 1,536 wickets (19.11), 332 catches.

Tom Cartwright joined Glamorgan in 1977, chiefly
to bolster the county's one-day side after over 25
years of first-class cricket with Warwickshire and
Somerset and five Tests for England. He was widely
regarded as one of the finest medium-pace seam
bowlers on the county circuit in the 1960s with a
repertoire of inswingers, outswingers and subtle
changes of pace. He took a career-best 8-39 for
Warwickshire against Somerset at Weston-super-
Mare in 1962, whilst Cartwright's best match figures
were achieved against Glamorgan when he claimed
15-89 in the game at Swansea in 1967. He was also
an aggressive middle-order batsman and scored 210
for Warwickshire against Middlesex at Nuneaton
in 1962. He achieved the 'double' that season and
the following year went on the MCC tour to East
Africa. He also toured South Africa in 1964-65 and
East Africa in 1973-74. In 1970 Cartwright joined
Somerset and also coached at Millfield School until
1976. He retired from county cricket at the end
of 1977 and became the Welsh county's first-ever
team manager. He held this post until 1980 when
he became coaching officer to the Welsh Cricket
Association. His son Jeremy plays for Neath and
has appeared for Glamorgan Seconds and Under-
25 team.

CHANDLESS, John
RHB; RM.
Born: Cardiff, 21 August 1884.
Died: Whitchurch, 1 June 1968.
Glamorgan debut: 1911 v Wiltshire at Trowbridge.
Career: 9 appearances in Minor County games
1911-20, with 1 first-class match in 1927.
HS for Glamorgan: 20 v Monmouthshire at
Swansea, 1911 and v Buckinghamshire at Ayles-
bury, 1911.

Chandless was one of Cardiff's leading batsmen in
the 1910s and 1920s.

Tom Cartwright, the former Warwickshire and England seamer who joined Glamorgan to strengthen the county's one-day side and coaching staff.

CLARK, John Gowan

All-rounder.
Born: Aberystwyth, September 1864.
Died: Cardiff, 28 November 1937.
Glamorgan debut: 1889 v Warwickshire at Cardiff Arms Park.
Career: 37 matches 1889-1903.
HS for Glamorgan: 95 v Monmouthshire at Newport, 1891.

BB for Glamorgan: 5-11 v Wiltshire at Cardiff Arms Park, 1892.

Gowan Clark was the secretary and accountant of the Rhymney Railway Company and captained Cardiff between 1897 and 1899. He served on the Glamorgan committee between 1895 and 1921 and was chairman of Cardiff from 1927 until his death. He was the uncle of Norman Riches and helped coach him in the 1890s.

CLARKE, Frank

RHB; RFM.
Born: Cardiff, 8 October 1936.
Education: Allensbank School.
Glamorgan debut: 1956 v Combined Services at Cardiff Arms Park.
Career: 31 matches 1956-60.
HS for Glamorgan: 31 v India at Swansea, 1959.
BB for Glamorgan: 5-66 v Middlesex at Lord's, 1959.

Clarke played for St Fagan's, Neath and Maesteg but his county career was interrupted by both injury and National Service when he played for the Army and the Combined Services. He was forced into retirement as a result of niggling injuries in 1960 and became a cabinet maker.

CLAY, John Charles

RHB; RFM/LB/OB.
Born: Bonvilston, 18 March 1898.
Died: St Hilary, 11 August 1973.
Education: Winchester.
Glamorgan debut: 1921 v Leicestershire at Swansea, 1921.
Career: 358 matches 1921-49; Captain 1924-27, 1929, 1946; Wales 1923-26; Treasurer 1933-38; England (1 Test in 1935); Gentlemen v Players, 1923, 1927, 1935; MCC 1923-24; 1927-28; Leveson-Gowers XI, 1927.
HS for Glamorgan 115* v New Zealand at Cardiff Arms Park, 1927.
BB for Glamorgan: 9-54 v Northamptonshire at Llanelli, 1935.

100 wickets (3); 176 wickets (17.34) 1937 best.
Full first-class record: 7,186 runs (15.45); 2 centuries 1,317 wickets (19.76); 177 catches.

Without the efforts of Johnnie Clay, Glamorgan might have folded during their lean years in the 1930s and he holds a special place in the annals of the club. He graduated into the Welsh side after club cricket with Chepstow, school cricket with Winchester and Minor County cricket with Monmouthshire. In his early years, he was a tearaway fast bowler, but he was affected by a series of injuries and in 1924 concentrated on off and leg spin. He took over the Glamorgan captaincy that season and steered them to a healthy 13th place in the championship. However, Clay had to give up the captaincy at the end of the 1927 season due to his work with his father's shipping line based at Cardiff Docks and family commitments following his marriage to the daughter of Colonel Homfray of Penll   ine Castle.

But he always answered Glamorgan's cries for help and turned out as often as he could during his summer holidays and shared the captaincy in 1929 with Norman Riches. Clay was also an aggressive lower-order batsman and in 1929 scored his maiden championship century against Worcestershire at Swansea, batting at number 10. His century came in only 95 minutes and, together with Joe Hills, added a record 203 for the ninth wicket. Despite only occasional games, Clay proved himself amongst the top off-spinners in the country during the 1930s and in 1934 took 103 wickets at 17 apiece, including match figures of 12-84 against Surrey at The Oval. The following year he was included in the squad for the Third and Fourth Tests against South Africa, before making his England debut in the Fifth Test at The Oval.

Clay took a record 176 wickets in 1937, including figures of 9-66 against Worcestershire at Swansea and 9-59 against Essex at Westcliff. He came close to selection for England the following year, but Clay did not want to be chosen and asked the selectors to pick a younger bowler. As a result of Clay's bowling, Glamorgan finished in seventh place in the championship in 1937. He also had a huge impact off the field and took over the role of treasurer in 1933. Together with his friend, Maurice Turnbull, they organized a host of fund-raising events and used their business contacts to drum up support. Their efforts silenced calls for the club to be wound up and they transformed Glamorgan from habitual losers with a sizable debt into a competitive team with a healthy bank balance.

Sadly, Turnbull was killed during World War Two, so when county cricket resumed in 1946, Clay accepted the captaincy and assembled a new squad so that his late friend's efforts were not in vain.

Together with Wilf Wooller, they fostered a good team spirit, which culminated in Glamorgan's first county title in 1948. By this time Clay had entered semi-retirement, but with the prospect of the championship looming on the horizon, Wooller cajoled the veteran off-spinner back into the team and it was Clay who bowled out Surrey and Hampshire to secure the title. Clay served as a Test

selector in 1947 and 1948 and played his final game for Glamorgan in 1949, appropriately back home on Monmouthshire soil against Yorkshire at Newport.

After retiring from county cricket, Clay played for Barry and Cowbridge and served on the county committee. He became a trustee in 1953 and was elevated to the post of president in 1960 and held this position until his death in 1973. Clay also served on the board of Wales Gas and was chairman of the board of the Park Hotel, Cardiff. He was also heavily involved in the horse-racing world, having hunted and ridden in point-to-points as a young man. He acted as secretary of the Glamorgan Hunt and then served as a director and steward of Chepstow Racecourse which had been laid out close to his family's home during the 1920s. A long distance steeplechase is run at the course in Clay's memory every year.

CLIFT, Phil Brittain
RHB; OB.
Born: Usk, 3 September 1918.
Glamorgan debut: 1937 v Kent at Tonbridge.
Career: 183 matches 1937-55; Cap 1947; Benefit 1959 (£3,000); Testimonial 1981.
HS for Glamorgan: 125* v Derbyshire at Cardiff Arms Park, 1949.
1,000 runs (3); 1,226 (26.08) 1949 best.
BB for Glamorgan: 3-6 v Sussex at Llanelli, 1951.
Phil Clift played for Usk, Abertillery and Neath and joined the Glamorgan staff in 1936. He

established himself as a free-scoring opening batsman and in 1948 was rated by Don Bradman as one of the finest young batsmen in the country. However, Clift suffered from bouts of illness which hampered his career and he missed the whole of the 1950 season after being taken ill on returning from a coaching post in South Africa. He retired in 1955 and became the county's coach, running the Indoor Schools at Cardiff and Neath and grooming the young colts in the second eleven. In 1959 he took over the duties of assistant secretary and continued to lead the second eleven during the 1960s. In 1969-70 he managed Glamorgan's tour to Bermuda and the West Indies and in 1978 he succeeded Wilf Wooller to the post of Secretary. Clift retired in 1982 but he maintained links with the club by scoring for the first and second teams and managing the Under-19 side.

CLOUGH
Batsman
Career: 1 match in 1909 against Monmouthshire at Newport scoring 15 in his only innings.
Clough was the professional with Cardiff, Llanelli and Hills Plymouth.

COLLEY, Robert Henry
Batsman.
Born: Clifton 1867.
Died: Cardiff, 3 June 1949.
Career: 1 match against Surrey II at The Oval, 1899 making 0 in his only innings.
Colley played for Cardiff and was a builder by trade.

COOPER, Edgar
RHB; RFM.
Born: Briton Ferry, November 1891.
Died: Kettering, 15 March, 1959.
Glamorgan debut: 1912 v Monmouthshire at Cardiff Arms Park.
Career: 1 Minor County match in 1912, 1913 and 1920, plus 4 first-class appearances during 1921.
HS for Glamorgan: 14 v Monmouthshire at Cardiff Arms Park, 1912.
BB for Glamorgan: 5-45 v Monmouthshire at Ebbw Vale, 1920.
Cooper played for Llanelli and Briton Ferry Steel.

COPE, John James
RHB.
Born: Ellesmere Port, 1 August 1908.
Glamorgan debut: 1935 v Kent at Tunbridge Wells.

Career: 3 matches in 1935.
HS for Glamorgan: 14* v Hampshire at Cardiff Arms Park, 1935.
Cope played for Monmouthshire in the early 1930s and also appeared for Glamorgan II in Minor County games in 1936. He was also a useful footballer and played in Lancashire.

CORDING, George Ernest
RHB; occ WK.
Born: Tredegar, 1 January 1878.
Died: St Mellons, 2 February 1946.
Glamorgan debut: 1900 v Berkshire at Cardiff Arms Park.
Career: 19 Minor County games 1900-14 plus 19

first-class appearances 1921-23.
HS for Glamorgan: 101 v Worcestershire at Swansea, 1921.
Cording only made sporadic appearances due to his teaching commitments in Cardiff. However, he used to invite some of his boys down to the Arms Park nets to bowl at 'Sir' and he generously rewarded them with a penny if they dismissed him. He captained Cardiff in 1921 and 1922 and during World War Two he acted as match secretary allowing Glamorgan to stage a number of fund-raising games to boost the war effort.

CORDLE, Anthony Elton
RHB; RFM.
Born: Bridgetown, Barbados, 21 September 1940.

West Indian Tony Cordle, who made over 300 appearances for Glamorgan.

Glamorgan debut: 1963 v Cambridge University at Margam, 1972.
Career: 312 appearances 1963-80; Cap 1967; Benefit 1977 (£8,000).
BB for Glamorgan: 9-49 v Leicestershire at Colwyn Bay, 1969.
HS for Glamorgan: 81 v Cambridge University at Swansea, 1972.

Cordle emigrated to Britain in the early 1960s after playing in club cricket in his native Barbados and worked initially with London Transport, before moving to South Wales and joining Cardiff. He made his county debut in 1963 and established a regular place in the side by the late 1960s. He formed an effective opening bowling partnership with Malcolm Nash and was a member of the 1969 championship winning side. Cordle was also a useful performer with both bat and ball in limited overs cricket and in 1979 took a hat-trick in the Sunday League match with Hampshire. After retiring, Cordle acted as the county's coach between 1981 and 1983, before emigrating to Canada to take up a coaching post. His uncle is Gerald Cordle, the Cardiff RFC winger. He is now playing rugby league.

COTTEY, Philip Anthony

RHB.
Born: Swansea, 2 June 1966.
Education: Bishopston Comprehensive, Swansea.
Glamorgan debut: 1986 v Oxford University at Oxford, 1990.
Career: 63 matches 1986-.
HS for Glamorgan: 156 v Oxford University at Oxford, 1990.
1,000 runs (1); 1,001 (33.36) 1990 best.
BB for Glamorgan: 1-49 v Warwickshire at Swansea, 1990.

Tony Cottey played professional football with Swansea City and won Welsh Youth soccer caps, but was released by Swansea in 1985 and switched to a career in cricket. He had been an outstanding schoolboy player for Swansea and appeared for Glamorgan II from 1982. He made his first-class debut in 1986, but did not win a regular place as a top order batsman until 1990 when he scored three centuries, including a maiden championship hundred against Leicestershire. Cottey is only 5ft 4in tall and is one of the best outfielders currently playing county cricket. His swift running and good throwing has been invaluable in Glamorgan's one-day side over the past two seasons. He has played grade cricket in Australia, but has spent the last few winters playing Welsh League football for Merthyr Town, Llanelli AFC and Maesteg Park.

Tony Cottey

COWLEY, Nigel Geoffrey

RHB; OB.
Born: Shaftesbury, 1 March 1953.
Education: Dutchy Manor Secondary School, Mere.
Glamorgan debut: 1990 v Oxford University at Oxford.
Career: 14 matches in 1990; Hampshire 1974-89 (257 matches, Cap 1978, Benefit 1988).
HS for Glamorgan: 76 v Kent at Swansea, 1990.
BB for Glamorgan: 3-84 v Lancashire at Colwyn Bay, 1990.
Full first-class record: 7,309 runs (23.35); 2 centuries; 437 wickets (34.04); 105 catches.

Former Hampshire off-spinner Nigel Cowley, who joined Glamorgan on a two-year contract in 1990 but was forced into retirement by injury at the end of his first season.

Nigel Cowley joined the Hampshire staff in 1973 after playing Minor County cricket with Dorset in 1972. He made his first-class debut in 1974 against Sussex and won a regular place as an aggressive middle-order batsman and off-spinner in the Hampshire side of the late 1970s and early 1980s. Cowley hit two centuries, with a top score of 109* at Taunton in 1977, whilst in 1982 he took a career-best 6-48 against Leicestershire at Southampton. His nagging accuracy also made him one of best spinners in limited overs cricket and his miserly off-spin was a key factor in Hampshire winning the Sunday League in 1986 and Benson & Hedges Cup in 1988. He joined Glamorgan on a two-year contract in 1990, but was forced to retire at the end of the season as a result of a pelvic injury and he settled with his family in South Africa where he had been coaching since 1981.

CREBER, Arthur Brynley
RHB; RM.

Born: Sketty, 11 October 1909.
Died: Colwyn Bay, 10 August 1966.
Career: 1 match against Leicestershire at Loughborough in 1929, scoring 4 and 3; Scotland 1937.
Full first-class record: 23 runs (11.25); 1 wicket and 1 catch.

He was the son of Harry Creber and later took up a professional post in Scotland, for whom he appeared in 1937, scoring 38 runs and taking 1-80. He had a short trial with Glamorgan in 1929 before taking up a professional position with the Longsight club in Manchester.

CREBER, Harry
RHB; LM/SLA
Born: Birkenhead, 30 April 1872.
Died: Uplands, Swansea, 27 March 1939.
Glamorgan debut: 1898 v Surrey II at The Oval.
Career: 192 Minor County matches 1898-1920, plus 33 first-class appearances in 1921 and 1922; Cap 1922; South Wales 1912.

Harry Creber, Birkenhead-born and the first bowler to take 100 wickets in a season for Glamorgan.

HS for Glamorgan: 53 v Monmouthshire at Newport 1900.
BB for Glamorgan: 9-56 v Carmarthenshire at Llanelli, 1908.
100 wickets (2); 100 (15.43) 1905; 112 (13.81) 1906 best.
Full first-class record: 157 runs (5.06); 98 wickets (27.25); 6 catches.

Creber played for Orton and Liverpool, before joining Swansea, for whom he played from 1896 until 1934. He was the groundsman at St Helen's, Swansea from 1899 until his death in 1939. Creber was the mainstay of the Glamorgan attack before World War One and in 1905 became the first Glamorgan bowler to take 100 wickets in a season. That year he bowled over 500 overs and his 100 wickets came at 15 apiece, including match returns of 13-82 against Wiltshire at Chippenham and 11-148 against the MCC at the Arms Park. He repeated the feat in 1906 when he claimed 112 wickets at 13.81 including returns of 12-88 against Durham, 11-110 against Northumberland and 13-85 against Wiltshire, all at the Arms Park. He was past his best when he appeared in first-class cricket, but even so was an accurate left arm spinner.

CROFT, Robert Damien Bale
RHB; OB.
Born: Morriston, 25 May 1970.
Education: St John Lloyd Catholic Comprehensive, Llanelli and West Glamorgan Institute of Higher Education.
Glamorgan debut: 1989 v Surrey at The Oval.

Career: 47 matches 1989-; England 'A' 1991-92.
HS for Glamorgan: 91* v Worcestershire at Abergavenny, 1990.
BB for Glamorgan: 5-62 v Warwickshire at Swansea, 1991.

Robert Croft is one of the most promising young spinners currently playing county cricket. He played his early cricket for Swansea and Glamorgan Colts and captained both Welsh Schools and England South in 1989. Towards the end of the season Croft made his first-class debut and he was a regular in the side from the middle of 1990 as a free scoring lower-order batsman and off-spinner. He has impressed many good judges with his loop and nagging accuracy and his promise was recognised by selection for the England 'A' tour to Bermuda and West Indies during 1991-92.

CROWTHER, Peter Gwynne
RHB; OB.
Born: Neath, 26 April 1952.

Education: Aberystwyth University.
Glamorgan debut: 1977 v Cambridge University at Cambridge.
Career: 9 matches in 1977 and 1978.

HS for Glamorgan: 99 v Cambridge University at Cambridge, 1977.

BB for Glamorgan: 1-22 v Cambridge University at Cambridge, 1977.

Crowther played for Maesteg and Neath and had the misfortune to score 99 on his county debut. He suffered from health problems and asked to be released from his contract midway through the 1978 season.

CULLEN, James S.

Batsman.

Born: Cardiff, 1869.

Career: 1 match in 1893 against Herefordshire at Hereford scoring 14 and 7.

Cullen played for Cardiff and St Pauls.

DALE, Adrian

RHB; RM.

Born: Germiston, Johannesburg, 24 October 1968.

Education: Chepstow Comprehensive and Swansea University.

Glamorgan debut: 1989 v Gloucestershire at Bristol.

Career: 31 matches 1989-; Combined Universities 1989.

HS for Glamorgan: 140 v Gloucestershire at Abergavenny, 1991.

BB for Glamorgan: 3-21 v India at Swansea, 1990.

Adrian Dale played his early cricket for Chepstow and represented Glamorgan at schoolboy level for soccer, basketball and swimming. He made his Glamorgan II debut in 1986 before going to Swansea University to read Economics. His all-round talents secured a place in the Combined Universities teams for the Benson & Hedges Cup in 1989 and in the middle of the season he made his championship debut. Dale's big break came in 1991 when he scored a maiden century on Glamorgan's pre-season tour of Zimbabwe. He was subsequently elevated to the number-three spot and responded with a match-winning innings in the NatWest Bank Trophy match at Worcester, two half centuries against the West Indies and a first championship century against Gloucestershire at Abergavenny.

DANIELS, Simon Anthony Brewis

RHB; RFM.

Born: Darlington, 23 August 1958.

Education: Sedbergh School and Newcastle Polytechnic.
Glamorgan debut: 1981 v Middlesex at Lord's.
Career: 16 matches 1981 and 1982.
HS for Glamorgan: 73 v Gloucestershire at Swansea, 1982.
BB for Glamorgan: 3-33 v Essex at Colchester, 1981.

Daniels appeared in Minor County cricket with Durham in 1979 and 1980 before joining the Glamorgan staff in 1981. He was a useful seam bowler and hard hitting lower order batsman who shared in a record tenth-wicket partnership with Terry Davies against Gloucestershire at Swansea in 1982. He played club cricket for Darlington and St Fagan's.

DAUNCEY, John Gilbert

RHB.
Born: Ystalyfera, 9 April 1936.
Glamorgan debut: 1957 v Gloucestershire at Swansea.
Career: 2 matches in 1957.
HS for Glamorgan: 34 v Gloucestershire at Swansea, 1957.

Gilbert Dauncey played club cricket for Swansea, Metal Box, Pontardawe, Clydach and Mumbles.

DAVID, Alexander Charles Robert MC

All-rounder.
Born: Cardiff, 5 November 1889.
Glamorgan debut: 1911 v Staffordshire at Stoke.
Career: 3 matches 1911-13.
HS for Glamorgan: 11 v Staffordshire at Stoke, 1911.
BB for Glamorgan: 1-30 v Staffordshire at Stoke, 1911.

He was the son of E.U.David and played for Cardiff and St Fagan's. He saw active service with the RFA during World War One and was awarded the Military Cross for single-handedly extinguishing an ammunition dump which had been accidently set alight.

DAVID, Arthur Cecil Griffith

RHB, WK.
Born: Narberth, 29 November 1888.
Died: Hove, 8 May 1952.
Education: Repton.
Career: 1 match in 1913 against Monmouthshire at Newport scoring 3 and 0.
Arthur David played for Cardiff.

DAVID, Edmund Ussher

RHB.
Born: St Fagan's, 24 April 1860.
Died: Nottage, 26 July 1942.
Education: Cheltenham College.
Glamorgan debut: 1889 v Warwickshire at Cardiff Arms Park (captaining Glamorgan's first ever team).
Career: 32 matches 1889-1900.
HS for Glamorgan: 85 v Monmouthshire at Newport, 1896.
BB for Glamorgan: 4-48 v Monmouthshire at Newport, 1896.

He was the son of William David, the rector of St Fagan's and brother of Arthur David, the chaplain of Dulwich College and archdeacon of Brisbane. E.U. played for St Fagan's, Fairwater, Cardiff and the South Wales CC and through his work as a land agent for the Margam Estate, he helped found Margam. He served on the Glamorgan committee between 1888 and 1907 and also was a member of the Port Talbot town council. David was president of the Land Agents Society in 1931.

DAVID, Rodney Felix Armine

RHB.
Born: Cardiff, 19 June 1907.
Died: Warbleton, Sussex, 2 July 1969.
Education: Wellington.
Glamorgan debut: 1925 v Leveson Gower's XI at Swansea.
Career: 1 match in 1925 and 2 in 1929.
HS for Glamorgan: 17 v Leveson Gower's XI at Swansea, 1925.

David was in the Wellington XI from 1923 until 1925, before pursuing a military career, where he rose to the rank of major. He played club cricket for Margam.

DAVIES, Charles Bernard

RHB; WK.
Born: Cardiff, 5 June 1894.
Killed in action, 9 June 1916.
Education: Cowbridge School and Llandovery College.
Career: 1 match in 1913 against Webb's XI at Cardiff Arms Park scoring 1 in his only innings.

C.B.Davies was in the Llandovery XI between 1910 and 1913 and was also a talented schoolboy rugby player. He played as a three-quarter for Swansea and Cardiff RFC, whilst his brother Ewan Davies won two Welsh caps in 1912. C.B.Davies won a place at Cambridge University for 1914-15, but opted to join up and serve with the Royal Dublin Fusiliers. On 8 June 1916 he was reported as 'wounded and a prisoner of the Prussian Guards'. He was subsequently reported to have died during captivity and buried in a German war cemetery which was later destroyed by bombing. He played club cricket for St Fagan's.

DAVIES, David ('Dai')

RHB; RM/OB.
Born: Llanelli, 26 August 1896.
Died: Llanelli, 16 July 1976.
Education: Pentip School, Sandy.
Glamorgan debut: 1923 v Nottinghamshire at Trent Bridge.
Career: 411 matches 1923-39; Benefit 1935 (£689); Players 1928.
HS for Glamorgan: 216 v Somerset at Newport, 1939
1,000 runs (7); 1,213 (32.78) 1928 best.
BB for Glamorgan: 6-50 v Essex at Westcliff, 1936.
Full first-class record: 15,390 runs (24.27); 16 centuries; 275 wickets (35.02); 195 catches.

Dai Davies was Glamorgan's first home-bred professional cricketer to make an impact at first-

class level and became one of the leading all-rounders in county cricket during the 1920s and 1930s. He initially played for Llanelli and worked at the town's steelworks, but in 1923 he was drafted into the Glamorgan side after a series of impressive performances for Carmarthenshire. His second appearance in 1923 came after a double nightshift

at the steelworks and he had to be woken up and driven to St Helen's for the match with Northants. In the next 17 seasons, Davies scored over 15,000 runs and took 271 wickets with his medium paced bowling and off-spin. Davies was also a good fielder, excelling in his early days as a cover point and was described by Jack Hobbs as the finest cover fielder he had ever seen.

In 1928 Davies scored three consecutive hundreds and won selection at the end of the season for the Players against the Gentlemen, whilst in 1932 he took part in a partnership of 220 for the third wicket with Maurice Turnbull at the Arms Park as the Nottinghamshire bowlers experimented with 'Bodyline'. In 1939 he registered a double-hundred at Newport in an ill-tempered game with Somerset. Glamorgan were enraged by the visitors' slow play so Turnbull told his batsmen to stay out in the middle for the rest of the game and Davies responded with a career-best 216.

Davies retired at the end of 1939 and despite coming out of retirement in Glamorgan's wartime friendlies, he opted to become an umpire after the war. His patriotic feelings towards Glamorgan were undimmed by his new post and were in evidence in 1948 when the Welsh county secured the championship title. As luck would have it, Davies was standing in the match at Bournemouth when Glamorgan won the title and when the last Hampshire wicket fell, Davies said: "That's out and we've won the championship."

Davies remained on the first-class list until 1961 and during that time he became one of the country's leading umpires, standing in 23 Tests between 1947 and 1958. Sadly, he was crippled with arthritis in his later years, but he was able to collaborate with his son-in-law John Edwards in the production of his memoirs called 'Dai Davies - Not Out 78' published in 1975.

DAVIES, David Aubrey

RHB; LB.
Born: Swansea, 11 July 1915.
Glamorgan debut: 1934 v Leicestershire at Hinckley.
Career: 46 matches 1934-38.

HS for Glamorgan: 55 v Surrey at The Oval, 1937.
BB for Glamorgan: 3-63 v Warwickshire at Edgbaston, 1938.

Aubrey Davies played for Swansea and also appeared for both Glamorgan II and Devon in the Minor County championship.

DAVIES, D.E.

Batsman.
Career: 1 match in 1892 v MCC at Cardiff Arms Park scoring 6 in his only innings.

Davies was a batsman with Cardiff.

DAVIES, David Emrys

LHB; SLA.
Born: Sandy, Carmarthenshire, 27 June 1904.
Died: Llanelli, 10 November 1975.
Glamorgan debut: 1924 v Gloucestershire at Cardiff Arms Park.
Career: 612 matches 1924-54; Cap 1928; South of England 1950; Benefit 1938 (£688); Testimonial 1947 (£1,800); Wales 1926-29; Combined Services 1946.
HS for Glamorgan: 287* v Gloucestershire at Newport, 1939 (county record)
1,000 runs (16); 1,954 runs (39.87) 1937 best.
BB for Glamorgan: 6-24 v Leicestershire at Newport, 1935.
100 wickets (2); 101 wickets (22.41) 1937 best. The double: 1935 and 1937.
Full first-class record: 26,566 runs (27.87); 32 centuries; 903 wickets (29.26); 217 catches.

Emrys Davies had a career with Glamorgan spanning 30 years during which time he paid yeoman service to the club and established a host of records. In all, he scored 26,102 runs and took 885 wickets for Glamorgan, yet Emrys had a quiet start to his career and despite winning his cap in 1928, he only established a regular place in the team during the 1930s. There were some calls for the batsman and left arm spinner to be released, but he repaid the faith Turnbull and Clay had in him by scoring a maiden century against Essex at the Arms Park in 1932. That year was a turning point in his career as he moved up to open the batting and started a partnership with Arnold Dyson that was to last until 1947.

The pair became one of the most consistent on the county circuit and in 1937 created a new county record of 274 against Leicestershire at Leicester. This was not the highest partnership in which Davies was involved as in 1948 he added 313 for the third wicket with Willie Jones at Brentwood. Davies made 215, which was one of two double hundreds the pugnacious batsman recorded during his career. The other was an unbeaten 287 against Gloucestershire at Newport in 1939. He batted for 7½ hours and may well have become the first Glamorgan batsman to score a triple hundred if Gloucestershire had not placed all their fielders on the boundary towards the end of his marathon vigil.

Davies also developed his bowling during the 1930s and in 1935 he became the first Glamorgan player to achieve the double, taking his 100th wicket in the final match of the season at Worcester. Davies went one stage further in 1937 by scoring 1,954 runs and taking 101 wickets and during the game with Leicestershire he took a hat-trick and scored a century. By the end of the 1930s, Davies was amongst the top batsmen and spin bowlers in the country and he won selection on the 1939-40 MCC tour to India. It seemed at long last he would gain recognition at the highest level, but the tour was cancelled due to the outbreak of war.

Davies played until he was 50 years old and despite a few grey hairs, he still remained nimble on his feet and the 'Rock of Glamorgan' was quick to dance down the wicket and drive the bowlers. His career came to an abrupt end in 1954 when playing Northamptonshire at Peterborough, as he found he could not pick up the fast bowling of Frank Tyson. He followed Dai Davies into

umpiring and stood in nine Tests between 1956 and 1959. Ill health forced him to resign from umpiring in 1960 and between 1961 and 1970 Davies coached at Llandovery College. In his early days he had played for Llanelli Steelworks, before joining Llanelli and in 1932 his brother Gwynfor also appeared for Glamorgan. Emrys' son Peter Davies won a Rugby Blue at Cambridge and captained Llanelli, as well as playing for and captaining Glamorgan II in the 1950s.

DAVIES, David Roy
RHB.
Born: Llanelli, 12 August 1928.
Education: Llanelli Grammar, Llandrindod Wells Grammar and Oswestery High School and Cardiff University.
Career: 1 match in 1950 against Somerset at Weston-super-Mare scoring 7 in his only innings.

Roy Davies was the brother of Haydn Davies. He played for St Fagan's from 1948 until 1956 before moving to Manchester and playing for Crosfields. He was an industrial chemist and fuel technologist, working for Unilever. Haydn Davies was also his legal father, as he was adopted by him when their parents died in World War Two. Roy also represented Wales at squash.

DAVIES, Gwynfor
RHB; RM.
Born: Sandy, Carmarthenshire, 12 August 1908.
Died: Llanelli, 10 March 1972.
Glamorgan debut: 1932 v Lancashire at Blackburn.
Career: 7 matches in 1932.
HS for Glamorgan: 44 v Surrey at Swansea, 1932.
BB for Glamorgan: 2-18 v Surrey at Swansea, 1932.

Gwyn was the younger brother of Emrys Davies and played for Glamorgan II in the Minor County championship in 1936 and 1937.

DAVIES, Gwynfor
RHB; RM.
Born: Cardiff, 10 June 1919.
Education: Cathays High School, Cardiff.
Glamorgan debut: 1947 v Lancashire at Cardiff Arms Park.
Career: 2 matches, 1 each in both 1947 and 1948.
HS for Glamorgan: 7 v Lancashire at Newport, 1948.

Gwyn Davies played for Cardiff.

DAVIES, Haydn George
RHB; WK.
Born: Llanelli, 23 April 1912.
Education: Llanelli Grammar School and Aberyst-

wyth University.
Glamorgan debut: 1935 v Sussex at Hastings.
Career: 423 matches 1935-38; Cap 1938; Benefit 1951 (£4,500); MCC 1947-48; The Rest 1946.
HS for Glamorgan: 80 v South Africa at Cardiff Arms Park, 1951.
BB for Glamorgan: 1-20 v Nottinghamshire at Trent Bridge, 1951.
Full first-class record: 6,613 runs (13.09); 1 wicket; 585 catches and 204 stumpings.

He was one of the finest wicketkeepers to represent Glamorgan and was amongst the best never to play for England. He appeared in the 1946 Test Trial, but was unlucky to be playing at the same time as Kent's Godfrey Evans and had his career interupted by World War Two. Haydn Davies first played for Llanelli as a batsman and failed to win a place behind the stumps. He moved to Morewoods where his neat wicketkeeping attracted the attention of the county's talent scouts.

Davies made his debut in 1935 and after some impressive performances in Minor County games, he won a regular place in the first team from 1939. Indeed, between 1947 and 1957 Davies did not miss a championship match. He also led the side during this time when Wooller was injured or unavailable,

talented squash player and after his retirement from county cricket, became the professional at Edinburgh Squash and Tennis club. He became their secretary in 1964 and later returned to South Wales to run a public house in Pembrokeshire. In his younger days Davies had also been a talented rugby player and won two Welsh Schoolboy caps in 1931. His brother Roy Davies made one appearance for Glamorgan in 1950, whilst his nephew Andrew Davies won a Blue at Cambridge in 1984 and also had trials with Glamorgan II.

DAVIES, Hugh Daniel

RHB; RM.
Born: Pembrey, 23 July 1932.
Education: Llanelli Boys Grammar School and Cardiff College of Education.

before retiring in 1958 with a career total of 581 catches and 203 stumpings. He was a technically correct lower order batsman who occasionally acted as emergency opener. He could also be a ferocious hitter and hit a career-best 80 in his Benefit Match with South Africa in 1951.

Davies was affectionately known as 'Panda' because of his heavy build and shambling walk, but he was lightening quick and agile behind the stumps and frequently made nonchalant stumpings as opposing batsmen misread the spin of Clay or McConnon. His vociferous appealing and penchant for hitting huge sixes made him a popular figure with Glamorgan supporters. Davies was also a

Glamorgan debut: 1955 v Gloucestershire at Swansea.
Career: 52 matches 1955-60.
HS for Glamorgan: 28 v Essex at Westcliff, 1958.
BB for Glamorgan: 6-85 v Yorkshire at Sheffield, 1957.

Hugh Davies played club cricket for Llanelli, Neath, Barry and the Steel Company of Wales. He joined

Glamorgan in 1953 after National Service with the RAF. He was also a schoolboy rugby international, but his cricket career was disrupted by a knee injury and he played on a part-time basis from 1957 whilst training to be a teacher. In 1960 he became a PE teacher and helped coach young players at Glamorgan's indoor school. Since 1982 he has been senior PE advisor for Mid Glamorgan.

DAVIES, John Anthony
RHB; LB.
Born: Pontypridd, 3 February 1926.
Education: Pontypridd County Boy School.
Career: 1 match in 1952 against Worcestershire at Cardiff Arms Park scoring 11 and 0.

John Davies played club cricket for Pontypridd, Cambridge, BAOR, Ludlow and the XL club. He also played for Herefordshire and worked as a bank manager with Midland Bank, and has recently appeared for Wales over 50s.

DAVIES, Mark
RHB; SLA.
Born: Neath, 18 April 1969.
Education: Cwrt Sart Comprehensive and Neath Tertiary College.
Career: 1 match in 1990 against Oxford University at Oxford, scoring 5* and taking 0-16.
Mark Davies was on the MCC groundstaff and

showed promise with Metal Box, Briton Ferry Town and Glamorgan Colts. He made his second team debut in 1986, but despite being a consistent wicket taker, his first team chances were limited to one game in 1990. Davies finished top of the second eleven averages in 1991, but was released from the staff at the end of the season and joined Gloucestershire for 1992. He has also played Minor County cricket for Wales.

DAVIES, Mark Nicholas
LHB; OB.
Born: Bridgend, 28 December 1959.
Education: Archbishop McGrath Comprehensive and Bridgend College of Technology.
Glamorgan debut: 1982 v Oxford University at Swansea.
Career: 2 matches in 1982, scoring 0 in his only innings against Oxford University.
Davies joined the Glamorgan staff in 1978 after

playing for Welsh Schools, but despite being a prolific run scorer in second team games, he only made two first-class appearances. He played club cricket for Maesteg Celtic.

DAVIES, Morean Kimsley

LHB; WK.
Born: Clydach, 13 October 1954.
Education: Cwmtawe Comprehensive School, Pontardawe.
Glamorgan debut: 1975 v Cambridge University at Swansea.
Career: 2 matches, 1 each in both 1975 and 1976.
HS for Glamorgan: 12 v Cambridge University at Swansea, 1975.

Kim Davies played for Clydach and was Eifion Jones' understudy in the 1970s. He also played rugby for Aberavon.

DAVIES, Terry

RHB; WK.
Born: St Albans, 25 October 1960.
Education: Townsend Secondary School, St Albans.
Glamorgan debut: 1979 v Sri Lanka at Swansea.
Career: 100 appearances 1979-86.

HS for Glamorgan: 75 v Middlesex at Sophia Gardens, Cardiff, 1985.

Davies was on the MCC groundstaff in 1977 and 1978, before joining Glamorgan as understudy to Eifion Jones. He made his debut in 1979 and held a regular place from 1984 when Jones retired. During his career, Davies played regularly in grade cricket in Sydney and he emigrated to Australia

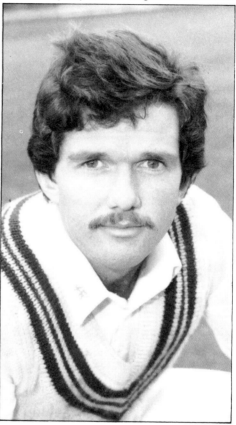

at the end of the 1986 season and has recently become a state selector with New South Wales. Davies was also a talented schoolboy footballer and played for Hertfordshire Under-16 and Watford Youth, besides having trials with West Ham, Tottenham Hotspur and Luton Town.

DAVIES, Thomas Clive

RHB; SLA.
Born: Pontrhydyfen, 7 November 1951.
Glamorgan debut: 1971 v Leicestershire at Sophia Gardens, Cardiff.
Career: 7 matches 1971-72.

HS for Glamorgan: 5 v Yorkshire at Swansea, 1971.
BB for Glamorgan: 3-22 v Leicestershire at Sophia Gardens, Cardiff, 1971.

Clive Davies was on the MCC groundstaff between 1969 and 1970 and played with some success for the second eleven between 1969 and 1972, but failed to make an impression at first team level.

DAVIES, William Arthur
Bowler.
Born: 1870.
Died: Margam, Port Talbot, 1 March 1960.
Education: Independent College, Taunton.
Glamorgan debut: 1893 v Herefordshire at Hereford.
Career: 3 matches in 1893.
BB for Glamorgan: 6-11 v Herefordshire at Hereford, 1893.

Arthur Davies played for Taibach and Aberavon and served on the Glamorgan committee between 1924 and 1926. He failed to score a run in his three innings' for Glamorgan.

DAVIES, William David Edward
RHB; LB.
Born: Briton Ferry, 28 June 1906.
Died: Briton Ferry, 1 October 1971.
Glamorgan debut: 1932 v Leicestershire at Cowbridge.
Career: 7 matches 1932-35.
HS for Glamorgan: 32 v Gloucestershire at Swansea, 1932.

William Davies played for Briton Ferry Town and also appeared for Glamorgan in Minor County games in 1937. He also played in wartime friendlies in 1943 for the Welsh county.

DAVIES, William George
RHB; RM.
Born: Barry, 3 July 1936.
Education: Barry Boys' School.
Glamorgan debut: 1954 v Warwickshire at Edgbaston.
Career: 32 matches 1954-60.
HS for Glamorgan: 64 v Somerset at Bath, 1960.
BB for Glamorgan: 2-23 v Warwickshire at Edgbaston, 1960.

Billy Davies played club cricket for Gorseinon, Maesteg Celtic, Clydach, Pontardawe, Hills Plymouth and Barry. His county career was interrupted by National Service in Germany and he failed to establish a regular place afterwards. He initially played as an opening batsman, but later developed into a medium pace bowler. He took a wicket with

his first ball in county cricket for Glamorgan at The Oval in 1958. Davies retired at the end of the 1960 season to take up a job in insurance with Refuge Assurance. He continued to play for Hills Plymouth and Barry, and in 1972 captained Wales.

DAVIES, William Henry
RHB; RM.
Born: Briton Ferry, 7 August 1901.

Glamorgan debut: 1922 v Leicestershire at Cardiff Arms Park.
Career: 5 matches 1922-27.
HS for Glamorgan: 8* v Nottinghamshire at Trent Bridge, 1924.
BB for Glamorgan: 2-35 v Leicestershire at Cardiff Arms Park, 1927.

Davies was a professional with Cardiff and Briton Ferry Steel during the 1920s.

DAVIS, Bryan Allan

RHB; LB.
Born: Belmont, Port of Spain, Trinidad, 2 May 1940.
Education: St Mary's College, Port of Spain.
Glamorgan debut: 1968 v Cambridge University at Colwyn Bay.
Career: 60 matches 1968-70; Cap 1969; Trinidad 1959-60 to 1970-71; West Indies 1964-65 (4 Tests).

HS for Glamorgan: 103 v Surrey at The Oval, 1969.
1,000 runs (2); 1,532 (31.26) 1970 best.
BB for Glamorgan: 1-2 v Trinidad at Port of Spain, 1969-70.

Full first-class record: 6,231 runs (34.81); 5 centuries; 9 wickets (48.22); 127 catches.

Bryan Davis made his debut in 1959-60 for Trinidad and soon established himself as a sound opening batsman. In 1964-65 he won four Test caps for the West Indies against Australia and on his debut added 116 and 91 for the first wicket with Conrad Hunte. He also toured India and Ceylon in 1966-67 with the West Indies, but failed to win any more Test caps. Whilst on tour, he took a career-best 4-79 with his leg breaks against the Indian Board Presidents XI at Nagpur and also that season scored 188* for North Trinidad against South Trinidad at Port of Spain. He joined Glamorgan in 1968 and established himself as a reliable top order batsman and slip fielder during the next two seasons. However, his family failed to settle in South Wales and returned to the West Indies. He wanted to continue playing for Glamorgan, but failed to find a job in Trinidad which would allow him to play county cricket during the summer and so reluctantly he retired. He was the brother of Charlie Davis of the West Indies and recently became a member of the West Indies Cricket Board.

DAVIS, Brian Henry Stevens (later Stevens-Davis)

RHB; RM.
Born: Beaconsfield, 16 January 1909.
Died: Docking, Norfolk, 2 February 1977.
Education: Lancing.
Career: 1 match in 1938 against Sir Julian Cahn's XI at West Bridgford, Nottingham scoring 23 in his only innings and taking 0-23.

Brian Davis was in the Lancing XI in 1926 before playing club cricket with Beaconsfield and making his Minor County debut for Buckinghamshire in 1928. He appeared for them until his job as a petroleum technologist took him to South Wales in 1938. He played for Cardiff and made his Glamorgan debut in the two-day friendly with Sir Julian Cahn's XI.

DAVIS, Francis John

RHB; SLA.
Born: Cardiff, 23 March 1939.
Education: Blundell's School and St John's, Oxford.
Glamorgan debut: 1959 v India at Swansea.
Career: 14 matches 1959-67.
HS for Glamorgan: 28* v Kent at Gravesend, 1966.
BB for Glamorgan: 5-72 v Warwickshire at Edgbaston, 1966.
Full first-class record: 552 runs (16.23); 52 wickets (32.57); 17 catches.

John Davis was in the Blundell's XI in the late 1950s and played for Cardiff, before making one appearance for Glamorgan in 1959. He went up to Oxford in 1963 where he was a Blue and recorded career-best performances of 63 against Northants at The Parks, plus 5-67 in the Varsity match at Lord's. He also took 10-126 in the friendly with the Free Foresters. Davis joined the Glamorgan staff and played occasionally between 1963 and 1967 before going into teaching. He is currently master i/c of cricket at Berkhamsted School, but plays regularly for the Old Blundellians and captain's their XI in the Cricketer Cup. He is the older brother of R.C.Davis.

DAVIS, John Darelan David

Batsman.
Born: Cardiff, March 1879.
Died: Neath, 27 November 1950.
Glamorgan debut: 1909 v Carmarthenshire at Swansea.
Career: 3 matches, 1 each in 1909, 1910 and 1911.

HS for Glamorgan: 27 v Buckinghamshire at Neath, 1911.

'JDD' was a leading figure with Neath, fulfilling the roles of captain and administrator during an association from 1905 until 1950 with the Gnoll

Park Club. He also served on the Glamorgan committee from 1907 until 1926. Davis was an engineer by profession and acted as secretary of the Welsh Engineers' Association.

DAVIS, Roger Clive
RHB; OB.
Born: Cardiff, 1 January 1946.
Education: Blundell's School.

Glamorgan debut: 1964 v Kent at Sophia Gardens, Cardiff.
Career: 213 matches between 1964 and 1976; Cap 1969; England Under-25 XI v England 1971.

HS for Glamorgan: 134 v Worcestershire at Sophia Gardens, Cardiff, 1971.

1,000 runs (1); 1,243 (31.07) 1975 best.

BB for Glamorgan: 6-62 v Gloucestershire at Cheltenham, 1970.

Full first-class record: 7,367 runs (21.60); 5 centuries; 241 wickets (32.33); 208 catches.

Roger Davis followed his elder brother John into the Blundell's XI in the early 1960s, before joining the county staff as a batsman and off-spinner. He was a member of the Glamorgan XI which won the second team championship in 1965, before securing a first team place as a sound and cool headed middle-order batsman. Roger later moved up to open the batting with Alan Jones and developed into an accurate off-spinner. He was also a fearless and brilliant short-leg and his close catching was a key factor in Glamorgan's championship success in 1969. It was also a position where he suffered a near fatal accident in 1971, when struck on the side of the head by Warwickshire's Neal Abberley. Davis collapsed and went into convulsions, but was given the kiss of life by a doctor who ran on to the field when Davis stopped breathing. He made a full recovery and regained his place in the side, as well as touring Zambia with Gloucestershire during the winter. Davis had his best ever season in 1975, but lost form in 1976 and it was a surprise when the committee opted not to retain him. During his career, Davis played for Llanelli, Briton Ferry Town, Bridgend, the Old Blundellians and Cardiff, for whom he served as captain and chairman. He has worked for an insurance company and estate agents in Cardiff and currently commentates on Glamorgan cricket for BBC Wales TV.

DAVIS, Winston Walter

RHB; RFM.

Born: Sion Hill, Kingstown, St Vincent, 18 September 1958.

Education: Emmanuel High School, St Vincent.

Glamorgan debut: 1982 v Pakistan at Swansea.

Career: 45 matches 1982-84; Windward Islands 1979-80; Wellington 1990-91; Combined Islands 1979-80 to 1980-81; West Indies 1983-87 (15 Caps); Northamptonshire 1987-89; Tasmania 1985-86.

HS for Glamorgan: 50 v Nottinghamshire at Trent Bridge, 1984.

BB for Glamorgan: 7-70 v Nottinghamshire at Ebbw Vale, 1983.

Full first-class record: 2,332 runs (14.21); 607 wickets (28.39); 57 catches.

Winston Davis played for West Indies Young Cricketers against Young England in 1976 and toured England in 1978. He made his first-class debut for the Windward Islands in 1980 before playing League cricket in north-east England for Sunderland and appearing for Durham against Scotland in 1980. He toured Zimbabwe with the West Indies 'B' team in 1981 and joined Glamorgan in 1982 following a back injury to Ezra Moseley. In 1983 he made his Test debut against India and subsequently won 15 caps, plus 35 one-day internationals including a performance of 7-51 against Australia at Headingley in the 1983 World Cup. He also toured India in 1983 and 1987-88, as well as Australia in 1984-85. Davis was summonded as a replacement to the West Indies party during their 1984 England tour and scored a career-best 77 in the Old Trafford Test. During his career with Glamorgan, Davis was plagued by run-up and no-ball problems and was released at the end of 1984 when the committee opted instead for the batting prowess of Javed Miandad. He played for Tasmania in 1985-86, before returning to county cricket with Northamptonshire, for whom he took a career-best 7-52 against Sussex at Northampton in 1988. He captained the Windward Islands in 1988 and has also played in domestic cricket in New Zealand for Wellington.

DENNIS, Simon John

RHB; LFM.

Born: Scarborough, 18 October 1960.

Education: Scarborough College.

Glamorgan debut: 1989 v Gloucestershire at Sophia Gardens, Cardiff.

Career: 32 matches 1989-91; Yorkshire 1980-88 (72 matches, Cap 1983); Orange Free State 1982-83.

HS for Glamorgan: 38 v Derbyshire at Derby, 1989.

BB for Glamorgan: 5-76 v Leicestershire at Sophia Gardens, Cardiff, 1990.

Full first record: 669 runs (9.42); 254 wickets (33.17); 26 catches.

Simon Dennis toured India with England Schools in 1978-79 and played for Young England against Australia in 1980. He made his county debut for Yorkshire in 1980 and won his cap in 1983 after several useful performances in one-day cricket and helping Yorkshire secure the Sunday League title. Dennis scored a career-best 53* against Nottinghamshire at Trent Bridge in 1984 and took 5-35 against Somerset at Sheffield in 1981, but he failed to gain a regular place in the Championship side and was released in 1988. He joined Glamorgan the following season, but once again was in and out of the team owing to loss of form and niggling injuries. He played for Orange Free State in 1982-83 and went on the MCC tours to North America in 1982 and Argentina in 1990. Dennis played club cricket for Scarborough for whom he

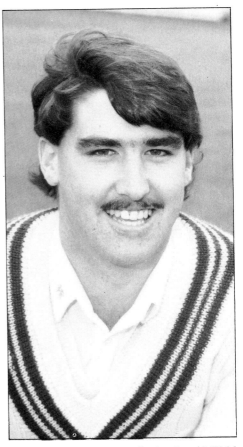

has also been assistant groundsman. He is the nephew of Yorkshire's Frank Dennis and the late Sir Len Hutton and is a cousin of Richard Hutton. He currently plays in the Staffordshire Leagues and retired at the end of the 1991 season to take up a career in computing.

DERRICK, John
RHB; RM.
Born: Cwmamman, 15 January 1963.
Education: Blaengwawr Comprehensive School.
Glamorgan debut: 1983 v Yorkshire at Middlesbrough.
Career: 95 matches 1983-91; Cap 1988; Northern Districts 1986-87.
HS for Glamorgan: 78* v Derbyshire at Abergavenny, 1986.
BB for Glamorgan: 6-54 v Leicestershire at Leicester, 1988.

John Derrick was an outstanding bowler with Welsh Schools and was attached to the MCC groundstaff between 1980 and 1982 where he developed his batting. He proved to be a useful 'bits and pieces' player in one-day cricket and won his county cap in 1988 after several good bowling performances in limited overs games. He played club cricket for Maesteg Celtic and Pontardulais and also represented Bay of Plenty in New Zealand, where he appeared for Northern Districts in 1986-87. However, he struggled with a knee injury from 1989 onwards and was released from the staff at the end of the 1991 season.

DEVEREUX, Louis Norman
RHB; OB.
Born: Heavitree, Exeter, 20 October 1931.
Glamorgan debut: 1956 v Kent at Canterbury.
Career: 106 matches between 1956 and 1960; Cap 1956; Middlesex 1949 (2 matches); Worcestershire

1950-55 (79 matches); Combined Services 1950-51.
HS for Glamorgan: 108* v Lancashire at Old Trafford, 1957.
1,000 runs (1); 1,039 (22.58) 1957 best.
BB for Glamorgan: 6-29 v Yorkshire at Middlesbrough, 1956.
Full first-class record: 5,560 runs (19.85); 1 century; 178 wickets (35.31); 107 catches.

Louis Devereux joined Glamorgan after spells with Middlesex and Worcestershire. Whilst in South Wales he played for the Gorseinon and Cardiff clubs. He made an early impact as a batsman and occasional off-spinner and was awarded his cap after his first season with the Welsh county. However, he lost form during the following seasons and was released at the end of 1960. He coached in South Africa and now keeps a public house in Aberystwyth. He was also a talented table tennis player and represented England in 1949.

DICKINSON, Harold John
RHB; RM.
Born: Barry, 26 November 1911.

Education: Barry County School.
Glamorgan debut: 1934 v Cambridge University at Cambridge.
Career: 7 matches in 1934-35.
HS for Glamorgan: 14* v Lancashire at Swansea, 1935.
BB for Glamorgan: 3-91 v Cambridge University at Cambridge, 1934.

Harry Dickinson played cricket for Barry and Maesteg and also played rugby for Barry Romilly RFC. He was an apprentice draughtsman with the GWR and after retiring took up a post in London.

DONNELLY, Charles W.
RFM.
Career: 1 match in 1890 against the MCC at Swansea scoring 0 and 0* and taking 1-13.
Donnelly was the professional with the Plymouth Works Club in Merthyr.

DONOVAN, John
Batsman.
Born: Cardiff, December 1859.
Died: Penarth, 20 August 1921.
Glamorgan debut: 1892 v Wiltshire at Swindon.
Career: 9 matches 1892-95.
HS for Glamorgan: 98* v Monmouthshire at Newport, 1892.

'Johnny' Donovan was the professional with the Cardiff club between 1883 and 1895. He also played for the Taff Vale club and the South Wales CC, in addition to coaching the Tynant club at Garth in 1894 and 1895. After retiring from cricket he worked as a rigger at Penarth Docks.

DONOVAN, Michael
Batsman.
Education: University College, Cardiff.
Glamorgan debut: 1891 v Gloucestershire at Cardiff Arms Park.
Career: 4 matches in 1891.
HS for Glamorgan: 2 v Gloucestershire at Bristol, 1891.

Michael Donovan played for Neath and the South Wales CC.

DOWNEY, John Edgar
All-rounder.
Career: 1 match in 1891 against Devon at Swansea, but he did not bat or bowl.
Downey was the professional with Neath and Llwynypia.

DUCKFIELD, Richard George

RHB; RM.
Born: Maesteg, 2 July 1907.
Died: Bridgend, 30 December 1959.
Glamorgan debut: 1930 v Yorkshire at Sheffield.
Career: 191 matches 1930-38; Players 1934.
HS for Glamorgan: 280* v Surrey at The Oval, 1936
1,000 runs (3); 1,343 (37.30) 1933 best.
Full first-class record: 7,000 runs (26.61); 10 centuries; 27 catches.

Dick Duckfield made his debut in 1930 and won a regular place in the middle order in the mid-1930s. In 1936 he scored an unbeaten 280 at The Oval which at the time was a club record. He hit 39 boundaries during a 5½ hour innings and seemed to have turned the corner. But during the next few years he lost form with the bat and more importantly Duckfield found it increasingly difficult to catch or field a ball. As a result of this problem, he retired at the end of the 1938 season, but reappeared in wartime friendlies in 1944. He also was a centre for Maesteg RFC and played in club cricket for Maesteg Town.

DUDLEY-JONES Robert David Louis

RHB; RM.
Born: Bridgend, 26 May 1952.
Education: Millfield School, Cardiff College of Education.
Glamorgan debut: 1972 v Hampshire at Portsmouth.

Career: 5 matches 1972-73.
HS for Glamorgan: 5 v Worcestershire at Sophia Gardens, Cardiff, 1973.
BB for Glamorgan: 4-31 v Hampshire at Portsmouth, 1972.

Bob Dudley-Jones was on the county staff in the early 1970s, but opted for a career in teaching. He also played rugby for Cardiff RFC.

DUNCAN, Anthony Arthur

RHB.
Born: Cardiff, 10 December 1914.
Education: Rugby School and Oxford University.
Glamorgan debut: 1934 v Gloucestershire at Llanelli.

Career: 2 matches in 1934; Oxford University 1935.
HS for Glamorgan: 15* v Somerset at Swansea, 1934.
Full first-class record: 18 runs (4.50).
Duncan was in the XI at Rugby in 1933 and played for Lord's Schools against The Rest. After leaving Oxford and the Army, he became one of the leading British golfers. He won the Welsh Amateur Championship in 1938, 1948, 1952 and 1954 and represented Wales between 1933 and 1959. He also played in the Walker Cup and against Australia in 1954. His family owned a number of newspaper companies based in Cardiff.

DUNFORD, William B.

Batsman.
Born: 1861.
Died: Pontypridd, September 1936.
Glamorgan debut: 1 match in 1895 against Herefordshire at Hereford scoring 0* in his only innings.
Dunford was a hairdresser and tobacconist and played for Cardiff and Cardiff Commercials.

DUNN, Frederick William Morgan

Batsman.
Born: Llanblethian, 1886.
Died: Gallipoli, 10 August 1915.
Education: Cowbridge Grammar School and University College, Cardiff.
Glamorgan debut: 1911 v Carmarthenshire at Llanelli.
Career: 2 matches in 1911.
HS for Glamorgan: 1 v Staffordshire at Cardiff Arms Park, 1911.

Dunn played for Cowbridge and Llanblethian and was one of the leading schoolboy batsmen in South Wales around the turn of the century. He served as a Lieutenant in the Welch Regiment during World War One, but was killed in action at Gallipoli in mid August. Five days later his older brother also lost his life. Both have no known graves and are commemorated at the Helles Memorial.

DYSON, Arnold Herbert

RHB; RM/occ WK.
Born: Halifax, 10 July 1905.
Died: Goldsborough, Yorkshire, 7 June 1978.
Glamorgan debut: 1926 v Leveson-Gowers XI at Cardiff Arms Park.
Career: 412 matches 1926-48; Cap 1929; Benefit 1939 (£529); Testimonial 1948 (£1,600); Cahn's XI 1938-39.

HS for Glamorgan: 208 v Surrey at The Oval, 1932.
1,000 runs (10); 1,885 (40.97) 1938 best.
BB for Glamorgan: 1-9 v Lancashire at Old Trafford, 1938.
Full first-class record: 17,922 runs (27.15); 24 centuries; 1 wicket; 243 catches and 1 stumping.

Dyson moved to South Wales in the mid-1920s after failing to gain a place in the Yorkshire side. He played for Neath whilst qualifying for Glamorgan and then made 305 consecutive appearances in championship games between 1930 and 1947. During this time he formed a reliable opening partnership initially with fellow Yorkshireman Billy Bates and then with Emrys Davies, with whom he shared 32 partnerships in excess of 100. He was a neat batsman in both style and appearance and on occasions could be a fast scorer, as testified by a century before lunch against Kent in 1937. In his younger days he was a good outfielder and in

later years became a safe catcher at slip. In   coaching in New Zealand and after retiring, coached
1938-39 he played for Sir Julian Cahn's XI whilst   at Oundle School.

EAGLESTONE, James Thomas

LHB.
Born: Paddington, 24 July 1923.
Glamorgan debut: 1948 v Essex at Cardiff Arms Park.
Career: 50 matches 1948-49; Cap 1948; Middlesex 1947 (9 matches).
HS for Glamorgan: 72 v Sussex at Swansea, 1948.
Full first-class record: 1,420 runs (15.77); 23 catches.

Eaglestone joined Glamorgan after failing to secure a place in the Middlesex side and was part of the championship winning side of 1948. He played for the MCC against Surrey at Lord's in 1947, when he scored a career-best 77. Eaglestone retired in 1949 and ran a newsagents business in London.

EDRICH, Brian Robert

LHB; OB.
Born: Cantley, Norfolk, 18 August 1922.
Glamorgan debut: 1954 v Surrey at Pontypridd.
Career: 52 matches 1954-56; Kent 1947-53 (128 matches); Oxfordshire 1966-70; Minor Counties 1967.
HS for Glamorgan: 74 v Leicestershire at Swansea, 1954.
Full first-class record: 5,529 runs (19.96); 4 centuries; 137 wickets (33.18); 130 catches.

Brian Edrich joined Glamorgan after seven seasons with Kent during which time he scored a career-best 193* against Sussex at Tunbridge Wells in 1949

and shared in a record partnership of 161 for the ninth wicket with Frank Ridgway. He also took 7-41 for Kent against Hampshire in 1949, but only bowled eight overs whilst with Glamorgan without taking a wicket and played as a middle-order batsman until 1956 when he became Glamorgan's assistant coach. Whilst in South Wales, Edrich played for Maesteg Town, Maesteg Celtic, Hills Plymouth, Swansea, Llanelli and Briton Ferry Steel. In 1964 he took up a coaching appointment at St Edwards, Oxford and subsequently played for Oxfordshire and the Minor Counties. He is the brother of Bill, Eric and Geoff Edrich and the cousin of John Edrich.

EDWARDS, Aubrey Mansel Edward

RHB; RM.
Born: Penygraig, 4 July 1918.
Career: 1 match in 1947 against Sussex at Hove scoring 0 in his only innings and taking 2-34 and 1-40.

Aubrey Edwards played for Glamorgan II in their Minor County games in 1947 and played club cricket for Cowbridge and Swansea. He subsequently emigrated to Canada after retiring from cricket.

EDWARDS, J.P.

All-rounder.
Glamorgan debut: 1895 v South Wales CC at Swansea.
Career: 3 matches in 1895.
HS for Glamorgan: 4 v South Wales CC at Swansea, 1895.
BB for Glamorgan: 2-35 v South Wales CC at Swansea, 1895.

Edwards played for Bridgend.

EDWARDS, William Armine

Batsman.
Born: Sketty, Swansea, 3 May 1892.
Died: Beersheba, Palestine, 1 November 1917.
Education: Harrow and Trinity Hall, Cambridge.
Glamorgan debut: 1913 v Surrey II at The Oval.
Career: 2 matches in 1913.
HS for Glamorgan: 37 v Surrey II at The Oval, 1913.

Edwards was not in the Harrow XI, but he did play for the school's rugby XV and appeared against Eton in 1909. He subsequently developed a knee injury and played little rugby whilst at Cambridge, where he attended Trinity Hall, but did not take a degree. Edwards played cricket for both Neath and Swansea and served in World War One with the Glamorganshire Yeomanry but died of wounds received whilst in Palestine.

ELDRIDGE, Alfred George

RHB; RM.
Born: Greenwich, 21 November 1863.
Glamorgan debut: 1891 v Gloucestershire at Cardiff Arms Park.
Career: 21 matches 1891-96.
HS for Glamorgan: 32 v Monmouthshire at Swansea, 1894.
BB for Glamorgan: 8-43 v Wiltshire at Swindon, 1894.

Eldridge was the professional attached to the Swansea and Neath clubs. He also held professional engagements with Trowbridge and Accrington and played Minor County cricket for Wiltshire from 1895 until 1898. Eldridge was a useful seam bowler who could make the ball move both ways and in 1896 he clean bowled all ten Monmouthshire batsmen in their match with Wiltshire at Usk. In 1894 he acted as 12th man for the West of England against the East at Portsmouth. He was a house decorator by profession.

ELERS, Charles George Carew

RHB; WK.
Born: Lyme Regis, 2 January 1867.
Died: Torpoint, 11 December 1927.
Glamorgan debut: 1910 v Carmarthenshire at Llanelli.
Career: 7 matches 1910-11; West of England 1910.
HS for Glamorgan: 151 v Carmarthenshire at Swansea, 1910.
Full first-class record: 4 runs (4.00); 5 catches and 1 stumping.

Charles Elers played for Seaton, before moving to South Wales and joining Bridgend. He appeared for Devon and the MCC and was renowned as a fierce hitter. He also served on the Glamorgan committee between 1912 and 1914.

ELLIS, Geoffrey Philip

RHB; RM.
Born: Llandudno, 24 May 1950.
Education: John Bright Grammar School, Llandudno; Cardiff College of Education.
Glamorgan debut: 1970 v Oxford University at Oxford.

Ellis was a leading batsman at The Perse and Trinity Hall. After coming down he began working as an architect in Cambridge before moving to South Wales in the 1890s and working in both Cardiff and Swansea. Ellis played cricket for Cardiff, Mumbles and Swansea, acting as the latter's captain in 1909. He was renowned as a big hitter in club cricket.

EMERY, William

RHB; RM.
Born: Pentrebach, Merthyr Tydfil, June 1897.
Died: Gowerton, December 1962.
Glamorgan debut: 1922 v Lancashire at Old Trafford.
Career: 2 matches in 1922; Wales 1925.
HS for Glamorgan: 5 v Nottinghamshire at Trent Bridge, 1922.
BB for Glamorgan: 1-41 v Nottinghamshire at Trent Bridge, 1922.
Full first-class record: 16 runs (3.20); 6 wickets (41.00).

Emery was attached to the Hills Plymouth club in the early 1920s and between 1923 and 1940 played for the Gowerton Club in the South Wales Leagues.

EVANS, David Gwilym Lloyd

RHB; WK.
Born: Lambeth, 27 July 1933.
Died: Llandyssul, 25 March 1990.
Education: Amman Valley Grammar School.
Glamorgan debut: 1956 v Combined Services at Cardiff Arms Park.
Career: 270 matches 1956-69; Cap 1959; Benefit 1969 (£3,500).
HS for Glamorgan: 46* v Oxford University at Oxford, 1961.

David Evans was born in London but was brought up near Ammanford where he played for the local club and won a place in the Glamorgan side in 1956. He followed in the footsteps of Haydn Davies and continued the high standards his predecessor established. David adopted a quiet and unobtrusive approach behind the stumps and strove endlessly for perfection. His hard work paid off with the award of a county cap in 1959 and during the 1960s Evans established himself in the top group of wicketkeepers in county cricket. His best season was 1963 when he took 89 victims to beat Haydn Davies' county record of dismissals in a season. In 1967-68 he was awarded the Churchill Scholarship and travelled the world studying coaching methods and delivering lectures. He retired after his Benefit in 1969 and took on a coaching post

Career: 75 matches 1970-76.
HS for Glamorgan: 116 v Middlesex at Sophia Gardens, Cardiff, 1974.
BB for Glamorgan: 2-20 v Lancashire at Swansea, 1975.

Ellis was one of the leading schoolboy cricketers in North Wales during the late 1960s and had a short county career after qualifying as a schoolteacher. Ellis has played for many sides in the South Wales Leagues including Swansea, Neath, Skewen, Llanelli and Ammanford and in 1979 he played for Wales in the I.C.C. Trophy. He has appeared for them in the Minor County championship and in 1983 captained Glamorgan II.

ELLIS, Henry Augustus

Batsman.
Born: Cambridge, 20 June 1872.
Died: Bishopston, Swansea, 30 October 1966.
Education: The Perse School, Cambridge and Trinity Hall, Cambridge.
Glamorgan debut: 1904 v Berkshire at Reading.
Career: 4 matches 1904-06.
HS for Glamorgan: 41 v Berkshire at Reading, 1904.

at The Hague. In 1971 he joined the first-class umpires lists and began a distinguished new career, showing the same close attention to detail he had paid in his playing days. He stood in nine Tests between 1981 and 1985 including the famous Headingley Test of 1981. David was also a fluent Welsh speaker and when not standing in games, he helped BBC Wales with their Welsh language broadcasts. However, he suffered with ill health and heart problems and had to stand down from the Test panel. During his career he played for Ammanford, Briton Ferry Steel and St Fagan's.

EVANS, Sir David William

Batsman.
Born: Dowlais, 4 November 1866.
Died: Cardiff, 17 March 1926.
Education: Llandovery School and Jesus College, Oxford.
Career: 1 match in 1891 against Devon at Exeter scoring 2 in his only innings.

Evans played cricket and rugby for Cardiff and captained Cardiff RFC in 1890-91 and 1891-92. He also played rugby for Oxford University and London Welsh, and won five Welsh caps between 1889 and 1891. Evans was one of the top solicitors in the Cardiff area and subsequently acted as legal advisor to King Edward VII, for which he was knighted in 1925. Evans also played in the 1891 Trial match at Cardiff Arms Park against a Colts XI.

EVANS, Gwynn

RHB; RM.
Born: Bala, 13 August 1915.
Education: St Asaph College and Brasenose College, Oxford.

Glamorgan Debut: 1939 v West Indies at Swansea.
Career: 7 matches in 1939; Oxford University 1938-39 (Blue 1939); Leicestershire 1949 (10 matches).
HS for Glamorgan: 36 v Surrey at Swansea, 1939.
BB for Glamorgan: 1-27 v West Indies at Swansea, 1939.
Full first-class reocrd: 824 runs (16.48); 72 wickets (34.13); 19 catches.

Evans won a Blue at Oxford in 1939 for whom he took 6-80 against Leicestershire. He played a few times for Glamorgan before doing his National Service. Evans reappeared for Leicestershire in 1949, winning his county cap and scoring an unbeaten 65 against Gloucestershire at Leicester.

EVANS, Herbert Price

RHB.
Born: Llandaff, 30 August 1894.
Died: Llandough, 19 November 1982.
Glamorgan Debut: 1920 v Monmouthshire at Ebbw Vale.
Career: 3 Minor County matches in 1920, plus one first-class match in 1922 against Worcestershire at Cardiff Arms Park scoring 0 and 9.
HS for Glamorgan: 49 v Monmouthshire at Ebbw Vale, 1920.

Evans played cricket for Cardiff and St Fagan's and was also a professional footballer with Cardiff City and Tranmere Rovers. After an amateur career with Cardiff Corinthians and one Welsh amateur cap in 1922, Evans joined Cardiff City for whom he made 94 appearances as a wing-half. He won six caps for the Welsh professional team but his career was dogged by leg injuries. In March 1924 he broke his left leg and in August 1927 broke his right leg. He joined Tranmere Rovers in 1926, but as a result of the second injury he was forced to retire. Evans was also a useful golfer and boxer and after retiring, worked for the Post Office.

EVANS, John Brian

RHB; RFM.
Born: Clydach, 9 November 1936.
Education: Pentrepoeth Secondary School.
Glamorgan Debut: 1958 v Nottinghamshire at Trent Bridge.
Career: 87 matches 1958-63; Cap 1960; Lincolnshire 1965-71; Minor Counties 1969.
HS for Glamorgan: 62* v Somerset at Weston-super-Mare, 1961.
BB for Glamorgan: 8-42 v Somerset at Cardiff Arms Park, 1961.

'Ginger' Evans played club cricket for Clydach

Briton Ferry Town, Swansea, Dafen and Pontardulais. He was a hostile fast bowler who formed an effective opening bowling partnership with Jeff Jones, but it was an all too brief pairing as Evans was plagued by injury and was forced into retirement from first-class cricket in 1964. He then worked at Velindre Steelworks, before moving to Lincolnshire to take a position as professional with the Ross Group of Grimsby. Evans made his Minor County debut in 1965 and in 1969 played for the Minor Counties against New Zealand. He is currently head groundsman at the Ross Sports Club and regularly umpires in the Lincolnshire Leagues.

EVANS, Talfryn

LHB; SLA.
Born: Sandy, Carmarthenshire, 10 June 1914.

Died: Llanelli, 31 March 1944.
Career: 1 match in 1934 against Kent at Gravesend scoring 0* and 0 and taking 0-25.

Evans had rheumatic fever as a child which prevented him from fully using his right arm. As a result, he concentrated on left-arm spin and his talents as a chinaman and googly bowler led to trials with Gloucestershire and later a place on the Glamorgan staff. He played club cricket for Elba and Llanelli and appeared for Glamorgan II in their Minor County games in 1936 and 1937.

EVANS, William H.

Batsman.
Career: 1 match in 1891 against Gloucestershire at Cardiff Arms Park scoring 2 and 0.

Evans played for the St Paul's club in Cardiff and also appeared for Glamorgan in a trial match in May 1891 against a Colts XX at the Arms Park.

EVANS-BEVAN, Sir David Martyn

Batsman.
Born: Neath, 4 March 1902.
Died: St Peter, Jersey, 9 September 1973.
Education: Uppingham.
Career: 1 match in 1920 against Carmarthenshire at Swansea, scoring 4 in his only innings.

Evans-Bevan's family owned the Vale of Neath and Swansea Valley Breweries and after leaving school, he had an illustrious business career, especially in the financial world where he served as a director of the Phoenix Assurance Company and Barclays Bank from 1938 until 1972. He was a High Sheriff of Breconshire in 1929-30 and Glamorganshire in 1951-52 and was created the First Baronet of Cadoxton-juxta-Neath in 1958. He acted as the Patron of Glamorgan CCC from 1951 until his death in 1973 and was also a borough councillor and Freeman of Neath, as well as being president of the town's rugby club.

EVERY, Trevor

RHB; WK.
Born: Llanelli, 19 October 1909.
Died: Newport, 20 January 1990.
Education: Llanelli Boys School.
Glamorgan debut: 1929 v Yorkshire at Cardiff Arms Park.
Career: 128 matches 1929-34.
HS for Glamorgan: 116 v Worcestershire at Stourbridge, 1932.

Every played club cricket for Gowerton, Maesteg and his native Llanelli, before establishing himself

Education: King Edward VII High School, Johannesburg.

Glamorgan debut: 1980 v Essex at Swansea.

Career: 45 matches 1980-81; Cap 1980; Middlesex 1968-79 (216 matches, Cap 1971, Benefit 1979); Transvaal 'B' 1967-68 to 1976-77; Transvaal 1969-70 to 1977-78; Northern Transvaal 1981-82.

HS for Glamorgan 113* v Hampshire at Bournemouth, 1981.

1,000 runs (2); 1,105 runs (32.50) 1981 best.

BB for Glamorgan: 5-90 v Somerset at Taunton, 1980.

Full first-class record: 13,922 runs (29.37); 12 centuries; 181 wickets (27.54); 277 catches.

as one of the best young wicketkeepers in county cricket. Sadly, he developed eye problems and lost his sight shortly after the start of the 1934 season. He subsequently trained as a stenographer and worked for the RNIB in Cardiff.

FARR, C.

Batsman

Career: 1 match in 1892 against Monmouthshire at Swansea scoring 2 in his only innings.

Farr played for Swansea.

FEATHERSTONE, Norman George

RHB; OB.

Born: Que Que, Rhodesia, 20 August 1949.

Featherstone joined Glamorgan in 1980 after his Benefit Year with Middlesex which raised £30,000. During his 12 seasons with Middlesex he made a career-best 147 against Yorkshire in 1975 at Scarborough and returned career-best bowling figures of 5-32 against Nottinghamshire at Trent Bridge in 1978. He retired from county cricket at the end of the 1981 season and went into business in his native South Africa.

FLETCHER, Edwin V.
Batsman.
Born: Cardiff, July 1867.
Career: 1 match in 1906 against Wiltshire at Trowbridge scoring 0 and 5.
Fletcher played for Cardiff and Cardiff YMCA.

FOSTER, Daren Joseph
RHB; RFM.
Born: Tottenham, 14 March 1966.
Education: Somerset School, Southgate Technical College and Harringay College.
Glamorgan debut: 1991 v Oxford University at Oxford.
Career: 28 matches in 1991; Somerset 1986-89.
HS for Glamorgan: 13* v Derbyshire at Chesterfield, 1991.
BB for Glamorgan: 6-84 v Somerset at Taunton, 1991.
Full first-class record: 161 runs (7.67); 74 wickets (40.86); 7 catches.
Daren Foster joined Glamorgan after a brief career with Somerset and trials with Derbyshire and Gloucestershire. Whilst with Somerset his best figures were 4-46 against Worcestershire at Worcester in 1988 and a career-best 20 against Hampshire at Southampton in 1988.

FRANCIS, David Arthur
RHB; OB.
Born: Clydach, 29 November 1953.

Education: Cwmtawe Comprehensive, Pontardawe.
Glamorgan debut: 1973 v Lancashire at Swansea.
Career: 138 matches 1973-84; Cap 1982.
HS for Glamorgan: 142* v Kent at Canterbury, 1982.
1,000 runs (1); 1,076 (38.42) 1982 best.
Arthur Francis played club cricket for Clydach, Gowerton and Briton Ferry Steel and since 1988 has played in the Minor County championship for Wales. He was on the MCC groundstaff in the early 1970s and began his county career as a middle-order batsman, before moving up to the number-three spot.

FREDERICKS, Roy Clifton
LHB; SLA.
Born: Blairmont, British Guiana, 11 November 1942.
Education: New Amsterdam Technical School, British Guiana.
Glamorgan debut: 1971 v Nottinghamshire at Trent Bridge.
Career: 45 matches 1971-73; Cap 1971; Guyana 1963-64 to 1982-83; West Indies 1968-69 to 1976-77 (59 Caps).
HS for Glamorgan 228* v Northamptonshire at Swansea, 1972.
1,000 runs (2); 1,377 (45.90) 1971 best.
BB for Glamorgan: 3-37 v Northamptonshire at Swansea, 1971.
Full first-class record: 16,384 runs (45.89); 40 centuries; 75 wickets (37.94); 177 catches.
Roy Fredericks was Glamorgan's first overseas Test star from the West Indies, for whom he scored a century off only 71 balls during an innings of 169 against Australia at Perth in 1975-76. Fredericks toured England with the West Indies in 1969, 1973 and 1976 as well as tours to Australia, New Zealand, India, Pakistan and Sri Lanka. His career-best score was 250 for Guyana against Barbados at Bridgetown in 1974-75, whilst his innings of 228* for Glamorgan was achieved during a county record opening partnership of 330 with Alan Jones. Fredericks joined the World Series Cricket team in Australia in 1977-78 and, after retiring, has followed a career in politics in Guyana, where he is currently the Minister for Sport.

FREETHY, Albert Edwin
RHB.
Born: Swansea, 27 April 1885.
Died: Cimla, 1966.
Glamorgan debut: 1908 v Wiltshire at Cardiff Arms Park.

Career: 11 Minor County matches between 1908 and 1920, plus 3 first-class matches in 1921.
HS for Glamorgan: 31 v Worcestershire at Swansea,

1921 and v Somerset at Weston-super-Mare, 1921.
Freethy was a stalwart of Neath and after retiring from cricket and rugby, he became one of the top

Roy Fredericks, Glamorgan's first overseas Test star from the West Indies.

Education: Alexander High School, Tipton; St Peter's, Wolverhampton and Durham University.
Glamorgan debut: 1990 v Oxford University at Oxford.
Career: 41 matches 1990-; Cap 1991; Surrey 1988-89 (13 matches)
HS for Glamorgan: 12 v Warwickshire at Edgbaston, 1990.
BB for Glamorgan: 7-99 v Gloucestershire at Cheltenham, 1991.
Full first-class record: 83 runs (2.86); 143 wickets (35.65); 6 catches.

rugby referees in Britain. In 1925 he sent off Brownlie of New Zealand during their international with England and thereby became the first referee to send off a player in an international in the UK. Freethy also refereed the 1928 Olympic Rugby Final. He later became a leading figure with the WRU and also served on the Glamorgan committee during the 1930s. Freethy died on 17 July 1966.

FROST, Mark
RHB; RFM.
Born: Barking, Essex, 21 October 1962.

Mark Frost graduated to the first-class game via League cricket in the Midlands with Himley, Dudley and Old Hill, university cricket with Durham and Minor County cricket with Staffordshire in 1987. He had trials with several counties including Lancashire, Gloucestershire and Worcestershire, before being offered a contract by Surrey. Despite being their leading seam bowler in second team cricket, he had limited opportunities at The Oval and joined Glamorgan in 1990. He has taken over 50 wickets in both of his seasons with Glamorgan and was awarded his cap in 1991. Frost is a committed Christian and has twice toured India with the Christians in Sport organization.

GABE-JONES, Arthur Royston

RHB; RM.
Born: Clydach Vale, 25 November 1906.
Died: Cardiff, 26 February 1965.
Education: Blundell's.
Career: 1 match in 1922 v Leicestershire at Cardiff
Arms Park scoring 6* in his only innings.

Royston Gabe-Jones holds the record for being the
youngest county cricketer this decade. The
Blundell's schoolboy played when he was only 15
years and 9 months old in the final match of the
1922 season after promising performances for the
Glamorgan Colts and Clydach Vale. He was also
an outstanding fly-half and after being in the
Blundell's XV, he went into business in South Wales
and played for Cardiff RFC.

GAGE, Henry F.

All-rounder.
Glamorgan debut: 1892 v Monmouthshire at
Swansea.
Career: 2 matches 1892-93.
HS for Glamorgan: 32 v Monmouthshire at
Swansea, 1892.
BB for Glamorgan: 2-26 v Monmouthsire at
Swansea, 1892.

Gage was a tobacconist in Swansea and played
cricket and rugby for the town club. Gage also took
5-23 and 3-10 for Glamorgan in the 1892 Trial match
against a Colts XI at Swansea.

GATEHOUSE, Peter Warlow

RHB; LFM.
Born: Caerphilly, 3 May 1936.
Education: Caerphilly Grammar School and
University College, Cardiff.
Glamorgan debut: 1957 v Nottinghamshire at
Llanelli.
Career: 19 matches 1957-62.

HS for Glamorgan: 20 v Derbyshire at Llanelli,
1960.
BB for Glamorgan: 7-94 v Middlesex at Lord's,
1958.

Gatehouse played club cricket for Cardiff and was

their captain during the club's centenary season in 1967. He also played rugby for Caerphilly, but did not pursue a career in sport owing to his studies in pharmacy, for which he was awarded a Ph.D.

GEARY, Frederick William

All-rounder.
Born: Hinckley, 9 December 1887.
Died: Hinckley, 8 January 1980.
Glamorgan debut: 1923 v Surrey at Cardiff Arms Park.
Career: 2 matches in 1923.
HS for Glamorgan: 2 v Surrey at Cardiff Arms Park, 1923.

Geary was a useful club cricketer in the Leicestershire area and whilst with Glamorgan was attached to the Port Talbot club.

GEMMILL, William Neilson

RHB; RM.
Born: Thio, New Caledonia, 14 June 1900.
Died: Canterbury, 18 September 1987.

Gemmill (right) goes out to bat with Abel.

Education: King's, Taunton.
Glamorgan debut: 1920 v Cheshire at Swansea.
Career: 4 Minor County matches in 1920, plus 47 first-class matches 1921-26.
HS for Glamorgan: 77 v Sussex at Hove, 1922.

BB for Glamorgan: 2-18 v Carmarthenshire at Swansea, 1920.

Gemmill played hockey and cricket for Swansea and won eight Welsh hockey caps between 1921 and 1924. He captained Swansea in 1924.

GEOGHEGAN, John P.A.

All-rounder.
Born: St Pancras, London, December 1867.
Died: Swansea, 11 April 1916.
Education: St Charles' College.
Glamorgan debut: 1891 v MCC at Swansea.
Career: 13 matches 1891-1901.
HS for Glamorgan: 82 v Cornwall at Swansea, 1898.
BB for Glamorgan: 4-57 v Monmouthshire at Newport, 1896.

'Jack' Geoghegan was brought up in the London area and played for Notting Hill and St Thomas' Hospital before winning a place in the Middlesex Colts team. He subsequently moved to the North-East and played for Whitehaven, before joining Swansea in 1890 and spending the rest of his life in South Wales.

GIBBS, Reginald Arthur

Batsman.
Born: Cardiff, June 1882.

Died: Cardiff, 28 November 1938.
Education: Queen's College, Taunton.
Glamorgan debut: 1902 v Wiltshire at Trowbridge.
Career: 33 matches 1902-14.
HS for Glamorgan: 95 v Monmouthshire at Newport, 1913.

Reggie Gibbs played rugby and cricket for both Cardiff and Penarth. He won 16 Welsh rugby caps between 1906 and 1911 and also played for the Barbarians. He went on the 1908 Anglo-Welsh tour to Australia and New Zealand, and was talented at billiards. Gibbs served on the Glamorgan committee between 1910 and 1926. His daughter Shelagh is a Welsh international golfer.

GIBSON, Arthur

Batsman and spin bowler.
Glamorgan debut: 1900 v MCC at Cardiff Arms Park.
Career: 57 matches 1900-09; Captain 1908.
HS for Glamorgan: 66 v MCC at Cardiff Arms Park, 1900.
BB for Glamorgan: 1-6 v Berkshire at Reading, 1905.

Arthur Gibson captained Cardiff between 1906-09 and served on the Glamorgan committee from 1904 until 1932, holding the post of secretary from 1923.

GIBSON, William D.

All-rounder.
Glamorgan debut: 1904 v Devon at Swansea.
Career: 1 match in 1904 and 1 in 1914.
HS for Glamorgan: 7* v Devon at Swansea, 1904.
BB for Glamorgan: 2-37 v Monmouthsire at Newport, 1914.

He was the younger brother of Arthur Gibson and played for Cardiff Alpha.

GLOVER, Edward Robert Kenneth

RHB; RFM.
Born: Worcester, 19 July 1911.
Died: Cardiff, 23 March 1967.
Education: Sherborne.
Glamorgan debut: 1932 v India at Cardiff Arms Park.
Career: 47 matches 1932-38.
HS for Glamorgan: 62 v Somerset at Downside, 1934.
BB for Glamorgan: 5-79 v Northamptonshire at Kettering, 1935.

Ted Glover was in the Sherborne XI in 1928 and 1929 and played for the Lord's Schools against the Rest in 1929. He played cricket for Cardiff and rugby for Glamorgan Wanderers. Glover was a sports journalist and married Ever Turnbull, the sister of his close friend Maurice Turnbull. During the late 1940s and early 1950s, Glover helped edit *The South Wales Cricketers' Magazine.*

GOOD, Dennis Cunliffe

RHB; RFM.
Born: Leeds, 29 August 1926.
Education: Denstone School and Sheffield University.
Glamorgan debut: 1947 v South Africa at Cardiff Arms Park.
Career: 3 matches in 1947; Worcestershire 1946 (1 match).
HS for Glamorgan: 21 v Derbyshire at Derby, 1947.
BB for Glamorgan: 2-34 v Derbyshire at Derby, 1947.
Full first-class record: 54 runs (13.50); 8 wickets (37.50); 1 catch.

Dennis Good was in the Denstone XI from 1941 until 1943. Good made one appearance for Worcestershire before joining Glamorgan in 1947. He subsequently played for the RAF and Rawdon and is currently living in Canada.

GREEN, Russell Christopher

RHB; RFM.
Born: St Albans, 30 July 1959.

Education: King Edward's Grammar School, Bury St Edmunds.
Glamorgan debut: 1984 v Worcestershire at Swansea.
Career: 2 matches in 1984.
HS for Glamorgan: 3* v Worcestershire, Swansea, 1984.
BB for Glamorgan: 2-65 v Worcestershire, Swansea, 1984.

Russell Green made his debut for Suffolk in 1982 and was capped the following year after taking 43 wickets at 19.37 apiece. He was on the Glamorgan staff in 1984 before returning to Suffolk. He played for the Minor Counties in the Benson & Hedges Cup from 1987 until 1989 and plays for the Bury St Edmunds club.

GRIFFITHS, Rt Hon LJ William Hugh MC

RHB; RFM.
Born: Marylebone, 26 September 1923.
Education: Charterhouse and St John's College, Cambridge.
Glamorgan debut: 1946 v Kent at Dover.
Career: 8 matches 1946-48; Cambridge University 1946-48 (Blue all three years); Free Foresters 1949.
HS for Glamorgan: 12 v Gloucestershire at Cheltenham, 1947.
BB for Glamorgan: 4-61 v Surrey at Cardiff Arms Park, 1947.

Full first-class record: 137 runs (3.91); 102 wickets (31.43); 7 catches.

The Right Honourable Lord Justice Griffiths was in the Charterhouse XI in 1940 and 1941, before serving in World War Two and being awarded the Military Cross for disarming a tank. After the war he went up to Cambridge where he was a Blue in all three years. During this time he achieved a career-best 6-129 against Lancashire at Fenners in 1946 and 19 in the 1948 Varsity match at Lord's. On coming down, he pursued a legal career and only occasionally played for Glamorgan. He subsequently has become a High Court Judge, Life Peer and Law Lord and gave judgement on the notorious 'Spycatcher' case in the 1980s. Lord Griffiths served as president of the MCC in 1990-91.

GWYNN, William Henry

Batsman and spin bowler.
Born: Swansea, June 1856.
Died: Bridgend, 1 April 1897.
Education: St John's College, Battersea.
Glamorgan debut: 1890 v MCC at Swansea.
Career: 2 matches in 1890.
HS for Glamorgan: 27 v MCC at Swansea, 1890.
BB for Glamorgan: 2-24 v MCC at Swansea, 1890.

Bill Gwynn was brought up in London where he played rugby for the Arrow club. He was a schoolmaster by profession and returned to his birthplace in 1880. He initially played for the Swansea Workingmen's Club and after some fine performances for them he was invited to join Swansea, whom he captained in 1890. He played rugby for Swansea and won five Welsh caps between 1884 and 1885. He served on the Glamorgan committee between 1888 and 1895 and was a good soccer player and referee. His brother David Gwynn also played rugby for Swansea and Wales, before turning professional with Oldham. In 1892 Gwynn became the first paid secretary of the Welsh Rugby Union, but in 1896 he suffered a mental breakdown and died in 1897 when in care.

GWYNNE, David Graham Pugsley

RHB.
Born: Swansea, 8 December 1904.
Died: Swansea, 11 December 1934.
Education: Swansea Grammar School and Llandovery College.
Glamorgan debut: 1922 v Derbyshire at Swansea.
Career: 3 matches 1922-23.
HS for Glamorgan: 12 v Hampshire at Southampton, 1922.

David Gwynne was in the Llandovery XI in 1918, 1919 and 1920 and played for Swansea, whom he captained between 1927 and 1929. He was the son of William Gwynne, who owned a glass importers business based in Swansea. Gwynne also played rugby for Swansea Grammar School and Swansea Uplands RFC.

HACKER, William Stamford

RHB; RM.
Born: Chipping Sodbury, 8 December 1876.
Died: Bristol, 8 December 1925.
Glamorgan debut: 1908 v Wiltshire at Cardiff Arms Park.
Career: 61 Minor County matches between 1908-20 and 21 first-class appearances 1921-23; Gloucestershire 1899-1901 (3 matches); South Wales 1912.
HS for Glamorgan: 64 v Monmouthshire at Cardiff Arms Park, 1909.
BB for Glamorgan: 9-75 v Wiltshire at Marlborough, 1920.
Full first-class record: 222 runs (8.60); 91 wickets (23.18); 8 catches.

Stamford Hacker was a tearaway fast bowler and was invited to play for Gloucestershire after impressing W.G.Grace. He subsequently played for Herefordshire, before joining the Hills Plymouth club and appearing for Glamorgan. Hacker also played for Briton Ferry Town and in 1921 made his first-class debut for Glamorgan at the age of 45, by which time he bowled at gentle medium pace.

HADLEY, Robert John

RHB; LFM.
Born: Neath, 22 October, 1951.
Education: Sandfields Comprehensive School, Port Talbot and St John's College, Cambridge.
Glamorgan debut: 1971 v Leicestershire at Leicester.
Career: 2 matches in 1971; Cambridge University 1971-73 (Blue all three years).
HS for Glamorgan: 4* v Leicestershire at Leicester, 1971.
BB for Glamorgan: 5-32 v Leicestershire at Leicester, 1971.
Full first-class record: 65 runs (3.25); 56 wickets (29.41); 8 catches.

Hadley was in the Cambridge XI for three years during which time he returned career-best figures of 5-31 against Sussex at Fenners in 1972 and the following year scored 17 against Northants at Fenners. Hadley also toured Malaysia and Singapore with an Oxbridge XI in 1972-73. He made two appearances for Glamorgan in August 1971, before concentrating on his medical studies and playing club cricket for Port Talbot and Bridgend.

HAINES, Claude Vincent Godby

RHB.
Born: Bristol, 17 January 1906.
Died: Lower Cwmtwrch, 28 January 1965.
Education: King's Canterbury.
Glamorgan debut: 1933 v Nottinghamshire at Trent Bridge.
Career: 12 matches 1933-34.
HS for Glamorgan: 59 v Sussex at Cardiff Arms Park, 1933.
BB for Glamorgan: 1-15 v Leicestershire at Cardiff Arms Park, 1933.

'Bob' Haines was the son of A.H.Haines of Gloucestershire and played for the Public Schools against The Rest in 1924. He also played for Devon, Kent II and the Gentlemen of Essex and during World War Two played for, as well as acting as match secretary for, the British Empire XI who raised money for the Red Cross. Haines played club cricket for Swansea and acted as their captain in 1950.

HANSFORD, Gordon
Batsman.
Died: Canton, Cardiff, 23 January 1957.
Glamorgan debut: 1920 v Capt J.H.P.Brains XI at Cardiff Arms Park.
Career: 2 matches in 1920.
HS for Glamorgan: 12 v Capt J.H.P.Brain's XI at Cardiff Arms Park, 1920.

Gordon Hansford played for Cardiff Alpha and was a regular tourist with the Glamorgan Nomads.

HARRIS, Alwyn
LHB.
Born: Aberdulais, 31 January 1936.
Education: Cadoxton Comprehensive School.
Glamorgan debut: 1960 v Kent at Blackheath.
Career: 49 matches 1960-64.
HS for Glamorgan: 110 v Warwickshire at Swansea, 1962.
1,000 runs (1); 1,048 (23.81) 1962 best.

Alwyn Harris played club cricket for Ynysygerwn Briton Ferry Steel, Ammanford, Gorseinon, Metal

Box and Llanelli. He joined Glamorgan after his National Service for the Royal Engineers and appeared in the Glamorgan side of the early 1960s. Harris was an opening batsman, but only played one full season during which he passed 1,000 runs. He also hit a century in 1962 against the Pakistan tourists at the Arms Park. After leaving Glamorgan he coached for a season at Christ College, Brecon before joining the Hills Plymouth club in Merthyr. He currently works for a gearbox company in Resolven.

HARRIS, George Joseph
RHB; RM.
Born: Underwood, Notts, 22 January 1904.
Died: Swansea, 28 December 1988.
Career: 1 match in 1932 against Surrey at Swansea scoring 0 in his only innings.

his success on a sound technique and his quick eye and nimble footwork made him one of Glamorgan's finest players of spin bowling, as testified by a brilliant 139 at Llanelli in 1957 against Nottinghamshire's Australian leg spinner Bruce Dooland. He was capped in 1954 after passing 1,000 for the first time and sharing in a match-winning partnership of 219 with Gilbert Parkhouse against Warwickshire. During his career, he took part in 14 century partnerships, including ten for the first wicket and in 1963 he scored Glamorgan's first ever century in one-day cricket hitting a hundred in their Gillette Cup match with Somerset. Hedges was also a gifted rugby player with Pontypridd and Swansea and came close to a Welsh cap by playing in a final Welsh trial. He retired in 1967 and joined Barclays Bank, but he has maintained his links with Glamorgan by coaching at the indoor school in Neath.

HEMP, David Lloyd

LHB; RM.
Born: Bermuda, 8 November 1970.
Education: Olchfa Comprehensive Swansea, Millfield School and West Glamorgan College of Higher Education.
Glamorgan debut: 1991 v Hampshire at Southampton, scoring 8 and 4*.

David Hemp was born in Bermuda but has been a UK resident since 1976. He has been a prodigious batsman in schoolboy cricket scoring four consecutive centuries for Welsh Schools in 1990. He plays for Swansea and Glamorgan Colts and in 1991 scored 258* for Wales against the MCC. He first appeared for Glamorgan in August 1991 in the Sunday League match with Surrey at The Oval.

HENDERSON, Stephen Peter

LHB; RM.
Born: Oxford, 24 September 1958.
Education: Downside, Durham University and Magdalene College, Cambridge.
Glamorgan debut: 1983 v Surrey at Swansea.
Career: 27 matches 1983-85; Worcestershire 1977-81 (24 matches); Cambridge University 1982-83 (Blue both years).
HS for Glamorgan: 135* v Warwickshire at Edgbaston, 1983.
BB for Glamorgan: 2-48 v Surrey at Swansea, 1983.
Full first-class record: 2,611 runs (26.37); 4 centuries; 3 wickets (72.67); 46 catches.

Henderson played for Dudley and Worcestershire before going up to Cambridge where he won a Blue in 1982 and 1983 and scored a career-best 209* against Middlesex at Fenners in 1982. He joined

Glamorgan after coming down and also toured North America and Canada with the MCC. After retiring from first-class cricket, he played for Hertfordshire and the Minor Counties and in 1989 played for MCC against France. He is the son of Derek Henderson who was a Blue in 1950 and Stephen now works in the City of London.

HEVER, Norman George

RHB; RFM.
Born: Marylebone, 17 December 1924.
Died: Oxford, 11 September 1987.

Glamorgan debut: 1948 v Essex at Cardiff Arms Park.
Career: 133 matches 1948-53; Cap 1948; Middlesex 1947 (9 matches).
HS for Glamorgan: 40 v Leicestershire at Leicester, 1950.
BB for Glamorgan: 7-55 v Hampshire at Swansea, 1952.
Full first-class record: 897 runs (9.34); 333 wickets (23.72); 63 catches.

Norman Hever was the son of Kent's H.L.Hever and joined the MCC groundstaff after World War Two. He returned match figures of 8-72 on his Middlesex debut against Hampshire at Lord's 1947, but was released at the end of the season and joined Glamorgan. 'Pete' Hever took 154 wickets in his first two seasons with the Welsh club and his presence strengthened their attack. He was used in short bursts by Wooller allowing Hever to develop into an effective shock bowler, taking 84 wickets at 17 apiece as Glamorgan won the 1948 championship. Hever was rewarded with his county cap and selection in the 1949 Test Trial at Edgbaston. He retired from first-class cricket in 1954, but continued to play club cricket for Ferndale, Clydach and Maesteg Town until the early 1960s. He became Northampton's groundsman in 1962 and won the 'Groundsman of the Year' award in 1964. He remained with Northamptonshire until 1973, when he took up a similar post at Wellingborough School.

HICKEY, Denis Jon

RHB; RFM.
Born: Mooropana, Victoria, 31 December 1964.
Education: Chisholm Institute of Technology.
Glamorgan debut: 1986 v Warwickshire at Edgbaston.
Career: 13 matches in 1986; Victoria 1985-86 to 1989-90; South Australia 1990-91.
HS for Glamorgan: 9* v Kent at Maidstone, 1986.
BB for Glamorgan: 5-57 v Oxford University at Oxford, 1986.
Full first-class record: 168 runs (8.40); 106 wickets (36.49); 8 catches.

Denis Hickey joined the Glamorgan staff in 1986 on an Esso Cricket Scholarship from Australia, primarily to play second team cricket. However, both Javed and Ezra Moseley were injured and Hickey became Glamorgan's overseas player for the majority of the season. He continued to play in Sheffield Shield cricket for Victoria but switched in 1990-91 to South Australia and won a regular place in their side. At the end of the season he was selected in the Australia 'A' party to tour Zimbabwe in 1991.

HICKLEY, Victor Allen

Batsman.
Born: Bridgwater, March 1874.
Died: Taunton, 5 January 1956.
Education: Radley College.
Glamorgan debut: 1894 v MCC at Cardiff Arms Park.
Career: 8 matches 1894-98.
HS for Glamorgan: 62 v Monmouthshire at Newport, 1897.

Hickley was a close acquaintance of the Brain family, who he played alongside for Cardiff and subsequently ran a brewery in Leeds.

HILDYARD, Revd Lyonel D'Arcy

RHB.
Born: Bury, 5 February 1861.
Died: Hull, 22 April 1931.
Education: Somerset County School and Magdalene College, Oxford.
Career: 1 match in 1891 against Gloucestershire at Cardiff Arms Park scoring 0 and 4; Somerset 1882-83 (7 matches); Oxford University 1884-86 (Blue all three years); Lancashire 1884-85 (8 matches).
Full first-class record: 811 runs (17.25); 26 catches.

The much travelled Lyonel Hildyard was a typical example of the amateur gentleman who played for Glamorgan in the 1890s. He made his Somerset debut in 1882, before going up to Oxford in the mid-1880s and becoming a close friend of the Brain family. Together with J.H.Brain, Hildyard played in the Oxford XI which defeated the Australians in 1884 and in 1885 he topped the Oxford averages and hit a career-best 62 against Surrey at The Oval. He was also a first rate cover fielder and safe catcher in the slips and played for his native Lancashire in 1884 and 1885, before becoming ordained into Holy Orders. He kept up his friendship with the Brain family and in 1891 invited down to play for Glamorgan. Between 1894 and 1908 Hildyard was a minor canon of Windsor, before becoming rector of Rowley in East Yorkshire.

HILL, Ernest Edward

Batsman.
Born: Bristol, 1869.
Died: Penylan, Cardiff, 6 December 1931.
Education: Lewisham House, Weston-super-Mare.
Career: 1 match in 1911 against Carmarthenshire at Llanelli scoring 18* in his only innings.

Hill played cricket for Cardiff and Monmouth and also played rugby for Cardiff and Somerset. He was an accountant and auditor by profession.

Born: Plumstead, Kent, 14 October 1897.
Died: Westbourne, Hants, 21 September 1969.
Glamorgan debut: 1926 v Surrey at The Oval, 1926.
Career: 104 matches 1926-31; Wales 1928-29.
HS for Glamorgan: 166 v Hampshire at Southampton, 1929.
Full first-class record: 3474 runs (21.57); 7 centuries; 93 catches and 5 stumpings.

Hills played club cricket for Barry and was a professional footballer with Cardiff City, Swansea Town and Fulham. However, he injured an elbow in 1931 whilst keeping goal and this forced him into retirement. He became an umpire with the Minor Counties in 1936 and was elevated on to the first-class list in 1939. He stood in the fourth Test between England and South Africa in 1947 and remained on the first-class list until 1956. During World War One he served with the Royal Engineers and in December 1918 won the Military Medal for gallantry.

HINWOOD, John William James

RHB; RFM.
Born: Wilton, Wiltshire, 8 April 1894.
Died: Swansea, 14 May 1971.
Glamorgan debut: 1920 v Cheshire at Aigburgh.

Career: 3 Minor County games in 1920, plus one first-class match in 1923 against Northamptonshire at Kettering, scoring 0 in both innings.
HS for Glamorgan: 10 v MCC at Swansea, 1920.
BB for Glamorgan: 3-99 v Cheshire at Aigburgh, 1920.

Hinwood captained Swansea in 1925, 1930 and 1934 and also played for Clydach and Llanelli.

HIRST, Joseph Owen

Middle-order batsman.
Born: Wakefield, June 1867.
Died: Cardiff, 12 March 1948.
Glamorgan debut: 1907 v Monmouthshire at Newport.
Career: 6 matches in 1907.
HS for Glamorgan: 43 v Cornwall at Penzance, 1907.

Hirst was a professional in Scotland from the 1890s and joined Cardiff in 1906 and acted as their professional until 1909. He subsequently joined Chippenham, but returned after World War One to work at Cardiff Mental Hospital. He is believed to have been a relation of George Hirst, the famous Yorkshire and England bowler.

HOARE, Walter Robertson

Batsman.
Born: Marlow Bucking, Hants, 27 October 1867.
Died: Lychpit, 1 July 1941.
Education: Eton and Trinity College, Cambridge.
Career: 1 match against South Africa at Cardiff Arms Park in 1901 scoring 14 and 0.

He was the son of Revd W.M.Hoare and followed his father to Eton where he made the XI in 1886. He then went up to Cambridge, but despite playing in the 1889 Seniors Match, he remained on the fringe of the Cambridge XI. After coming down, he went into the brewing business and played for MCC, Free Foresters, Norfolk and the Eton Ramblers. His single appearance for Glamorgan was the result of his romance with Constance Hill, the sister of V.T.Hill and daughter of Sir Edward Hill of Llandaff. During the summer of 1901 Hoare spent time in South Wales wooing Miss Hill and joined Cardiff. After some good performances, he was included in the Glamorgan side to play South Africa, but only scored 14 runs. However his time in the area was successful, as he later got married to Constance Hill.

HOBBS, Robin Nicholas Stuart

RHB; LB.
Born: Chippenham, 8 May 1942.
Education: Raines Foundation School, Stepney.
Glamorgan debut: 1979 v Oxford University at Oxford.
Career: 41 matches 1979-81; Captain 1979; Essex 1961-75 (325 matches, Cap 1964, Benefit 1974 - £13,500); England 1967-71 (7 Caps).
HS for Glamorgan 49* v Hampshire at Swansea, 1981.

BB for Glamorgan 5-67 v Worcestershire at Hereford, 1981.

Full first-class record: 4,940 runs (12.10); 2 centuries; 1,099 wickets (27.09); 295 catches.

Hobbs joined Glamorgan as their captain in 1979 after a long and distinguished career with Essex and England. His appointment came as a surprise to many because he had retired from Essex in 1975 and had been playing only Minor County cricket for Suffolk between 1976 and 1978. Hobbs went on MCC tours to East Africa in 1963-64, South Africa 1964-65 and to Pakistan 1966-67 and 1968-69. He also went to Jamaica with the International Cavaliers in 1963-64, the West Indies in 1969-70 with the Duke of Norfolk's XI, South Africa with D.H.Robins XI and Pakistan with a World XI in

1973-74. He stepped down from the Glamorgan captaincy in 1980 and the following year retired from county cricket and went into a banking career. Ironically, both of his career-best performances were for Essex against Glamorgan. In 1968 he hit 100 at Ilford and in 1966 he took 8-63 at Swansea.

HODGES, Albert Edward

RHB.
Born: Newport, 29 January 1905.
Career: 1 match in 1936 against Gloucestershire at Newport scoring 3 and 0; Wales 1930.
Full first-class record: 14 runs (3.50).

Hodges played for Newport and played for Glamorgan II in their Minor County games in 1935. He made his first-class debut in 1930 for Wales scoring 8 and 3.

HOLMES, Geoffrey Clarke

RHB; RM.
Born: Newcastle upon Tyne, 16 September 1958.

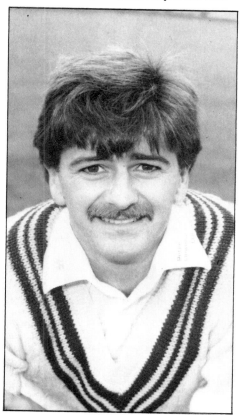

Education: West Denton High School.
Glamorgan debut: 1978 v Warwickshire at Sophia Gardens, Cardiff.
Career: 203 matches 1978-91; Cap 1985; Benefit 1991; Border 1989-90.
HS for Glamorgan: 125 v Somerset at Sophia Gardens, Cardiff, 1990.
1,000 runs (3); 1,129 (30.51) 1985 best.
BB for Glamorgan: 5-38 v Essex at Colchester, 1988.
Full first-class record: 8,092 runs (28.49); 11 centuries; 88 wickets (45.03); 85 catches.

Geoff Holmes joined Glamorgan after being on the MCC groundstaff in 1977 and won a regular place in the side during the mid-1980s. He proved to be a useful 'bits and pieces' player, batting anywhere from three to six, besides opening the innings in one-day games. He has also recorded some exceptional bowling performances in limited overs games. He took 5-2 in the Sunday League match with Derbyshire at Ebbw Vale in 1984 and recorded a hat-trick at the same ground against Nottinghamshire in 1987. He has regularly played and coached in Cape Town during the winter months and in 1989-90 hit a career-best 182 for Border against Western Province 'B' at East London. He currently plays club cricket for Neath, but a back injury forced him to retire from county cricket at the end of 1991.

HOLMES, T.

Batsman.
Career: 1 match in 1894 against Monmouthshire at Newport, scoring 4 and 0.

HOPKINS, John Anthony

RHB; occ WK.
Born: Maesteg, 16 June 1953.
Education: Ynysawdre Comprehensive and Trinity College, Carmarthen.
Glamorgan debut: 1970 v Leicestershire at Leicester.
Career: 299 matches 1970-88; Cap 1977; Benefit 1986 (£35,250); Eastern Province 1981-82; MCC 1978.
HS for Glamorgan: 230 v Worcestershire at Worcester, 1977
1,000 runs (7); 1,500 (33.33) 1984 best.
Full first-class record: 13,742 runs (27.32); 18 centuries; 213 catches and 1 stumping.

John Hopkins was born within 100 yards of Maesteg Celtic's ground, so it was not surprising that he followed a career in cricket. He was attached to the MCC groundstaff in 1969 and 1970, whilst his brother Jeff was on the Middlesex staff between 1969 and 1972. 'Ponty' made his first-class debut

in 1970 before going to college and playing during his vacations as a batsman/wicketkeeper. He won a regular place as an opening batsman from 1977 onwards and in his first-season scored a career-best double hundred during a stand of 253 with his opening partner Alan Jones. He scored over 2,700 runs in his first two seasons of regular county cricket and was tipped as a possible England player. In 1977-78 he won a Whitbread Scholarship to Australia and was selected in the MCC side which played Pakistan in May 1978. He also spent a winter playing in South Africa for Eastern Province. Hopkins played some forceful innings in limited-overs cricket and in 1983 scored 130 in the Sunday League match with Somerset at Bath, which remains the highest score in the competition for Glamorgan. He trained as a teacher, but now works for a national building society and plays club cricket for Maesteg Celtic.

HORDLEY, Thomas Joseph

All-rounder.
Glamorgan debut: 1892 v Wiltshire at Swindon.
Career: 9 matches 1892-94.
HS for Glamorgan: 8 v Monmouthshire at Swansea, 1892.
BB for Glamorgan: 4-19 v MCC at Cardiff Arms Park, 1892.
Hordley played for the Plymouth Works club in Merthyr.

HORSFALL, Richard

RHB.
Born: Todmorden, Yorkshire, 26 June 1920.
Died: Halifax, 25 August 1981.

Glamorgan debut: 1956 v Kent at Canterbury.
Career: 5 matches in 1956; Essex 1947-55 (207 matches, Cap 1948); South of England 1948.
HS for Glamorgan: 21 v Essex at Ilford, 1956.

Full first-class record: 9,777 runs (29.09); 17 centuries; 1 wicket and 87 catches.

Dick Horsfall played for Todmorden, before joining Essex where he made his debut in 1947. He won his county cap the following season, as well as playing for the South of England against Glamorgan at the Arms Park. Horsfall was affected by back trouble in 1949 and 1950, but recovered in 1951 and hit a career-best 206 against Kent at Blackheath during a partnership of 343 for the third wicket with Paul Gibb. In 1953 he scored the fastest century of the season, hitting 100 in 85 minutes against Warwickshire at Edgbaston. He was hindered by a back injury again in 1954 and lost form, resulting in his release by Essex at the end of 1955. He joined Glamorgan in 1956, but his career with the Welsh side was cut short by illness and he was forced to retire midway through the season after having a nervous breakdown.

HORSPOOL, James J.

Born: Burton, September 1874.
Died: Cardiff, 10 September 1960.
Glamorgan debut: 1905 v Northumberland at Swansea.
Career: 5 matches in 1905 and 1 in 1913.
HS for Glamorgan: 11* v Surrey at The Oval, 1905.

Horspool played for Hills Plymouth, before joining Cardiff, for whom he served as captain between 1913 and 1919 and secretary from 1924 until 1945. He was also on the Glamorgan committee in 1920.

HOWARD, Alan Raymond

LHB; LM.
Born: Leicester, 11 December 1909.
Glamorgan debut: 1928 v Worcestershire at Worcester.

Career: 59 matches 1928-33; Wales 1930.
HS for Glamorgan: 63 v Derbyshire at Swansea, 1930.
Full first-class record: 1,181 runs (12.17); 35 catches.

Alan Howard was the son of Leicestershire's Arthur Howard and the brother of Jack Howard. He played club cricket for Hills Plymouth and St Fagan's and appeared for Glamorgan II in their Minor County matches in 1936.

HOWELLS, Percy

Batsman.
Career: 1 match against Monmouthshire at Newport in 1900 scoring 0 and 6.

Howells played for Cardiff and was a late replacement for the match with Monmouthshire when only 10 Glamorgan players turned up.

HUGHES, David Wilfred

RHB; RFM.
Born: Ebbw Vale, 12 July 1910.
Died: Southampton, 21 April 1984.
Education: Ebbw Vale Boys School and University College of North Wales, Bangor.
Glamorgan debut: 1935 v South Africa at Cardiff Arms Park.
Career: 22 matches 1935-38.
HS for Glamorgan: 70* v South Africa at Cardiff Arms Park, 1935.
BB for Glamorgan: 5-70 v Leicestershire at Leicester, 1936.

Wilf Hughes played as a fast bowler for Ebbw Vale

Wilf Hughes (left) on his debut against South Africa when he shared a last wicket partnership of 131 with Smart (right), Dai Davies is in the middle.

and Monmouthshire in the late 1920s, before reading physics and chemistry at Bangor University. He qualified as a science teacher and took a post at a school in Northamptonshire believing he was not good enough to break into county cricket. He joined Kettering and earned a reputation as a fiery bowler and fierce hitter of the ball. Glamorgan's officials heard of his feats and in 1935 he was given a trial during the school holidays. Hughes had a fairy-tale start to his career sharing a partnership of 131 for the tenth wicket with Cyril Smart against the touring South Africans. Hughes' contributions was a beligerent 70 which included four sixes. He continued to appear during his school holidays until 1938 and opened the bowling with Jack Mercer. During World War Two, he was adjutant of the School of Artillery at Larkhill and after being demobbed he taught in Dorset and played for Poole. Hughes also appeared in Minor County cricket for Dorset between 1946 and 1949 before moving to schools in Eastern England. He ended his teaching career by being headmaster of a boys' school in Peterborough.

HUGHES, Francis E.

Batsman.
Career: 1 match against Herefordshire at Cardiff Arms Park scoring 0 in his only innings.

Hughes played for Cardiff and was in a solicitor's practice with his club and county colleague W.S.R.Sweet-Escott.

HUGHES, Gwyn

RHB; SLA.
Born: Cardiff, 26 March 1941.
Education: Cardiff High School and Queen's College, Cambridge.

Glamorgan debut: 1962 v Pakistan at Swansea.
Career: 17 matches 1962-64; Cambridge University 1965 (Blue).
HS for Glamorgan: 92 v Australia at Cardiff Arms Park, 1964.
BB for Glamorgan: 3-20 v Cambridge University at Fenners, 1964.
Full first-class record: 457 runs (12.35); 31 wickets (44.12); 22 catches.

Gwyn Hughes played club cricket for Cardiff, St Fagan's and Briton Ferry Town. He won a cricket Blue at Cambridge and also represented the university in their rugby XV in 1964. His career-best bowling figures were 4-31 against New Zealand at Fenners in 1965. He went into teaching and currently teaches economics at St Paul's School, where he also coaches cricket.

INGLEDEW, Hugh Murray

All-rounder.
Born: Cardiff, 26 October 1865.
Died: Cardiff, 1 February 1937.
Education: St Edwards, Oxford and Merton College, Oxford.

Glamorgan debut: 1891 v MCC at Swansea.
Career: 5 matches in 1891.
HS for Glamorgan: 20 v Monmouthshire at Newport, 1891.
BB for Glamorgan: 2-37 v Devon at Exeter, 1891.

Ingledew played cricket and rugby for Cardiff and won three caps for Wales at fly-half in 1890 and 1891. He was also an original member of the Barbarians RFC and took an active role in the affairs of Glamorgan, serving on the county's committee from 1892 and acting as honorary treasurer between 1904 and 1912. He was a prominant solicitor in Cardiff and played a leading role in the acquisition by Cardiff Athletic Club of the Arms Park from the Bute Estate during the 1920s. His son Kenneth was a well known hockey administrator.

JACOB, Norman Ernest

RHB; RM.
Born: Neath, 9 July 1901.
Died: Grimsby, 12 March 1970.
Education: Tonbridge.
Glamorgan debut: 1920 v Carmarthenshire at Llanelli.
Career: 1 Minor County match in 1920, plus 7 first-class matches in 1922.
HS for Glamorgan: 19 v Lancashire at Old Trafford, 1922.

Norman Jacob was in the Tonbridge XI in 1918 and after leaving school played for Neath, Port Talbot and Penarth. He was one of Wales' leading golfers in the 1920s and 1930s, winning the Glamorgan and West Wales Championship in the 1930s and representing Wales in their Home Internationals between 1932 and 1936. He subsequently acted as secretary of Dinas Powis Golf Club and the Glamorgan County Golf Union.

JAMES, David Harry

RHB; RM.

Born: Briton Ferry, 3 March 1921.
Education: Cwrt Sart School, Neath.
Career: 1 match in 1948 against Nottinghamshire at Trent Bridge scoring 17 and taking 1-59.

He was the son of E.H.James and played with great success for both Briton Ferry Town and Briton Ferry Steel.

JAMES, Edward Hugh

LHB; SLA.
Born: Briton Ferry, 14 April 1896.
Died: Briton Ferry, 15 March 1975.
Glamorgan debut: 1920 v Cheshire at Swansea.
Career: 4 Minor County games in 1920, plus 3 first-class matches in 1922.
HS for Glamorgan: 41 v Capt J.H.P.Brain's XI at Cardiff Arms Park, 1920.
BB for Glamorgan: 7-44 v Devon at Neath, 1920.

He was the father of D.H.James and played for Briton Ferry Steel, Gowerton and Maesteg.

JAMES, Evan Llewellyn

RHB; RM.
Born: Barry, 10 May 1918.

Education: Gladstone Road School, Barry.
Glamorgan debut: 1946 v Warwickshire at Edgbaston.
Career: 9 matches 1946-47.
HS for Glamorgan: 62* v India at Swansea, 1946.
BB for Glamorgan: 1-8 v Essex at Cardiff Arms Park, 1947.

Evan James played for Glamorgan in their wartime friendlies in 1944 and 1945 and played club cricket for Cardiff and Maesteg Town. He was a middle-order batsman and occasional seam bowler.

JAMES, Stephen Peter

RHB.
Born: Lydney, 7 September 1967.
Education: Monmouth School, Swansea University and Hughes Hall, Cambridge.

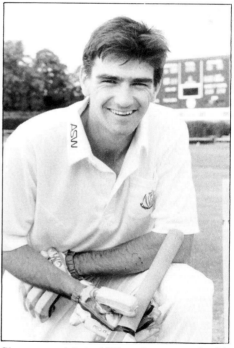

Glamorgan debut: 1985 v Sussex at Sophia Gardens, Cardiff.
Career: 33 matches 1985-; Cambridge University 1989-90 (Blue both years); Combined Universities 1989-90.
HS for Glamorgan: 106 v Oxford University at Oxford, 1987.
1,000 runs; (1) in all matches for Cambridge University, Combined Universities and Glamorgan in 1990.

Full first-class record: 2,840 runs (28.12); 8 centuries; 43 catches.

Stephen James had a prodigious record as a schoolboy cricketer and rugby player whilst at Monmouth School. He captained Welsh Schools and made his Glamorgan debut at the end of 1985, although he never got on to the field of play because of rain. He has only made sporadic appearance since then owing to his university studies. James read Classics at Swansea before taking a postgraduate degree at Cambridge, where he was a Blue as an opening batsman. He represented the Combined Universities in 1989 and 1990 and scored a career-best 151* against Warwickshire at Fenners in 1989. In his final year he also played a match-winning innings of 131* as the Universities beat New Zealand. Whilst up at Cambridge, he hit six centuries, but so far he has only scored one for Glamorgan, during a record partnership of 249 for the second wicket with Hugh Morris against Oxford University in 1987. James has also represented Cambridge University, Gloucestershire and Lydney at rugby and was on the bench in the 1988 and 1989 Varsity match. He joined the staff on a full-time basis in 1991 after a winter's coaching in Zimbabwe.

JARRETT, Harold Harvey

RHB; LB.
Born: Johannesburg, 23 September 1907.
Died: Pontypool, 17 March 1983.
Education: Highgate School.
Career: 1 match in 1938 against Sir Julian Cahn's XI at Newport scoring 0 and taking 1-27 and 3-18; Warwickshire 1932-33 (14 matches).
Full first-class record: 228 runs (15.20); 51 wickets (32.35); 6 catches.

Jarrett joined Glamorgan after appearing for Warwickshire and a spell coaching and playing in Scotland. He played for Newport and took a wicket with his first ball for Glamorgan against Sir Julian Cahn's XI at Newport in 1938. He later played for Glamorgan in their wartime friendlies in 1944 and edited *The South Wales Cricketers' Magazine* between 1948 and 1951. He was the father of K.S.Jarrett and acted as groundsman at Rodney Parade, Newport after World War Two. His career-best score was 45 on his debut for Warwickshire against India at Edgbaston in 1932, whilst his best figures were 8-187 against Leicestershire at Hinckley in 1932.

JARRETT, Keith Stanley

RHB; RM.
Born: Newport, 18 May 1948.

Education: Monmouth School.
Glamorgan debut: 1967 v India at Sophia Gardens, Cardiff.
Career: 2 matches in 1967.
HS for Glamorgan: 18* v Pakistan at Swansea, 1967.

Keith Jarrett won greater fame on the rugby pitch than on the cricket field. He made 82 appearances for Newport RFC between 1966 and 1969, plus ten Welsh caps in 1967, 1968 and 1969. He also played for Abertillery and London Welsh, and toured South Africa with the British Lions in 1968, before turning professional with Barrow and Widnes and winning a place in the Great Britain side. He is currently a marketing director in the Newport area.

JAVED MIANDAD, Khan

RHB; LB.
Born: Karachi, 12 June 1957.
Education: CMS Secondary School, Karachi.
Glamorgan debut: 1980 v Essex at Swansea.
Career: 83 matches 1980-85; Cap 1980; Captain 1981-82; Habib Bank 1976-77; Pakistan 1976-77 to 1991 (104 Tests); Karachi 1973-74 to 1975-76; Sind 1973-74, 1975-76; Sussex 1976-79.
HS for Glamorgan: 212* v Leicestershire at Swansea, 1984.
1,000 runs (4); 2,083 (69.43) 1981 best.
BB for Glamorgan: 3-52 v Warwickshire at Edgbaston, 1982.

Full first-class record: 27,468 runs (54.07); 78 centuries; 191 wickets (33.48); 328 catches and 3 stumpings.

Javed Miandad was one of the top Test batsman of the 1980s and joined Glamorgan in 1980 after a short career with Sussex where he shared the overseas position. During his career with Glamorgan he set county records of eight centuries and 2,083 runs in 1981 and in the early 1980s the gifted Pakistani delighted the Welsh crowds with his attractive stroke play. He struck 17 centuries

BB for Glamorgan: 1-41 v Worcestershire at Worcester, 1970.
Full first-class record: 36,049 runs (32.89); 56 centuries; 3 wickets; 288 catches.

Alan Jones is the finest batsman never to have played Test cricket for England, aggregating over 36,000 first-class runs during his 27 year career. He made his debut in 1957 and moved up to open

the batting in the early 1960s. The left-hander proceeded to share a host of opening stands in excess of a hundred with a variety of partners including Bernard Hedges, Gilbert Parkhouse, Roger Davis, Roy Fredericks and John Hopkins. He combined a solid technique with admirable powers of concentration and his record of 1,000 runs in 23 successive seasons highlighted his consistency and makes even more surprising his absence from the England team. Jones played in the series against the Rest of the World in 1970, which at the time was considered to be worthy of Test status. He was given a cap and England blazer, but the bureaucrats at Lord's later stripped the series of Test status. It has been suggested that a shoulder injury which restricted his fielding, was the reason for the selectors ignoring the elegant left-hander, but his outstanding record of scoring a century against every county apart from Middlesex makes impressive reading. Despite his sadness at never playing in Test cricket, Jones was a model professional during his long career and led the county in the late 1970s, including their Gillette Cup Final appearance in 1977. He also served as vice-captain and senior professional from 1979 until his retirement in 1983.

He made his maiden century against Sussex at Hastings in 1962 and the following year scored 187* and 105* against Somerset at Glastonbury. One of his finest innings came in 1966 when he dispatched the West Indies attack, which included the fiery Wes Hall, for 161* at Swansea. In 1969 he put on 224 with Roger Davis for the first wicket at Derby, whilst in 1972 he shared in a record opening partnership of 330 with Roy Fredericks against Northamptonshire at Swansea. He also shared two double century opening partnerships with John Hopkins in 1977 and 1978 and with 4,702 runs, holds the record for the most runs by a Glamorgan batsman in the Sunday League. He also scored the first ever Glamorgan century in that competition, by making 110* against Gloucestershire at Sophia Gardens in 1978 and earlier in 1976 he became the highest scorer in the Gillette Cup for Glamorgan with 124* against Warwickshire at Edgbaston.

Jones also played in first-class cricket overseas. He played for Western Australia in 1963-64 and appeared for an Australia XI against South Africa at Perth. He toured Malaysia, Ceylon and Singapore with the MCC in 1969-70 and went on Glamorgan's tours to the West Indies in 1969-70 and Zambia in 1972. He also played in South Africa during the mid-1970s, appearing for Northern Transvaal and Natal.

He has received many honours for his loyal and wholehearted service to Glamorgan. Jones was one of Wisdens Cricketers of the Year in 1977 and in 1982 he received an MBE in the Queen's Honours List. He is also a fluent Welsh speaker and was admitted to the Gorsedd of the Welsh National Eisteddfod in 1983. He has been the county coach since 1984 and currently captains the Glamorgan Colts side. His autobiography *Hooked on Opening* was published in 1984.

JONES, Alan Lewis

LHB.
Born: Alltwen, 1 June 1957.
Education: Ystalyfera Grammar School and Cardiff College of Education.
Glamorgan debut: 1973 v Gloucestershire at Bristol.
Career: 160 matches 1973-76; Cap 1983.
HS for Glamorgan: 132 v Hampshire at Sophia Gardens, Cardiff, 1984.
1,000 runs (2); 1,811 (36.95) 1984 best.
BB for Glamorgan: 1-60 v Yorkshire at Sophia Gardens, Cardiff, 1984.

A.L.Jones played for Young England in 1974 and toured New Zealand with D.H.Robin's XI in 1974-75 and 1979-80. He was groomed during the 1970s as the successor to Alan Jones as the county's opening batsman and A.L. went from strength to strength after winning a regular place in the team in the early 1980s following the completion of his teacher training. Even so, he went 11 seasons before

Wicketkeeper Eifion Jones, who made a county record 933 dismissals.

club cricket for Llangennech, Dafen, Llanelli and Pontardulais and was an opening bowler and tail-end batsman, who could have had a more illustrious county career had it not been for the war.

JONES, Hopkin Bevan Thomas

Batsman.
Born: Neath, December 1884.
Died: Neath, 2 August 1956.
Education: Queens College, Taunton.
Career: 1 match in 1920 against Carmarthenshire at Llanelli, scoring 1 and 2.

Hopkin Jones played cricket for Taibach, Margam, Neath and Port Talbot, who he captained between 1920 and 1925. He also played rugby for Aberavon and was a leading member of the Royal Porthcawl Golf Club. He also had a career in local politics and was the mayor of Aberavon and Port Talbot in 1925-26.

JONES, Ivor Jeffrey

RHB; LF.
Born: Dafen, 10 December 1941.
Education: Stebonheath School, Llanelli.
Glamorgan debut: 1960 v Kent at Blackheath.
Career: 157 matches 1960-68; Cap 1965; England 1963-64 to 1967-68 (15 Tests).
HS for Glamorgan: 20 v Sussex at Cardiff Arms Park, 1965.
BB for Glamorgan: 8-11 v Leicestershire at Leicester, 1965.
100 wickets: 100 wickets in all first-class games for England and Glamorgan in 1967.
Full first-class record: 513 runs (3.97); 511 wickets (25.98); 46 catches.

Jeff Jones was one of the fastest bowlers in English cricket in the early 1960s. The left arm quickie joined the staff in 1960 and became the regular opening bowler in 1962. His fast high action enabled him to extract both pace and bounce from the wickets and during the season he took a hat-trick against Yorkshire at Harrogate. In 1963 he took 58 wickets and was selected for the MCC tours to East Africa and India, despite the fact that he was still an uncapped player. Indeed, he won his England cap before his Glamorgan one by appearing in the Second Test at Bombay in 1963-64. Jones was injured in 1964, but returned to form in 1965 and produced figures of 13-9-11-8 on a damp green wicket at Leicester as the home side were dismissed for 40. This form won him a place on the MCC tour to Australia and New Zealand in 1965-66. He played in all the Tests and finished as leading wicket-taker on the tour with 48 victims. He was an automatic selection for the West Indies tour in 1967-68

and once again played in all five Tests. However, he played a vital role as a batsman in the last Test at Georgetown, blocking out the final over from Lance Gibbs to save the match and win the series for England. Earlier on tour, he had also scored a career-best 21 against Guyana at Georgetown. Jones returned home looking forward to the 1968 series with Australia, but he damaged shoulder and elbow ligaments at Ilford early in the season and missed the rest of the summer. Even worse was

to follow as a specialist found arthritus in his elbow joint and a wearing of the bone. Despite trying to make a comeback and change his action, Jones was forced to retire from county cricket. During his career he played club cricket for Pontardulais, Dafen, Llanelli, Bridgend, Briton Ferry Town and Briton Ferry Steel. He is a representative for a brewery and still plays as a spin bowler in Carmarthenshire for Felinfoel and Trostre.

JONES, James M.
LHB; WK.
Died: Bristol, 1945.

Glamorgan debut: 1928 v Surrey at The Oval.
Career: 8 matches 1928-29; Somerset 1922-23 (7 matches); Wales 1929.
HS for Glamorgan: 75 v Essex at Leyton, 1928.
Full first-class record: 846 runs (18.80); 23 catches and 13 stumpings.

Jimmy Jones joined Gowerton in 1924 after a brief career with Somerset. Whilst in South Wales he also played for Neath and Briton Ferry Town and after retiring from county cricket he coached at several public schools including Denstone from 1932 until 1934 before becoming a publican in Staffordshire and the West Country.

JONES, John Walter
RHB; SLA.
Glamorgan debut: 1910 v Hertfordshire at Swansea.
Career: 11 matches 1910-20.
HS for Glamorgan: 108* v Monmouthshire at Newport, 1913.
BB for Glamorgan: 2-7 v Surrey II at The Oval, 1912.

He played for Neath and Briton Ferry Town.

JONES, Revd Owen
RHB; RFM.
Born: Pontllanycharan, Aberystwyth, 1860.
Died: Llangan, Bridgend, 20 December 1923.
Education: Llandovery College and Jesus College, Oxford.
Glamorgan debut: 1891 v MCC at Swansea.
Career: 17 matches 1891-97.
HS for Glamorgan: 79 v Monmouthshire at Swansea, 1892.
BB for Glamorgan: 5-34 v MCC at Lord's, 1894.

Owen Jones was reputed to be the fastest bowler in South Wales in the 1880s and 1890s. He went up to Oxford in 1878, but was suspended from the university after causing damage to a railway carriage and travelling in a first-class compartment on a third-class ticket. Despite this, he entered the church and was ordained in 1887. He taught at Abingdon Grammar School and the Royal Medical School, Epsom before moving to South Wales to become curate of Cadoxton in 1890. He also served as rector of Llansannor, Llanfrynach and Penlline and was rector of Llangan from 1908 until his death in 1923. Owen Jones played for the South Wales CC, Cadoxton, Cowbridge, Bridgend and the Gentlemen of Surrey.

JONES, Dr Rees Gabe (later GABE-JONES)

All-rounder.
Born: Merthyr Tydfil, December 1861.
Died: Clydach Vale, 9 November 1927.
Education: London University.
Glamorgan debut: 1891 v Devon at Exeter.
Career: 4 matches 1891-93.
HS for Glamorgan: 17* v Herefordshire at Hereford, 1893.
BB for Glamorgan: 5-42 v Monmouthshire at Newport, 1891.

Dr Gabe Jones played for Cardiff and Clydach Vale and was the father of A.R.Gabe-Jones. He also played rugby for London Welsh and was a founding member of Rhondda Golf Club.

JONES, Thomas Charles

RHB.
Born: Pontypool, 1 April 1901.
Died: Westminster, 19 July 1935.
Education: Shrewsbury School.
Glamorgan debut: 1925 v Somerset at Cardiff.
Career: 3 matches 1925-28.
HS for Glamorgan: 21 v Warwickshire at Edgbaston, 1928.

Jones was in the Shrewsbury XI in 1918 and 1919, but only played occasionally in the 1920s due to his career in the Army.

JONES, Watkin Edward ('Watt')

RHB; RFM.
Born: Gwauncaegurwen, 6 July 1917.
Education: Gwancaegurwen School.
Glamorgan debut: 1946 v Lancashire at Cardiff Arms Park.
Career: 5 matches 1946-47.
BB for Glamorgan: 7-92 v Kent at Newport, 1947.

Watt Jones played club cricket for Pontardawe, Pontardulais and Clydach and was a policeman in the Swansea Valleys. He played five times, but only had one innings in which he was dismissed for a duck.

JONES, Wilfred Edward

LHB; SLA.
Born: Pontardawe, 2 February 1912.
Glamorgan debut: 1929 v South Africa at Pontypridd.
Career: 50 matches 1929-33.
HS for Glamorgan: 27 v Sussex at Cardiff Arms Park, 1931.

BB for Glamorgan: 6-93 v New Zealand at Cardiff Arms Park, 1931.

Wilf Jones played club cricket for Pontardawe and Neath and was a lower-order batsman and left arm spinner who met with reasonable success when given an extended run in the first XI. He was released on financial grounds in 1933 and could have developed into a useful bowler had Glamorgan been a wealthier side.

JONES, William Edward

LHB; SLA.
Born: Carmarthen, 31 October 1916.
Glamorgan debut: 1937 v Hampshire at Swansea.
Career: 340 matches 1937-38; Cap 1946; South 1949-56; Benefit 1953 (£4,460).
HS for Glamorgan: 212* v Essex at Brentwood, 1948
1,000 runs (7); 1,656 (42.46) 1948 best.
BB for Glamorgan: 5-50 v Kent at Gravesend, 1949.
Full first-class record: 13,535 runs (27.12); 11 centuries; 192 wickets (30.11); 120 catches.

Willie Jones played for Glamorgan II in Minor County cricket in the mid 1930s after impressive performances for Carmarthen and in 1937 he made his first-class debut. The young amateur was included in the side again in 1938 as Turnbull strove to improve the team's fielding. Jones was a swift runner and a talented fly-half with Llanelli, Neath and latterly Gloucester where he holds the record of 17 dropped goals in a season (1946-47). He also won a Welsh cap during wartime internationals.

His prowess at rugby was clearly evident in his deep fielding where his fast running allowed him to make a host of fine catches and save many runs. Jones served with the RAF during World War Two, but played for Glamorgan in wartime friendlies and joined the county's staff on a full-time basis in 1946.

Jones had previously batted in the middle-order, but he moved up the order after the war and confirmed Wooller's belief in him as a gifted strokemaker, with a penchant for the square cut. Despite knee trouble Jones had his best-ever season in 1948 and hit two double-hundreds within a

fortnight, scoring 207 against Kent at Gravesend and then an unbeaten 212 against Essex at Brentwood during a record-breaking stand of 313 for the third wicket with Emrys Davies. Besides scoring 1,655 runs in 1948, Jones also took 47 wickets with his left-arm spin and delivered several important spells as the Welsh county won the Championship.

Jones was a modest man and had he shown a little more belief in his own abilities as a spinner he could have become a true all-rounder. He was selected in the 1949 Test Trial, but just when he seemed to be on the verge of the England team, he was injured and missed the rest of the season. He returned to fitness in 1950 and during the next few seasons continued to be a reliable top order batsman and dashing strokemaker, although his knee problems restricted his bowling to occasional spells. Jones retired at the end of 1958 and became coach at Dean Close School, Cheltenham.

JONES, William Maxwell

RHB; RM.
Born: Alltwen, 11 February 1911.
Died: Denbigh December 1941.
Glamorgan debut: 1933 v Worcestershire at Llanelli.
Career: 11 matches 1933-38.
HS for Glamorgan: 51* v Worcestershire at Llanelli, 1933.
BB for Glamorgan: 3-11 v Sir Julian Cahn's XI at Newport, 1938.

William Jones was a successful all-rounder with Pontardawe, who played occasionally for Glamorgan in the mid 1930s.

JOSEPH, Arthur Frederick

RHB; LB.
Born: Neath Abbey, 13 March 1919.

Career: 1 match in 1946 against Derbyshire at Chesterfield scoring 8 and 0.

Joseph appeared in Minor County games for Glamorgan II in 1946 and played for Briton Ferry Town and Neath.

JUDGE, Peter Francis

RHB; RFM.
Born: Cricklewood, 23 May 1916.
Education: St Paul's.
Glamorgan debut: 1939 v Northamptonshire at Kettering.
Career: 54 matches 1939-47; Middlesex 1933-34 (8 matches); Bengal 1944-45, 1945-46; Europeans 1944-45.
HS for Glamorgan: 40 v Worcestershire at Ebbw Vale, 1946.
BB for Glamorgan: 8-75 v Yorkshire at Bradford, 1939.
Full first-class record: 454 runs (7.69); 173 wickets (27.02); 33 catches.

Peter Judge was in the St Paul's XI in 1933 and played for The Rest against the MCC Schools at Lord's. He made his Middlesex debut in 1933, before joining Buckinghamshire and playing in League cricket for Burnley, Scarborough, Elland and Carlisle. The well-travelled Judge joined the Glamorgan staff in 1939 and took 69 wickets in his first season. During the war he served with the RAF in Middlesex and Gloucestershire before going overseas and appearing in domestic cricket in India. Judge rejoined Glamorgan in 1946 and took 64 wickets as their opening bowler. He was a tail-end batsman and holds the unique distinction of being dismissed by two consecutive balls within a minute. This strange event occurred in the match with India at the Arms Park in 1946 as he was dismissed off the last ball of Glamorgan's first innings. With the game heading for a draw, the batting order was reversed and Judge was bowled by the first ball of the second innings! Sadly, he aggravated a foot injury after three games in 1947 and was forced to retire.

KINDERSLEY, Revd Cyril Edwin

Batsman.
Born: Dorchester, 13 September 1865.
Died: Clyffe Knowle, Dorset, 12 January 1938.
Education: Harrow and Trinity College, Cambridge.
Career: 1 match in 1891 against Gloucestershire at Cardiff Arms Park, scoring 0 in both innings.

Cyril Kindersley was in the Harrow XI in 1884 before going up to Cambridge where he became

friends with several Welsh sportsmen. After leaving Cambridge he entered the clergy and served as the curate of Rotherham in Yorkshire from 1891 until 1893, the Harrow Mission from 1893 until 1895 and Belvedere, Kent from 1895 until 1898, before moving to Dorset where he served as vicar of Fleet, Sturminster Newton and Wimborne.

KING, Collis Llewellyn

RHB; RM.
Born: Fairview, Barbados, 11 June 1951.
Education: Metropolitan High School, Bridgetown.
Glamorgan debut: 1977 v Somerset at Taunton.
Career: 16 matches in 1977; West Indies 1976-81 (9 Caps); Barbados 1972-73, 1981-82; Worcestershire 1983-86; Natal 1983-.
HS for Glamorgan: 78 v Surrey at Sophia Gardens, Cardiff, 1977.
BB for Glamorgan: 4-31 v Worcestershire at Worcester, 1977.
Full first-class record: 6,770 runs (38.24); 14 centuries; 128 wickets (34.21); 98 catches.

Collis King made his Test debut for the West Indies during their tour of England in 1976 and he joined Glamorgan the following season but was hampered by a series of niggling injuries. He played World Series Cricket between 1977 and 1979, before touring Australia, New Zealand and England with the West Indies. He went on the 'rebel' West Indies tours to South Africa in 1982-83 and 1983-84 and has subsequently played in the Currie Cup for Natal, besides a short career with Worcestershire and League cricket with Nelson, Colne and Pontblyd-den. His career-best score was 163 against Northamptonshie during the 1976 West Indian tour, whilst his best bowling figures are 5-91 for Barbados against Jamaica at Bridgetown in 1975-76.

KINGSTON, Graham Charles

RHB; RM.
Born: Newport, 1 November 1950.
Education: St Julians High School, Newport.
Glamorgan debut: 1967 v Worcestershire at Colwyn Bay.
Career: 9 matches 1967-71.
HS for Glamorgan: 26 v Oxford University at B.P.Llandarcy, 1971.
BB for Glamorgan: 2-18 v Worcestershire at Neath, 1970.

Kingston played for Newport, Swansea, Briton Ferry Town and Llanelli and went on Glamorgan's tour to Bermuda and the West Indies in 1969-70. He was a useful seam bowler in limited overs cricket and took 6-36 in the Sunday League match with

Derbyshire at Ebbw Vale in 1969. His father was an international soccer referee and since leaving the Glamorgan staff in 1971 he has worked as an estate agent and is currently an area sales director for Abbey National.

LAMBERT, William
RHB; RM.
Born: Hatfield, 19 April 1843.
Died: St Fagan's, 4 March 1927.
Glamorgan debut: 1897 v Monmouthshire at Cardiff Arms Park.
Career: 12 matches 1897-98; Middlesex 1874-77 (7 matches).
HS for Glamorgan: 7* v Cornwall at Swansea and at Penzance, 1898.
BB for Glamorgan: 9-86 v Wiltshire at Swindon, 1897.
Full first-class record: 112 runs (10.18); 1 wicket; 9 catches.

Lambert played for Hertfordshire and Northumberland after a brief career with Middlesex. In the 1890s he moved to South Wales to become the professional with Bridgend. His brother George was tennis champion of England. Lambert's highest first-class score was 34* against Surrey at The Oval in 1874.

LANDERS, E.
Batsman.
Career: 1 match in 1890 against Warwickshire at

Cardiff Arms Park scoring 0 and 7.
Landers played for Swansea and the South Wales CC.

LAVIS, George
RHB; RM.
Born: Sebastopol, Monmouthshire, 17 August 1908.
Died: Pontypool, 29 July 1956.
Glamorgan debut: 1928 v Derbyshire at Ilkeston.
Career: 206 matches 1928-49; Testimonial 1950 (£2,248); Coach 1946-56.
HS for Glamorgan: 154 v Worcestershire at Cardiff Arms Park, 1934.
BB for Glamorgan: 4-55 v Sussex at Cardiff Arms Park, 1933.

Lavis played club cricket for Panteg and Barry, before securing a regular place in Turnbull's Glamorgan side of the 1930s. However, he lost his place in 1938 and moved to Dundee where he played for Broughty Ferry and acted as professional for Forfarshire. Lavis returned to South Wales during the war and played for Glamorgan in their wartime friendlies. He was appointed the county coach in 1946 and reappeared for the Welsh team in their championship matches until retiring in 1949. He became a highly respected coach and worked

George Lavis, who lost his first-team place in 1938 but returned to play in the Championship-winning side ten years later.

tirelessly in the Indoor School at the Arms Park, grooming the junior members of the Glamorgan staff and young players such as Jim McConnon. His premature death in 1956 after a short illness came as a huge blow to the club.

LAWLOR, Peter John

RHB; OB.
Born: Gowerton, 8 May 1960.
Education: Gowerton Comprehensive School.
Career: 1 match in 1981 against Sri Lanka at Sophia Gardens, Cardiff scoring 8 and 0 and taking 1-36 and 0-14.

Lawlor has played for Welsh Schools and Wales

in the Minor County championship. He has also represented Glamorgan at badminton and currently plays for St Fagan's, for whom he appeared in the 1991 Haig Village Cup Final at Lord's.

LETCHER, Harold Bertie

All-rounder.
Born: Swansea, 4 June 1871.
Died: Bermuda, 15 June 1942.
Education: Wycliffe College and London University.
Glamorgan debut: 1890 v Monmouthshire at Cardiff Arms Park.
Career: 108 matches 1890-1908.

Tony Lewis, the first Glamorgan player to lead England in a Test Match and now a well-known broadcaster and adminstrator, currently Glamorgan CCC's chairman.

HS for Glamorgan: 156 v South Wales CC at Swansea, 1895.

BB for Glamorgan: 7-66 v Monmouthshire at Cardiff Arms Park, 1891.

Letcher played for Cardiff and the Public School Nondescripts. He served on the county committee between 1895 and 1900 and acted as the club's secretary from 1904 until 1908. After retiring from cricket he became the manager of an insurance company based in Belfast.

LEWIS, Anthony Robert

RHB; LB.

Born: Uplands, Swansea, 6 July 1938.

Education: Neath Grammar and Christ's College, Cambridge.

Glamorgan debut: 1955 v Leicestershire at Cardiff Arms Park.

Career: 315 matches 1955-74; Captain 1967-72; Chairman 1988-; Benefit 1973; England 1972-73 (9 Caps); Cambridge University 1960-62 (Blue all three years); Combined Services 1958-59; Gentlemen 1962.

HS for Glamorgan: 223 v Kent at Gravesend, 1966.

1,000 runs (9); 2,052 (41.87) 1966 best.

BB for Glamorgan: 3-18 v Somerset at Neath, 1967.

Full first-class record: 20,495 runs (32.42); 30 centuries; 6 wickets (72.00); 193 catches.

Although born in Swansea, Tony Lewis was brought up close to The Gnoll where he regularly watched rugby and cricket. He showed great talent with Neath Grammar School and Neath, and made his county debut in 1955 whilst still at school and ironically whilst preparing to go on the Welsh National Youth Orchestra's summer tour as a violinist. After doing his National Service with the RAF and playing for the Combined Services, Lewis went up to Cambridge to read History. He represented the university at rugby and cricket and won a Blue all three years, besides captaining the XI in 1962. He was also a talented full-back and played in the 1959 Varsity match. Lewis also appeared for Neath, Pontypool and Gloucester, before a knee injury forced him to concentrate on his blossoming cricket career.

Lewis became a regular in the Glamorgan side from 1963 onwards and established himself as a dashing middle-order batsman and an elegant driver and cutter.

His most successful season was 1966 when he hit 2,052 runs with five centuries including a career-best 223 against Kent with 32 fours and two sixes. He also shared in a record partnership of 238 for the second wicket against Sussex at Hastings in 1962 with Alan Jones. Throughout his early career he was groomed as a future captain by Wilf Wooller

and in 1967 he took over the leadership from Ossie Wheatley. Glamorgan's championship success in 1969 highlighted Lewis' excellent leadership skills. He was a sound tactician and was able to get the best out of his players and was tipped as a future England leader. In 1969-70 he led the MCC side to Ceylon and the Far East and in 1972 when England skipper Ray Illingworth was unavailable for the winter tour, Lewis was appointed captain of the side to India, Pakistan and Sri Lanka. He made his Test debut in the First Test at Delhi and became the first Glamorgan player to lead England in a Test match. He scored 70 in the second innings and steered England to a six wicket win. During the Fourth Test at Kanpur he scored 125 and Lewis kept his place in the side in 1973 against New Zealand under Ray Illingworth. However, he aggravated his old knee injury and withdrew from the side for the Second Test. Sadly, the problems with his knee failed to clear up and he was forced to retire from county cricket in 1974.

During his career Lewis also appeared for the Gentlemen and toured South America in 1964-65 and North America in 1982 with the MCC, besides captaining the Arabs to Barbados in 1973-74. Since retiring he has become a leading broadcaster with the BBC, acting as 'anchor-man' with their cricket coverage, as well as being cricket correspondent of The Sunday Telegraph. He has also written several books including his autobiography Playing Days, Cricket in Many Lands and Double Century to celebrate the bi-centenary of the MCC. He has remained closely involved with Glamorgan and has served as club chairman since 1988.

LEWIS, Brian

RHB; OB.

Born: Maesteg, 18 July 1945.

Glamorgan debut: 1965 v Lancashire at Swansea.

Career: 37 matches 1965-68.

HS for Glamorgan: 38 v Nottinghamshire at Swansea, 1968.

BB for Glamorgan: 7-28 v Hampshire at Southampton, 1968.

Lewis played for Maesteg Celtic, Pontardulais, Ammanford and Gorseinon. He was a lower middle-order batsman and off-spinner, who appeared in the Glamorgan side in 1968 which defeated Australia. Despite taking seven wickets in this famous victory, he was released at the end of the season.

LEWIS, David Wyndham

RHB; LB.

Born: Cardiff, 18 December 1940.

Born: Llanelli, 31 January 1942.
Glamorgan debut: 1961 v Somerset at Weston-super-Mare.
Career: 95 matches 1961-66; Cap 1965; Sussex 1967-69 (86 matches, Cap 1967). MCC.
HS for Glamorgan: 80 v Sussex at Cardiff Arms Park, 1965.
BB for Glamorgan: 8-89 v Kent at Swansea, 1965.
Full first-class record: 3,487 runs (14.06); 341 wickets (27.23); 131 catches.

Education: Wycliffe College.
Glamorgan debut: 1960 v Northamptonshire at Cardiff Arms Park.
Career: 12 matches 1960-69; Transvaal 1972-73.
HS for Glamorgan 29* v Northamptonshire at Swansea, 1968.
BB for Glamorgan: 4-42 v Oxford University at Colwyn Bay, 1968.
Full first-class record: 122 runs (9.38); 21 wickets (45.61); 3 catches.

David Lewis has played for Gowerton, SCOW, Radyr, MCC and Cardiff. He went on Glamorgan's tour to Bermuda and the West Indies in 1969-70 and has also played in domestic cricket in South Africa. He has served on the county committee and is the son of Wyndham Lewis, an entertainment entrepreneur in South Wales.

LEWIS, Euros John

LHB; OB.
Born: Llanelli, 31 January 1942.

Euros Lewis made his debut in 1961 opening the batting with Bernard Hedges and the free-hitting left-hander showed great promise with scores of 23 and 40. He was also a useful leg-spinner and gradually worked at his bowling so that he was able to supplement the spin of Don Shepherd and Jim Pressdee. In 1963 he took 51 wickets to win his county cap. The following year he represented the MCC against the West Indies at Lord's, but his relationship with the Welsh club became strained and in 1966 he left to join Sussex. He was capped by his new county in 1967, but was released in 1969. Lewis played club cricket for Dafen, Llanelli, Pontardulais, SCOW, Llangennech and Ammanford.

LEWIS, Harry Tamplin

Batsman.
Career: 1 match in 1903 against Devon at Exeter scoring 12 and 8.

Lewis played for Bridgend and Llwynypia and was a solicitor in the Bridgend area.

LEWIS, Kenneth Humphrey
RHB; RFM.
Born: Penygladdfa, Newtown, 10 November 1928.
Education: Newtown Grammar School.
Glamorgan debut: 1950 v Combined Services at Cardiff Arms Park.
Career: 36 matches 1950-56.
HS for Glamorgan: 34 v Hampshire at Cardiff Arms Park, 1956.
BB for Glamorgan: 4-25 v Kent at Cardiff Arms Park, 1953.

Ken Lewis played for Newtown, Neath, Clydach, Ammanford, Llanelli and Swansea. He had a trial with Worcestershire and Glamorgan in 1949, after doing his National Service before joining the staff in 1950. Whilst serving with the Royal Artillery at Woolwich, he took 10-21 against Charterhouse. He soon showed that he was able to bowl genuinely fast, but his career was hampered by a series of niggling injuries and Lewis was never able to play on a regular basis. He broke down with a serious leg injury during the 1956 season and was forced to retire from first-class cricket. Lewis worked for an assurance company and a garage and played in club cricket for Welshpool, Shropshire Gents and Montgomeryshire. He is currently president of Newtown cricket club.

LEWIS, Robert Ajax
LHB; SLA.
Born: Pontypridd, September 1868.
Died: Ferryside, Carmarthenshire, 13 December 1913.
Education: Christ College, Brecon.
Glamorgan debut: 1890 v Monmouthshire at Newport.
Career: 9 matches 1890-92.
HS for Glamorgan: 52 v Somerset at Bath, 1890.
BB for Glamorgan: 3-9 v Gloucestershire at Bristol, 1891.

Lewis was in the Christ College XI between 1883 and 1886 and played club cricket for Cardiff and the South Wales CC. He served on the county committee from 1892 until 1895.

LEWIS, S.A.
Batsman.
Career: 1 match against Carmarthenshire at Llanelli in 1906 scoring 4 in his only innings.

LEWIS, William Edgar
Batsman.
Born: Bridgend, 26 September 1862.
Died: Bridgend, 26 December 1936.
Education: Charterhouse.
Glamorgan debut: 1889 v Warwickshire at Cardiff Arms Park.
Career: 3 matches 1889-90.
HS for Glamorgan: 10 v Warwickshire at Cardiff Arms Park, 1889.

Lewis was a solicitor in Bridgend and played for Bridgend, Penarth and Cardiff, as well as the South Wales CC. He was in the Charterhouse XI in 1880 and was also a good racquets player.

LEWIS, W.L.
Career: 1 match against Monmouthshire at Cardiff Arms Park in 1903, without batting or bowling.

He played for Cardiff and was a late substitute for the match in 1903 with Monmouthshire.

LINDLEY, James V.
All-rounder.
Born: Nottingham, 18 July 1844.
Died: Mansfield, 15 October 1911.
Glamorgan debut: 1889 v Warwickshire at Cardiff Arms Park.
Career: 5 matches 1889-90.
HS for Glamorgan: 31* v Surrey II at The Oval, 1889.

BB for Glamorgan: 7-45 v MCC at Cardiff Arms Park, 1889.

Lindley was on the Nottinghamshire staff in 1874, before moving to South Wales to become the professional with Cardiff and Swansea. He also played for the South Wales CC and St Andrews.

LING, Anthony John Patrick
LHB.
Born: Skewen, 10 August 1910.
Died: Eastbourne, 12 January 1987.
Education: Stowe.
Glamorgan debut: 1934 v Cambridge University at Cambridge.

Career: 9 matches 1934-36; Somerset 1939 (5 matches).
HS for Glamorgan: 41* v Leicestershire at Swansea, 1934.
Full first-class record: 256 runs (16.00) and 2 catches.

Tony Ling captained the Stowe XI in 1928, before winning a place in the Wiltshire side in the Minor County championship and proving himself to be an attractive left-handed batsman. He made his Glamorgan debut in 1934 as Maurice Turnbull introduced a number of young Welsh amateurs in the Glamorgan side. He played on an occasional basis for the next three seasons, as well as playing for the second eleven in Minor County games in 1936 and 1937. Business took him back to the West Country and in 1939 he made five appearances for Somerset.

LINTON, James Edward Fryer DSO
RHB; RM.
Born: Llandaff, 7 May 1909.
Died: Cozumel Island, Mexico, 27 December 1989.
Education: Charterhouse and Woolwich.
Glamorgan debut: 1932 v Middlesex at Cardiff Arms Park.
Career: 2 matches in 1932.
HS for Glamorgan: 2 v Hampshire at Bournemouth, 1932.
BB for Glamorgan: 1-34 v Middlesex at Cardiff Arms Park, 1932.

Linton was in the Charterhouse XI in 1926 and 1927, where he captained the school, but he opted for a military career and had a gallant service record with the Royal Artillery. He was awarded the DSO in 1944 after escaping from a PoW camp, as well as courageous fighting in the Battle of Arnheim when he had to swim naked across a river to gain safety. After the war he was a senior instructor in anti-tank warfare at the School of Artillery and was elevated to the rank of brigadier.

LLEWELLYN, John Griffith
Batsman.
Career: 1 match in 1896 against Monmouthshire at Newport, scoring 2 and 3*.
Llewellyn played for the Penarth club.

LLEWELLYN, Michael John
LHB; OB.
Born: Clydach, 27 November 1953.
Glamorgan debut: 1970 v Oxford University at The Parks.
Career: 136 matches 1970-82; Cap 1977.
HS for Glamorgan: 129* v Oxford University at The Parks, 1977.
BB for Glamorgan: 4-35 v Oxford University at The Parks, 1970.

Llewellyn showed great promise as a schoolboy batsman and off-spinner in the South Wales leagues and was attached to the MCC groundstaff in 1970

Full first-class record: 834 runs (22.54); 1 century; 15 catches.

Willie Llewelyn was the son of J.T.D.Llewelyn and was the bright young thing of the early Glamorgan sides. He was in the XI at Eton and won the Public Schools Racquets competition in 1886 and 1887, before winning a Cricket Blue at Oxford where he scored a career-best 116 in 1890 against A.J.Webbe's XI. He captained the Glamorgan team during the 1890 and 1891 seasons and acted as their treasurer

and 1971. Despite taking four wickets on his county debut, Llewellyn developed into an aggressive middle-order batsman. He played some forceful innings at times but failed to maintain a regular place. He clearly showed his preference for slow bowling rather than fast by hitting John Emburey for a mighty six on to the roof of the Lord's pavilion during the 1977 Gillette Cup Final when he top scored with 62. He was released at the end of 1982 and played for a couple of seasons with Wiltshire in Minor County cricket. During his career, Llewellyn played club cricket for Skewen, Clydach and Maesteg Celtic.

LLEWELYN, William Dillwyn

RHB; RM.
Born: Ynysygerwn, 1 April 1868.
Died: Penllergaer, 24 August 1893.
Education: Eton and New College, Oxford.
Glamorgan debut: 1889 v MCC at Lord's.
Career: 14 matches 1889-93; Oxford University 1890-91 (Blue both years).
HS for Glamorgan: 99 v Monmouthshire at Cardiff Arms Park, 1893.
BB for Glamorgan: 5 wickets v Devon at Swansea, 1893.

in 1893. He was a playing member of the MCC and seemed on the verge of an illustrious career, but tragically took his life in August 1893 by shooting himself in the grounds of his father's mansion, a few weeks before his marriage to the daughter of Lord Dynevor.

LLOYD, Barry John

RHB; OB.
Born: Neath, 6 September 1953.
Education: Llangatwg Comprehensive School, Neath and Bangor Normal College.
Glamorgan debut: 1972 v Gloucestershire at Bristol.
Career: 147 matches 1972-73; Cap 1982; Captain 1982.

HS for Glamorgan: 48 v Sussex at Sophia Gardens, Cardiff, 1982.
BB for Glamorgan 8-70 v Lancashire at Sophia Gardens, Cardiff, 1981.

Barry Lloyd first appeared in the Glamorgan side of the early 1970s and was tipped to take over the off-spin mantle of Don Shepherd. He was attached to the MCC groundstaff in 1971 and 1972, but then went to college and only played regular county cricket from 1978 onwards after completing his teacher training. He was not a big spinner of the ball, but his greatest virtue was a nagging accuracy and he developed into a highly effective spinner in one-day cricket. He shared the captaincy duties

in 1982 with Javed Miandad, but lost his place in the side during the following season when Mike Selvey joined the club as captain. He made one appearance in a Sunday League game in 1984 but was released at the end of the season and joined the South Wales Police. He has subsequently gone back into teaching and has played for Wales in the Minor County championship. Barry has played club cricket for Neath and Pontardulais.

LONG, John P.

Glamorgan debut: 1891 v Gloucestershire at Cardiff Arms Park.
Career: 6 matches 1891-93.

HS for Glamorgan: 20 v Devon at Exeter, 1892.
Long played for Swansea and was a schoolmaster in the town, acting as principal of Arnold College.

LOWE, Richard

RHB; LM.
Born: Kirkby-in-Ashfield, 18 June 1869.
Died: Kirkby-in-Ashfield, 3 July 1946.
Glamorgan debut: 1896 v MCC at Cardiff Arms Park.
Career: 59 matches 1896-1901; Nottinghamshire 1891 (1 non first-class friendly); Sussex 1893-94 (14 matches); Lord Sheffields XI 1891.
HS for Glamorgan: 87 v Wiltshire at Swindon, 1897.
BB for Glamorgan: 8-54 v MCC at Swansea 1898.
Full first-class record: 183 runs (10.76); 22 wickets (26.27); 5 catches.

Richard Lowe joined Cardiff as their professional, after brief spells with Nottinghamshire and Sussex. He was the younger brother of Sam Lowe and showed great promise as an all-rounder during his early career with Glamorgan. However, an injury restricted his bowling after 1898 and he became more of a middle-order batsman who occasionally bowled.

LOWE, Samuel

RHB; RFM.
Born: Kirkby-in-Ashfield, 1867.
Died: Nottingham, 31 May 1947.
Glamorgan debut: 1895 v South Wales CC at Swansea.
Career: 76 matches 1895-1902; Nottinghamshire 1894 (1 match).
HS for Glamorgan: 36* v Surrey II at Cardiff Arms Park, 1901.
Full first-class record: 8 runs (4.00).

Like his older brother, Sam Lowe also played for Cardiff after a brief county career with Nottinghamshire. Sam appeared regularly for Glamorgan from 1897 and proved to be a hostile seam bowler, especially on his home wicket at the Arms Park. In 1901 he took a career-best 8-37 against Wiltshire on the ground, plus 7-77 against South Africa, as well as match figures of 12-97 in the game with Monmouthshire. He finished the year with his best ever haul of 80 wickets at a cost of 11 apiece. He also performed the first ever hat-trick for Glamorgan during their match against Cornwall at Swansea in 1897. Lowe was offered a lucrative contract with a South African club in 1902, but he opted instead to stay in South Wales and played for Cardiff until retiring in 1906.

LYONS, Kevin James

RHB; RM.
Born: Cardiff, 18 December 1946.
Education: Lady Mary High School, Cardiff.
Glamorgan debut: 1967 v Hampshire at Swansea.
Career: 62 matches 1967-77; Assistant Coach 1973-83.
HS for Glamorgan: 92 v Cambridge University at Cambridge, 1972.
BB for Glamorgan: 1-36 v Worcestershire at Sophia Gardens, Cardiff, 1972.

Kevin Lyons joined the Glamorgan staff in the mid-1960s and played initially as a middle-order batsman. He moved up the order in the early 1970s, but at the end of 1972 he announced his retirement from first-class cricket to become the county's assistant coach and second team captain. Kevin also coached regularly in South Africa during the 1970s and acted as coach to Western Province. Lyons briefly reappeared in the Glamorgan side in 1976 and 1977 when the county were hit by injuries and he held the post of coach until 1984 when he became a first-class umpire. In 1989-90 he stood in an international between England and the West Indies in New York. During his career, Lyons played for Cardiff, St Fagan's, Maesteg Celtic, Maesteg Town

and Llanelli. He retired from umpiring at the end of the 1991 season to become coach of Worcestershire CCC.

McCONNON, James Edward

RHB; OB.
Born: Burnopfield, County Durham, 21 June 1922.
Education: Brooms School, Durham.
Glamorgan debut: 1950 v Surrey at The Oval.
Career: 243 matches 1950-61; Cap 1951; Benefit 1961; England 1954 (2 Tests).
HS for Glamorgan: 95 v Middlesex at Cardiff Arms Park, 1958.
BB for Glamorgan: 8-36 v Nottinghamshire at Trent Bridge, 1953.
100 wickets (3); 136 (16.07) 1951 best.
Full first-class record: 4,661 runs (14.38); 819 wickets (19.88); 152 catches.

Jim McConnon was a late entry into county cricket after a short career as a professional footballer. He played for Aston Villa in wartime friendlies in 1944-45, but after a knee injury the centre-half moved to South Wales to play for Lovells Athletic. He also joined Newport and showed promise as an attacking batsman and fast bowler. He went to Glamorgan's indoor cricket school at the Arms Park where George Lavis converted him into an off-spinner utilizing his tall, flowing action and long fingers. McConnon spent hours learning the art of spin, flight and length and his practice was rewarded by a regular place in Glamorgan's side in 1950.

In his second season of county cricket, McConnon took 136 wickets and his finest performance came in the match with South Africa at Swansea where he took 6-27 including a hat-trick as the tourists collapsed from 54-0 to 83 all out. McConnon also showed promise as an aggressive middle-order batsman and his height and reach allowed him to develop into a fine gully fielder. Sadly, he aggravated his knee injury in 1952 and missed much of the season, but he was restored to full fitness in 1953 and took 97 wickets, including a career-best 8-36 at Trent Bridge, to confirm his ability as a match-winning bowler and a place as an aspiring Test spinner. He toured India with the Commonwealth XI in 1953-54, but his injured knee flared up and he had to return early. However, he was fit for the start of the season and took 105 wickets, besides winning a place in England's side for the last two Tests against Pakistan at Old Trafford and The Oval. He began his England career with a spell of 3-12 in 6 overs and held four catches to win a place ahead of Jim Laker on the MCC tour to Australia in 1954-55. However, the spinner failed to recapture his best form and broke the little finger of his right hand, forcing him home early. He then broke a bone in his left hand and missed much of the 1955 side. Sadly, his relationship with Glamorgan started to turn sour and he left the staff when they insisted he underwent a medical before being offered a new contract. McConnon joined Burnley and helped them win the Lancashire League in 1956. This success lifted his morale and he returned to Glamorgan with a new contract. Over the next five seasons, he formed an effective partnership with Don Shepherd, taking 113 wickets at 18 apiece in 1959 including 8-62 against Worcestershire at Swansea. He took a Benefit in 1961, but picked up several small injuries and at the end of the season, announced his retirement. McConnon took up a job with Guinness in Manchester and played Minor County cricket for Cheshire between 1962 and 1964, before taking up a coaching post at Stonyhurst School.

McFARLANE, Leslie Leopold
LHB; RFM.
Born: Portland, Jamaica, 19 August 1952.
Glamorgan debut: 1985 v Oxford University at Oxford.

Career: 13 matches in 1985; Northamptonshire 1979 (8 matches); Lancashire 1982-84 (23 matches).
HS for Glamorgan: 8 v Somerset at Sophia Gardens, Cardiff, 1985.
BB for Glamorgan: 4-100 v Derbyshire at Derby, 1985.
Full first-class record: 127 runs (5.77); 102 wickets (40.58); 13 catches.

Les McFarlane joined Glamorgan in 1985 after spells with Northants and Lancashire. He was released at the end of the season and went back to play for Bedfordshire in the Minor Counties. His career-best performances were both for Lancashire at Southport, 15* against Northants in 1984 and 6-59 against Warwickshire in 1982.

MACK, Andrew James
LHB; LFM.
Born: Aylsham, Norfolk, 14 January 1956.
Glamorgan debut: 1978 Oxford University at Oxford.

Career: 21 matches 1978-80; Surrey 1976-77 (10 matches).
HS for Glamorgan: 18 v India at Swansea, 1979.
BB for Glamorgan: 4-28 v Worcestershire at Worcester, 1978.
Full first-class record: 102 runs (4.63); 44 wickets (42.93); 4 catches.

The 6ft 5in Mack played in five Sunday League games for Surrey in 1975 and made his first-class debut in 1976. He left The Oval in 1978 and joined Glamorgan, but he was plagued by injury and left the Glamorgan staff at the end of 1980 and joined the Metropolitan Police, before returning to cricket in 1989 with Norfolk. Despite a gap of nine years, he finished the season as the second highest wicket

taker and won a place in the Minor Counties squad for their games in the Benson & Hedges Cup in 1990 and 1991. He currently plays for Norwich Barleycorns.

McKAY, John Frederick

All-rounder.
Career: 1 match against Monmouthshire at Usk, 1895 scoring 2 and taking 1-8.
McKay played for Cardiff and was a tailor.

MADDEN-GASKELL, John Charles Pengelley MBE, OBE

RHB.

Born: Pontypool, 1 March 1896.
Died: Lowertown, Cornwall, 4 February 1975.
Education: Haileybury.
Career: 1 match in 1922 against Yorkshire at Headingley scoring 7 and 32. Somerset 1928-30 (9 matches).
Full first-class record: 300 runs (15.78); 5 wickets.

John Madden-Gaskell was a promising sportsman whilst at Haileybury playing in the rugby XV between 1911 and 1913 and in the cricket second XI in 1912 and 1913. On leaving school he went into the services and played one match for his native Glamorgan whilst playing for Penarth. He also appeared occasionally for Somerset between 1928 and 1930 and in 1928 scored 42 and 63 against Nottinghamshire at Taunton. Madden-Gaskell repeatedly drove the fast bowling of Larwood and showed that he would have held a regular place in either the Glamorgan or Somerset side had he chosen a career in cricket. He had a long and distinguished career in the Army, rising to the rank of major and was awarded the MBE in 1945 followed by the OBE in 1955.

MAJID JAHANGIR, Khan
RHB; RM/OB.

Born: Ludhiana, India, 28 September 1946.
Education: Aitchison College, Lahore; Punjab
University and Emmanuel College, Cambridge.

Glamorgan debut: 1968 v Northamptonshire at
Northampton.
Career: 154 matches 1968-76; Cap 1968; Captain
1973-76; Lahore 1961-62 to 1982-83; Punjab 1964-
65 to 1967-68; PIA 1968-69 to 1980-81; Cambridge
University 1970-72 (Blue all three years, Captain

1971-72); Pakistan 1964-65 to 1982-83 (63 Tests); Queensland 1973-74.
HS for Glamorgan: 204 v Surrey at The Oval, 1972.
1,000 runs (5); 1,547 runs (39.67) 1969 best.
BB for Glamorgan: 4-48 v Hampshire at Portsmouth, 1972.
Full first-class record: 27,328 runs (42.90); 73 centuries; 224 wickets (32.12); 408 catches.

Majid Khan was one of the most elegant and graceful batsmen ever to wear a Glamorgan sweater. He spent nine seasons in county cricket displaying his talents as a gifted strokemaker and useful seam bowler or off-spinner and it was a tragedy that his career with Glamorgan should end in discord during the middle of 1976.

He was the son of Dr Jahangir Khan, the former Indian Test Cap and Cambridge Blue and at the age of 15, young Majid scored 111* and took 6-67 on his first-class debut for Lahore 'B'. He was a heavy scorer and brisk opening bowler with Punjab University and toured England with the Pakistan Eaglets in 1963. He made his Test debut in 1964-65 against Australia at Karachi and later that season added 217 for the sixth wicket with Hanif Mohammed against New Zealand. The following season he scored a career-best 241 for Lahore against Bahawalpur at Lahore and won a place in the Pakistan party for the tour to England in 1967. In the game at Sophia Gardens he hit a superb 147 in 89 minutes before lunch, hitting Roger Davis for five sixes in one six-ball over. Wilf Wooller had been a close friend of his father whilst at Cambridge so Wooller persuaded the county to sign the dashing strokemaker. He scored 1,372 runs in his first season and became a valuable member of the championship winning side. His greatest asset was an ability to bat on the most difficult of wickets, as testified by 156 out of a total of 256 at Sophia Gardens as Glamorgan beat Worcestershire to win the county title and a breathtaking 147 before lunch against the West Indies at Swansea in 1969.

He went up to Cambridge in 1970, captaining the side in 1971 and 1972 and in the latter year led Cambridge to the first Varsity success for 14 years. After coming down, he also won the Lawrence Trophy for scoring 100 against Warwickshire in only 70 minutes. Majid led Glamorgan in 1973, before touring England with Pakistan in 1974. He returned to the county scene in 1975 and during the Sunday League match with Northants scored 50 off only 22 balls. He had a very laid-back style to captaincy which met with criticism from certain factions and he found it difficult to communicate with the young Welsh players. Things came to a head in 1976 as Glamorgan had a poor season and finished at the bottom of the championship for the first time since 1929. Majid also lost form and in

the middle of the season quit the county club.

Majid continued to play for Pakistan and toured Australia, New Zealand and the West Indies during the 1970s, before returning to England on the 1982 Pakistan tour. He retired from Test cricket at the end of the 1982-83 series with New Zealand and went into a career in broadcasting. Majid is currently controller of sport for Pakistan TV, but returned to England as manager of the Pakistan Under-19 team. He is a cousin of Pakistan's Imran Khan and Javed Burki.

MALONE, Steven John

RHB; RFM.
Born: Chelmsford, 19 October 1953.
Education: King's School, Elyand St Edmunds, Ipswich.
Glamorgan debut: 1985 v Oxford University at Oxford.
Career: 9 matches in 1985; Essex 1975-78 (2 matches); Hampshire 1980-84 (46 matches).
HS for Glamorgan: 2 v Oxford University at Oxford, 1985.
BB for Glamorgan: 5-38 v Hampshire at Southampton, 1985.
Full first-class record: 182 runs (5.87); 118 wickets (35.89); 13 catches.

'Piggy' Malone joined Glamorgan in 1985 after spells with Essex and Hampshire. He represented the Minor Counties in the Benson & Hedges Cup in 1986 after joining Durham and he has also played for Dorset and Wiltshire. His career-best performances were both achieved for Hampshire, 23 against Kent at Bournemouth in 1981 and 7-55 against Oxford University at The Parks in 1982.

MANN, Albert Henry

Batsman.
Born: Cardiff, November 1863.
Glamorgan debut: 1896 v Herefordshire at Hereford.
Career: 4 matches in 1896.
HS for Glamorgan: 58 v Herefordshire at Hereford, 1896.

Mann played for Cardiff.

MARLEY, Kenneth Ramsden

Batsman.
Born: Darlington, March 1865.
Died: Brentford, December 1915.
Career: 1 match in 1894 against Wiltshire at Cardiff Arms Park scoring 33 and 49.

Marley played for Cardiff and the Water Rats.

MARSH, William Edward

RHB; RFM.
Born: Newbridge, 10 September 1917.

Maynard failed to recapture his earlier form and with an immediate Test recall unlikely, he opted to tour South Africa with Mike Gatting's English XI in 1989-90. The presence of Viv Richards in the 1990 Glamorgan side helped Maynard curb his impetuous instincts and his batting matured in 1991.

He recorded double hundreds against Nottinghamshire and Hampshire, centuries in two limited overs matches and a century on his debut for Northern Districts in New Zealand in 1990-91 where he played for the Bay of Plenty club.

MEGGITT, Frank Claxton

RHB; WK.
Born: Barry, 17 February 1901.
Died: Radyr, 9 October 1945.
Education: Mill Hill and Emmanuel College,
Cambridge.
Career: 1 match in 1923 against Nottinghamshire
at Swansea scoring 0 and 4.

Frank Meggitt played for Barry and was the son
of the town's ex-mayor who owned a timber
importing business. He was also a leading hockey
player and after winning a Blue in 1925, he played
for Cardiff and Glamorgan and won three Welsh
caps in 1925. In later life, Meggitt became a useful
golfer and captained Radyr Golf Club besides
appearing   in   the   Glamorgan   Amateur
Championship.

MENDELSON, Wallingford

Batsman, occ WK.
Born: Temuka, New Zealand, 29 December 1872.
Died: Durban, South Africa, 19 August 1902.
Education: Christ College, Christchurch; Otago
University and Jesus College, Cambridge.
Glamorgan debut: 1896 v Surrey II at Cardiff Arms
Park.
Career: 2 matches in 1896; Canterbury 1894 (1
match).
HS for Glamorgan: 19 v Herefordshire at Cardiff
Arms Park, 1896.
Full first-class record: 7 runs (7.00).

Wally Mendelson was the son of a Polish Jew and
was brought up in Christchurch, New Zealand. He
was an outstanding schoolboy sportsman excelling
at athletics, rugby and cricket for Christ College;
He read Law at Otago University and won a place
in their XV in 1891 and 1892. He also represented
the university at cricket and was selected for
Canterbury against Hawkes Bay in 1894 scoring
seven in his only innings. Soon afterwards he moved
to England to continue his studies and had an
outstanding first-term at Cambridge, winning a
place at full-back for the 1894 Varsity match.
However, he aggravated an old knee injury and
had to give up rugby. Despite this, he continued
to excell at athletics and won a long jump Blue
in 1895 and even beat the immortal C.B.Fry despite
having two bad knees. He also was a half-Blue in
billiards, but never made the University cricket XI.
Mendelson spent his vacations with relatives in
Cardiff and played for the town club. He produced
some good performances with the bat and excelled
as a fielder and was drafted into the Glamorgan
side when J.H.Brain was injured out riding the night
before the match with Surrey II. After going down

from Cambridge, Mendelson moved to London to
complete his legal training, before returning to New
Zealand to set up a practice at Timaru in 1898.
In 1902 he moved to South Africa to seek new
opportunities, but within a couple of months, he
was found dead at a boarding house in Durban.

MERCER, John ('Jack')

RHB; RFM.
Born: Southwick, Sussex, 22 April 1895.
Died: London, 31 August 1987.
Glamorgan debut: 1922 v Oxford and Cambridge
XI at Cardiff Arms Park.
Career: 412 matches 1922-39; Benefit 1936 (£729);
Sussex 1919-21 (12 matches); Wales 1923-30;
Northamptonshire 1947 (1 match); Players 1926-34;
South of England 1928.
HS for Glamorgan: 72 v Surrey at The Oval, 1934.
BB for Glamorgan: 10-51 v Worcestershire at
Worcester, 1936.
100 wickets (6); 137 (20.35) 1929 best.
Full first-class record: 6,076 runs (11.77); 1,591
wickets (23.38); 144 catches.

Jack Mercer played club cricket for Southwick and
joined the Sussex staff in 1913 as a swing bowler.
But he left the following season and travelled across
Europe to Russia. He returned to Britain to serve
with the Royal Sussex during World War One and
rejoined the Sussex staff in 1919. However, his
opportunities were restricted due to the presence
of Maurice Tate and at the end of 1921 he accepted
an offer from Glamorgan and qualifed for the Welsh
county by playing for Barry. He took 4-41 as
Glamorgan defeated the 1923 West Indians and the
following season secured a regular place in the
county side. He had a modest start to his career,
taking 40 wickets at 21 apiece, but came into his
own from 1925 onwards and in the next 12 seasons
recorded the following annual total of victims; 96,
129, 96, 98, 137, 111, 90, 115, 79, 44, 109 and 127.

Mercer became the mainstay of Glamorgan's
limited new ball attack and he might have taken
more than 1,460 wickets had he received more
support at the other end or had more athletic
fielders. He based his success on a priceless ability
to swing the ball either way and when the shine
was off the ball, or on unhelpful wickets, Mercer
cut down on his pace and reverted to off-cutters.
Had he played for a more fashionable team, Jack
would have come close to the Test side, but even
so he toured India, Burma and Ceylon with the
MCC in 1926-27 and went with Sir Julian Cahn's
XI to Jamaica in 1928-29, besides making regular
appearances for the Players. Mercer was also an
aggressive lower-order batsman, striking 31 runs off
an eight-ball over against Worcestershire in 1939

outstanding returns including 8-41 at Worcester in 1930 and 8-42 at Edgbaston in 1931. He took a hat-trick at The Oval in 1932, but his finest performance of all came in his Benefit Year when at the age of 41 he took all ten wickets at Worcester in 1936. This was the first and only time this feat has been achieved by a Glamorgan bowler. All this hard work took its tole and he lost some of his pace in the late 1930s. He announced his retirement at the end of 1939, but reappeared for Glamorgan in their wartime friendlies in 1943.

In 1947 Mercer was appointed coach to Northamptonshire and during his first season was even drafted into the county side. He held that position until 1963 when he became the club's scorer and he continued to be a popular figure on the county circuit until retiring in 1981. He was also a noted card player and magician and was a member of the Magic Circle. Mercer also enjoyed more than the odd flutter and is reputed to have read of his selection on the MCC tour in 1926-27 whilst at Longchamp Races.

METSON, Colin Peter
RHB; WK.
Born: Goffs Oak, Herts, 2 July 1963.

and hitting Wilfred Rhodes for four mighty sixes during a half-hour 50 at Bradford in 1924.

During his career Mercer produced a number of

Education: Enfield Grammar; Stanborough School, Welwyn Garden City and Durham University.
Glamorgan debut: 1987 v Warwickshire at Edgbaston.
Career: 119 matches 1987; Cap 1987; Middlesex 1981-86 (24 matches).
HS for Glamorgan: 84 v Kent at Maidstone, 1991.
Full first-class record: 2,564 runs (17.81); 338 catches and 25 stumpings.

Colin Metson spent six seasons with Middlesex as Paul Dowton's understudy. He played for Young England against India in 1981, when he also made his first-class debut, before going to Durham University to read Economic History. Metson captained their side in the UAU in 1984 and later in the season hit a career-best 96 for Middlesex at Uxbridge against Gloucestershire. He joined Glamorgan in 1987 and won his county cap during his first full season of county cricket. He has established himself as one of the best specialist wicketkeepers in county cricket and broken several county records. Metson took seven catches in an innings against Derbyshire at Chesterfield in 1991 and finished the season as the leading keeper in the country with 76 victims. His neat style has won many admirers and it is surprising that he has never been selected for an England 'A' tour.

MILLER, Hamish David Sneddon
RHB; RM.
Born: Blackpool, 20 April 1943.
Education: Rondebosch High School; University of Cape Town and the University of Wales.

Glamorgan debut: 1963 v Hampshire at Swansea.
Career: 27 matches 1963-66; Western Province 1962-63; Orange Free State 1969-70, 1970-71.
HS for Glamorgan: 81 v Gloucestershire at Cheltenham, 1964.
BB for Glamorgan: 7-48 v Nottinghamshire at Trent bridge, 1964.
Full first-class record: 589 runs (11.54); 76 wickets (28.94); 23 catches.

Miller made his first-class debut in South Africa, before moving to South Wales where he had a university place. Whilst on the Glamorgan staff, he played for Ebbw Vale, St Fagan's and Briton Ferry Town. Miller returned to South Africa in 1967 and subsequently appeared for Orange Free State and toured South America in 1971-72 with a Country Districts XI.

MIR, Parvez Jamil
RHB; RM/OB.
Born: Sutrapur, Pakistan, 24 September 1953.
Education: Lahore University.
Career: 1 match in 1979 against Sri Lanka at Swansea scoring 10 and 6; Rawalpindi 1970-71; Lahore 1971-72; Punjab 1972-73, 1975-76; Universities 1973-74, 1974-75; Derbyshire 1975 (1 match); Habib Bank 1975-76, 1980-81.
Full first-class record: 3,353 runs (30.76); 5 centuries; 164 wickets (26.01); 61 catches.

Parvez Mir appeared for Derbyshire in 1975 after playing in domestic cricket in Pakistan and touring Sri Lanka with the national team in 1975-76. He subsequently played League cricket and made his debut for Norfolk in 1981, for whom he played until 1987. His single appearance for Glamorgan was the result of a double hundred in a benefit game and same outstanding batting performances for the second XI. He was also a useful squash player and is currently the director of the North American Cricket Authority for whom he organized games in 1990 between England and the West Indies. His highest first-class score was 155 for Punjab against Sind at Lahore in 1977-78, whilst his best bowling figures were 6-31 for Lahore at Rawalpindi in 1982-83. He appeared for the MCC against Wales and Scotland in 1991.

MIZEN, Charles A.
All-rounder.
Glamorgan debut: 1891 v Gloucestershire at Cardiff Arms Park.
Career: 2 matches in 1891.
HS for Glamorgan: 12 v MCC at Swansea, 1891.
He played for Cardiff and was a carpenter by trade.

MONKHOUSE, Steven

RHB; LFM.
Born: Bury, 24 November 1962.
Education: Derby Technical Grammar School and Peel College, Bury.
Glamorgan debut: 1987 v Oxford University at Oxford.
Career: 9 matches 1987-88; Warwickshire 1985-86 (2 matches).
HS for Glamorgan: 15 v Northamptonshire at Swansea, 1987.
BB for Glamorgan: 3-37 v Cambridge University at Fenners, 1988.
Full first-class record: 30 runs (4.28); 18 wickets (32.00); 2 catches.

MONTGOMERY, Stanley William

RHB.
Born: West Ham, 7 July 1920.
Education: Brew Road School, West Ham.
Glamorgan debut: 1949 v Derbyshire at Cardiff Arms Park.
Career: 29 matches 1949-53.
HS for Glamorgan: 117 v Hampshire at Bournemouth, 1949.
BB for Glamorgan: 3-29 v Hampshire at Bournemouth, 1952.

Monkhouse joined Glamorgan after a brief spell on the Warwickshire staff, but he was released at the end of the 1988 season. He has subsequently played club cricket for Ramsbottom and Minor County cricket with Staffordshire since 1989.

Montgomery played football for Hull in 1944, before joining Southend United as a centre-half. He made 96 appearances for them between 1946 and 1948 and during that time was on the staff of Essex CCC. In 1948 he joined Cardiff City for whom he made 231 appearances until 1955, before playing a season with Newport County and Llanelli. He made his first-class debut in 1949 and whilst in South Wales played for Briton Ferry Steel, Merthyr Tydfil, Hills Plymouth and Maesteg Celtic.

He subsequently became a football coach with Norwich, Cardiff and Cardiff University and in 1969 took up a coaching appointment at Bradfield School. In recent times he has returned to Cardiff and been a sports organizer with the Boys' Clubs of Wales and has acted as a talent scout for Bristol Rovers.

MOORE-GWYN, Howell Gwyn MC, CdeG, DSO
RHB.
Born: Duffryn Clydach, Neath, 7 July 1886.
Died: Midhurst, Eastbourne, 31 July 1956.
Education: Winchester and Sandhurst.
Glamorgan Debut: 1903 v Berkshire at Reading.
Career: 8 matches 1903-12; Army 1923; Punjab Governors XI 1929-30.
HS for Glamorgan: 63 v Devon at Devonport, 1906.
Full first-class record: 91 runs (30.33); 1 catch.

Howell Moore-Gwyn was in the Winchester XI between 1903 and 1905 before pursuing a military career and winning a place at Sandhurst. He was awarded the MC, Croix de Guerre and DSO for gallantry during World War One whilst serving with the Rifle Brigade. He subsequently became a staff officer with the King's African Rifles and served in India where he also appeared in domestic cricket. He played for Neath, MCC, I Zingari and Greenjackets and won the Army racquets double championships eight times between 1920 and 1933. He was the brother of Joseph Moore-Gwyn and grandson of Howel Gwyn, an MP for Neath.

MOORE-GWYN, Joseph Gwyn
Batsman.
Born: Neath, 15 May 1879.
Died: Liss, Hampshire, 17 February 1937.
Education: Winchester and Hertford College, Oxford.
Career: 1 match in 1906 against Devon at Devonport scoring 4 and 0.

Joseph Moore-Gwyn also played for Neath and was a Major in the Glamorgan Yeomanry. He served on the county committee between 1902 and 1909 and was the brother-in-law of Jestyn Williams.

MORGAN, Aubrey Niel
RHB; RM.
Born: Llandaff, 30 January 1904.
Died: Washington, USA, 14 September 1985.
Education: Charterhouse and Jesus College, Cambridge.
Glamorgan debut: 1928 v Oxford University at Oxford.

Career: 5 matches 1928-29; Wales 1929.
HS for Glamorgan: 35 v Oxford University at Oxford, 1928.
BB for Glamorgan: 2-93 v Yorkshire at Hull, 1929.
Full first-class record: 95 runs (8.63); 6 wickets (56.00); 1 catch.

Aubrey Morgan was the older brother of J.T.Morgan and was in the Charterhouse XI in 1922. He played for Cardiff and went into business in the Welsh capital.

MORGAN, Edward ('Teddy')
All-rounder.
Born: Abernant, 22 May 1880.
Died: North Walsham, 1 September 1949.
Education: Christ College, Brecon and Guy's Hospital.
Glamorgan debut: 1903 v Devon at Exeter.
Career: 1 match in 1903 and 2 appearances in 1913.
HS for Glamorgan: 5 v Devon at Exeter, 1903.
BB for Glamorgan: 3-18 v Devon at Exeter, 1903.

'Doctor Teddy' Morgan won 16 Welsh rugby caps as a winger between 1902 and 1908 and scored the famous try in 1905 which led to the defeat of the New Zealand All Blacks for the first time by Wales. He also played for Cardiff, London Welsh, Newport, Sketty, Surrey, Kent and Guy's Hospital and played cricket for Sketty. He was the uncle of E.N. and W.G.Morgan and had a doctor's practice in Swansea. He was also a useful golfer with the Pennard club and played in the Glamorgan Amateur Championship. He lost the sight of his right eye in a shooting accident in October 1938.

MORGAN, Edward Noel
RHB.
Born: Garnant, 22 December 1905.
Died: Cardiff, 27 August 1975.
Education: Christ College, Brecon.
Career: 1 match in 1934 v Essex at Neath scoring 1 in his only innings.

Noel Morgan played rugby and cricket for Cardiff and was the elder brother of W.G.Morgan. He had a fine schoolboy record at Christ College and was considered to be the school's outstanding athlete in the first half of this century. Noel pursued a career in banking and worked in Exeter, Hereford and Cardiff.

MORGAN, Frederick William
All-rounder.
Career: 1 match v Monmouthshire at Newport in 1896 scoring 3 and taking 1-33.

He was a timber merchant who played for Penarth and was a useful all-rounder. In 1888 he returned the figures of 8-8 against Barry Dock and in 1889 took 8-10 in Penarth's match with St Mary's. It was therefore surprising he was not called upon more often by Glamorgan.

MORGAN, Herbert Edward

Batsman and spin bowler.
Born: Cardiff, December 1870.
Died: Lower Penarth, 5 February 1933.
Glamorgan debut: 1889 v MCC at Lord's.
Career: 92 matches 1889-1905.
HS for Glamorgan: 254 v Monmouthshire at Cardiff Arms Park, 1901.
BB for Glamorgan: 3-50 v Wiltshire at Cardiff Arms Park, 1894.

Herbie Morgan played cricket and rugby for Penarth and in 1890 became the first Glamorgan batsman to score a century. His feat came in the match with Monmouthshire at the Arms Park, but only because Daniel Jones was unavailable. Morgan had scored a fine 52 for Penarth against Cardiff the previous weekend, so he was drafted into the

Glamorgan side as a late replacement. He went in at number seven and hit 147 with four sixes and 15 fours. In 1901 he also became the first Glamorgan batsman to score a double century, amassing 254 out of Glamorgan's total of 538 against Monmouthshire. He lived up to his nickname of 'The Penarth Slogger' by smashing one six and 40 fours. Morgan was a farmer in the Penarth area and served on the committee between 1898 and 1909.

MORGAN, Howard William

RHB; OB.
Born: Maesteg, 29 June 1931.
Education: Maesteg Grammar School.
Glamorgan debut: 1958 v Leicestershire at Newport.
Career: 2 matches in 1958.
HS for Glamorgan: 5 v Leicestershire at Newport, 1958.
BB for Glamorgan: 1-27 v Warwickshire at Swansea, 1958.

Howard Morgan was a batsman and off-spinner who joined the Glamorgan staff in the mid-1950s. He produced some good bowling performances in the second team, but had few opportunities in the

John Trevil Morgan (left) and William Guy Morgan.

first XI due to McConnon and Shepherd. He eventually made two appearances in the middle of 1958, but was released at the end of the season and became a school teacher in Cardiff, teaching geography and PE. He played club cricket for Maesteg Celtic, Neath and Briton Ferry Town and from 1960 until 1985 acted as a selector for the Welsh Schools Under-19 side.

MORGAN, John Trevil
LHB; RM; occ WK.
Born: Llandaff, 7 May 1907.
Died: Clifton, 18 December 1976.
Education: Charterhouse and Jesus College, Cambridge.
Glamorgan debut: 1925 v Essex at Leyton.
Career: 39 matches 1925-34; Cambridge University 1927-30 (Blue 1928-30); Wales 1928.
HS for Glamorgan: 103* v South Africa at Swansea, 1929.
BB for Glamorgan: 3-16 v Warwickshire at Edgbaston, 1933.
Full first-class record: 2,339 runs (21.07); 4 centuries; 26 wickets (51.65); 60 catches and 12 stumpings.

John Morgan was in the Charterhouse XI between 1922 and 1928, before going up to Cambridge where he won a Blue in 1928, 1929 and 1930 and captained the university during his final year in residence. He returned to South Wales and joined the family's business, David Morgan's of Cardiff. He retired from first-class cricket at the end of the 1934 season to become the coach and captain of Glamorgan's second eleven who played in the Minor County championship. He fulfilled this role until 1947 and in later years became a director of the Welsh National Opera. J.T. played club cricket for Cardiff and was the brother of A.N.Morgan. His career-best score was 149 in the 1929 Varsity match.

MORGAN, Thomas Rees
RHB; OB.
Born: Pontypridd, 11 April 1893.
Education: Monmouth School.
Glamorgan debut: 1913 v Kent at Bromley.
Career: 18 Minor County matches between 1913 and 1920, plus 39 first-class games from 1921 until 1925.
HS for Glamorgan: 87* v Leicestershire at Leicester, 1923.
BB for Glamorgan: 2-35 v Carmarthenshire at Swansea, 1920.

Morgan played club cricket for Cardiff and was renowned for his correct, if ultra-cautious, approach, hence his nickname of 'Stonewall'.

MORGAN, William
All-rounder.
Born: Nantgarw, 1862.
Died: Porthleven, 22 October 1914.
Education: Weston School, Bath.
Glamorgan debut: 1889 v MCC at Lord's.
Career: 24 matches 1889-1901; West of England 1894.
HS for Glamorgan: 91 v MCC at Lord's, 1892.
BB for Glamorgan: 7-79 v MCC at Lord's, 1892.
Full first-class record: 34 runs (6.80); 3 wickets; 2 catches.

William Morgan was a leading figure in club and county cricket during the 1880s and 1890s, appearing for Cardiff, Llwynypia, Lansdown, MCC, I Zingari and the South Wales CC. He served on the Glamorgan committee from 1888 and after a move to the West Country, filled a similar position with Somerset.

MORGAN, William Guy (later STEWART-MORGAN by marriage in May 1941)
RHB; RM.
Born: Garnant, 26 December 1907.
Died: Carmarthen, 29 July 1973.
Education: Christ College, Brecon; St Catherine's, Cambridge and Guy's Hospital.
Glamorgan debut: 1925 v Somerset at Cardiff Arms Park.
Career: 45 matches 1925-38; Cambridge University 1927-29; Wales 1929.
HS for Glamorgan: 91* v Sussex at Horsham, 1929.
BB for Glamorgan: 1-15 v Essex at Swansea, 1928.
Full first-class record: 1,071 runs (17.55); 3 wickets; 8 catches.

Guy Morgan was a talented all-rounder, playing cricket and rugby for Cambridge University, Cardiff and Swansea, besides winning eight Welsh rugby caps between 1926 and 1929. During his rugby career he also appeared for Guy's Hospital, London Welsh and the Barbarians. He was also a rugby Blue whilst up at Cambridge and acted as 12th man in the Varsity match. Sadly, he was crippled with rheumatoid arthritis from his late-30s, but taught for 32 years with great fortitude at Radley, despite being confined to a wheelchair in his later years. He had also been a talented golfer and was the brother of E.N.Morgan and the nephew of Dr Teddy Morgan.

MORGAN, William Percival
RHB; RM.
Born: Abercrave, 1 January 1905.

Died: Neath, 3 March 1983.
Education: Christ College, Brecon.
Career: 1 match in 1925 v Nottinghamshire at Swansea scoring 0 and 4.

He played cricket for Swansea who he captained in 1933 and also for Neath. Morgan was an accountant by profession and also played rugby for Neath.

MORRIS, Alexander William

LHB; LM.
Born: Cardiff, August 1863.
Education: Cowbridge Grammar School.
Glamorgan debut: 1889 v Warwickshire at Cardiff Arms Park.
Career: 13 matches 1889-97.
HS for Glamorgan: 91 v Monmouthshire at Cardiff Arms Park, 1890.
BB for Glamorgan: 2-14 v Monmouthshire at Cardiff Arms Park, 1890.

Alex Morris was one of the leading batsman with the South Wales CC during the 1880s and captained Cardiff in 1890 and 1891. He also captained the county side in 1890 and served on the committee between 1888 and 1900.

MORRIS, Frank Hall (later Byng-Morris)

Batsman.
Born: Bridgend, September 1869.
Died: Tonbridge, 21 October 1954.
Education: Malvern.
Glamorgan debut: 1893 v Monmouthshire at Cardiff Arms Park.
Career: 3 matches 1893-96.
HS for Glamorgan: 16 v Monmouthshire at Cardiff Arms Park, 1893.

Morris was in the Malvern XI in 1888 and played club cricket for Swansea and Monmouth.

MORRIS, Hugh

LHB; OB.
Born: Cardiff, 5 October 1963.
Education: Blundell's School and South Glamorgan Institute.
Glamorgan debut: 1981 v Leicestershire at Sophia Gardens, Cardiff.
Career: 179 matches 1981-; Cap 1986; Captain 1987-89; England 1991 (3 Caps); MCC; England 'A'.
HS for Glamorgan: 160* v Derbyshire at Sophia Gardens, Cardiff, 1990.
1,000 runs (5); 2,276 (55.51) 1990 best.
BB for Glamorgan: 1-6 v Oxford University at Oxford, 1987.
Full first-class record: 10,539 runs (36.84); 24 centuries; 2 wickets (161.50); 104 catches.

Hugh Morris had an outstanding record, as a schoolboy with Blundell's and Cardiff. He broke every batting record at the famous West Country school with a total of over 3,000 runs whilst in the XI including 1,032 in his final year at an average of 149. The gritty opening batsman was selected for the English Schools and went on their tours to the West Indies in 1980-81 and Sri Lanka in 1982-83.

Morris made his second eleven debut when still only 15 and made his first-class debut in 1981, but his subsequent appearances were limited by his studies for a Human Movement degree. However, he was selected for Young England against the Young West Indies in 1982 and the following year led Young England against their Australian counterparts. Morris played several attractive innings' in Glamorgan's middle order in 1983 and in 1984 recorded his maiden first-class century against Yorkshire at Sophia Gardens. Morris also established himself as a swift outfielder as befitted a talented fly-half with South Glamorgan Institute, Aberavon and Newport and in 1986 he passed 1,000 runs for the first time and was awarded his county cap.

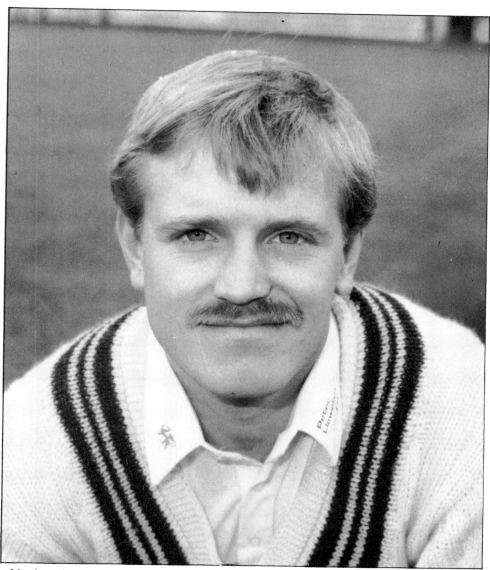

Morris took over the Glamorgan captaincy in July 1987 and when he led the side at Leicester became the club's youngest ever captain at 22 years and ten months. He celebrated with a maiden Sunday century, but the pressure of leading the side, who often struggled for consistency, affected Morris' own form. He failed to pass the 1,000 mark in 1988 and midway through 1989 stood down from the captaincy to concentrate on his own batting. 1990 saw a welcome return to form as Morris broke two of Javed Miandad's county records, by scoring 2,276 runs and hitting ten centuries — the most in a season for Glamorgan. He continued to form a reliable opening partnership with Alan Butcher and became the most consistent pairing in the country. His return to form attracted the attention of the England selectors and he was appointed captain of the England 'A' tour to Pakistan and Sri Lanka in 1990-91. Before this however, Hugh was called up to Australia to join the Test party as cover for Graham Gooch who had an injured hand. Despite scores of 33 and 50 in two limited overs games, Morris was surplus to requirements and flew back to lead the 'A' tour. Political unrest disrupted the Pakistan leg of the tour, but a full series was possible in Sri Lanka, where Morris hit 118 in the third one-day international. In 1991 Morris led the MCC against the county champions and then become the first player in the country to score 1,000 runs. He won overdue selection for the Test side later in the season and scored 50 runs in four innings' against the West Indies. Despite scores of 42 and 23 against Sri Lanka and over 1,500 championship runs, Morris lost his place for the New Zealand tour and was selected once again for the 'A' tour to Bermuda and the West Indies in 1991-92.

MORRIS, Ian

RHB; SLA.
Born: Maesteg, 27 June 1946.
Education: Maesteg Grammar School.
Glamorgan debut: 1966 v Hampshire at Cardiff Arms Park.
Career: 14 matches 1966-68.

HS for Glamorgan: 38 v Hampshire at Cardiff Arms Park, 1966.
BB for Glamorgan: 2-30 v Northamptonshire at Swansea, 1968.

Ian Morris was an all-rounder with Maesteg Celtic and Ynysygerwn who played occasionally during the mid-1960s, but never established a regular place and returned to play for and coach, Maesteg Celtic.

MORRIS, Vernon Leslie

RHB; RM.
Born: Briton Ferry, 13 June 1894.
Died: Exmouth, 11 January 1973.
Glamorgan debut: 1920 v Monmouthshire at Briton Ferry.
Career: 2 Minor County matches in 1920, plus 18 first-class matches 1921-29.
HS for Glamorgan: 46 v Wiltshire at Marlborough, 1920.

Morris played club cricket for Swansea and Briton Ferry Town and batted in the middle order for Glamorgan during the 1920s.

MORRIS, William Percy

RHB; RM.
Born: Swansea, 19 June 1881.
Died: Swansea, 30 July 1975.
Glamorgan debut: 1906 v Monmouthshire at Swansea.
Career: 46 Minor County matches between 1906 and 1920 and 8 first-class games from 1921 until 1925; South Wales 1912.
HS for Glamorgan: 56 v Wiltshire at Cardiff Arms Park, 1911.
BB for Glamorgan: 4-28 v Surrey II at Cardiff Arms Park, 1920.
Full first-class record: 159 runs (9.35); 2 wickets; 6 catches.

Percy Morris was a leading batsman with Swansea and captained them in 1911 and 1921. He was the father of R.J.Morris who played for Kent in 1950 and was a Blue at Cambridge in 1949.

MOSELEY, Ezra Alphonsa

RHB; RFM.
Born: Waldrons Village, Barbados, 5 January 1958.
Education: Christ Church High School, Barbados.
Glamorgan debut: 1980 v Essex at Swansea.
Career: 35 matches 1980-86; Cap 1981; Barbados 1981-82; Eastern Province 1985-; West Indies 1990 (5 Tests).
HS for Glamorgan: 70* v Kent at Canterbury, 1980.
BB for Glamorgan: 6-23 v Australia at Swansea, 1981.

Full first-class record: 1,379 runs (18.63); 243 wickets (24.27); 20 catches.

Ezra Moseley joined Glamorgan in 1980, despite not having played any first-class cricket for Barbados. He soon made an impact with the Welsh county, but his fiery bowling was hindered by a severe back injury and he was forced to return home in 1982. He recovered and toured South Africa with the 'rebel' West Indies in 1982-83 and 1983-84. Moseley returned to the UK to play for Littleborough in the Central Lancashire League and in 1986 reappeared for Glamorgan after an injury to Javed Miandad. After several successful seasons in the domestic competitions, Moseley finally won a place in the West Indies team for the one-day internationals and Test matches against England in 1989-90. He also turned down a contract with Surrey for the 1990 season, preferring instead to play League cricket with Oldham.

MOSS, Ernest

RHB.
Career: 1 match in 1923 against Lancashire at Blackpool scoring 5 and 10 and taking 2-70.

He was the son of Sam Moss and created Lancashire League bowling records whilst playing for Todmorden and Ramsbottom. Moss was drafted into the Glamorgan side when they found themselves with only ten fit players for the game at Blackpool.

MOYNAN, Dr William Arthur

Batsman.
Education: Dublin University.
Career: 1 match in 1898 against Monmouthshire at Newport scoring 4 in his only innings.

Dr Moynan played for Penarth and Barry and was an expert on criminal lunacy, serving at various asylums in South Wales and the West Country.

MULLENS, David

All-rounder.
Glamorgan debut: 1896 v Worcestershire at Cardiff Arms Park.
Career: 1 match in 1896 and 1 in 1900.
HS for Glamorgan: 6 v Berkshire at Cardiff Arms Park, 1900.
BB for Glamorgan: 2-55 v Worcestershire at Cardiff Arms Park, 1896.

He played for Cardiff, Canton and Taff Vale and was a painter by trade.

MULLINS, Alfred Edward

All-rounder.
Born: Chepstow, September 1858.
Died: Tidenham, 30 November 1913.
Education: Monmouth School.
Career: 1 match in 1890 against the MCC at Swansea scoring 3 and 8 and taking 2-44.

Mullins played for Chepstow and Monmouthshire and was a prominent figure in Monmouthshire 'society'. He also played for the XXII of Chepstow and District which challenged, and defeated, the United XI of All-England at Piercefield Park in 1882. He scored 14 and 11 and took 1-42 and 4-24.

MUNCER, Bernard Leonard

RHB; LB; OB.
Born: Hampstead, 23 October 1913.
Died: Camden, 18 January 1982.
Glamorgan debut: 1947 v Yorkshire at Swansea.
Career: 224 matches 1947-54; Cap 1947; Benefit 1954 (£3,556); Middlesex 1933-46 (82 matches, Cap 1935); MCC 1935-57; Players 1948.
HS for Glamorgan: 135 v Somerset at Swansea, 1952.

BB for Glamorgan: 9-62 v Essex at Brentwood, 1948.
1,000 runs (1); 1,076 (24.45) 1952 best.
100 wickets (4); 156 (17.12) 1948 best.
The Double 1952.
Full first-class record: 8,646 runs (20.88); 4 centuries; 755 wickets (20.90); 144 catches.

Len Muncer played his early club cricket with Hampstead and Reading before joining the MCC groundstaff in 1929, primarily as a leg-spinner and making his Middlesex debut in 1933. However, he failed to command a regular place and during World War Two was a PoW in South-East Asia and forced to undertake labouring on the Burma-Siam Railway. He reappeared for Middlesex in 1946, but his long-term future looked unattractive, so he moved to Glamorgan in 1947. As Johnnie Clay went into semi-retirement, Muncer opted to concentrate on off-spin and he made an immediate impact with 107 wickets in 1947, followed by 156 in the Championship season of 1948. Muncer possessed

Muncer also added a record 230 for the sixth wicket with Willie Jones at Worcester in 1953, but at the age of 40 all this hard work, never mind his experiences as a PoW, began to tell and he missed six weeks of the 1953 season with a groin strain. With McConnon emerging on the scene, Muncer was prepared to take a back seat and at the end of his Benefit season in 1954, he announced his retirement. He played club cricket for Crewe in the Staffordshire Leagues and appeared for the MCC, but from 1955 he served as head coach at Lord's. He held this position until 1978 and whilst at Lord's recommended many young players to Glamorgan. He was a popular and jovial figure and received a testimonial of £2,114 from the MCC in 1971.

MURRAY, T.

Batsman.
Career: 1 match in 1911 against Staffordshire at Stoke scoring 23 and 78*.

He was the professional with Plymouth Merthyr and judging by his performance against Staffordshire could have been called upon more often by Glamorgan.

NASH, Albert ('Jack')

RHB; RM; OB.
Born: Blean, Kent, 18 September 1873.
Died: Battersea, 6 December 1956.
Glamorgan debut: 1900 v MCC at Cardiff Arms Park.

the three virtues of length, flight and spin and proved to be almost unplayable on the turning wickets of South Wales. Amongst his outstanding returns in 1948 were 15-51 against Essex at Brentwood and 15-201 against Sussex at Swansea and his cunning off-spin proved to be an indispensable weapon at Wooller's disposal. Muncer was also a fine catcher close to the wicket and took 31 catches in the leg trap or at slip during 1948.

He took 105 wickets in 1949 and in 1951 performed the match double of 107* and 10-57 at Chesterfield against Derbyshire. In 1952 he achieved the Double of 100 wickets and 1,076 runs after being moved up the batting order and hitting his career-best against Somerset from the number-four spot.

Malcolm Nash. Perhaps best known outside Wales as the man hit for six sixes in an over by Gary Sobers, Nash was himself a fine striker of the ball as well as a being a particularly economical bowler in limited-over cricket.

Career: 123 Minor County matches 1900-20, plus 36 first-class appearances in 1921 and 1922.

HS for Glamorgan: 44 v Monmouthshire at Cardiff Arms Park, 1908.

BB for Glamorgan: 9-33 v Oxford Harlequins at Cardiff Arms Park, 1908.

Nash joined Cardiff as their professional and groundsman in 1900 and played regularly for Glamorgan from 1902. Over the next ten years he bore the brunt of the bowling, firstly as a medium-pace bowler and latterly as an off-spinner. Amongst his best match returns were 10-94 v MCC at the Arms Park and 12-77 against Berkshire at Swansea in 1903, besides 11-62 at Newport in 1904 and 11-118 against Devon at Swansea in 1906. He also produced figures of 8-31 against Devon at Exeter in 1904, plus 9-56 against Somerset at the Arms Park in 1910 and his nagging accuracy and powers of spin were two of the factors behind Glamorgan's success in the early 1900s. In 1912 he joined Haslington in the Lancashire League, but returned in 1920 to Neath. He rejoined Cardiff in 1921 and looked after the Arms Park wicket until 1925. Nash was past his best when Glamorgan entered the county championship but still took 15-116 against Worcestershire at Swansea in 1921.

NASH, Malcolm Andrew

LHB; LM, occ SLA.

Born: Abergavenny, 9 May 1945.

Education: Wells Cathedral School.

Glamorgan debut: 1966 v Cambridge University at Cardiff Arms Park.

Career: 335 matches 1966-83; Cap 1969; Benefit 1978 (£18,000); Captain 1980-81; The Rest 1976.

HS for Glamorgan: 130 v Surrey at The Oval, 1976.

BB for Glamorgan: 9-56 v Hampshire at Basingstoke, 1975.

Full first-class record: 7,129 runs (17.73); 2 centuries; 993 wickets (25.87); 148 catches.

Malcolm Nash played as a youngster for Abergavenny and made his Glamorgan debut as a left-arm seam bowler in 1966. He shot to fame in 1968 when Gary Sobers of Nottinghamshire hit Nash, who was experimenting with slow left-arm spin, for six sixes in an over at Swansea. He won a regular place in the side the following year and took 80 wickets at 19.50 as Glamorgan won the Championship. During the 1970s Nash developed into one of the best new ball bowlers in county cricket, swinging the ball both in and away from the batsman and he had the priceless habit of dismissing the best batsman in the country.

Amongst his best returns were 14-137 against Hampshire at Basingstoke in 1975 and 12-131 against Gloucestershire at Sophia Gardens in 1975,

whilst his best season was 1977 when he took 81 wickets at 24 apiece and dismissed Mike Brearley with his first ball in the Gillette Cup Final. Nash was a fine bowler in limited overs cricket, bowling his allocation of overs on a Sunday straight through at a minimal cost, as testified by figures of 8-4-8-2 and 8-4-8-1 against Lancashire in 1980 and 1973 respectively. Nash also took a hat-trick in the Sunday League match with Worcestershire in 1975. He was also an aggressive tail-end batsman who could on his day produce a violent innings. In 1976 he scored a century off only 61 balls before lunch at The Oval and became the first Glamorgan centurion in the Benson & Hedges Cup by making an unbeaten 103 against Hampshire at Swansea.

Nash led the county side in 1980 and 1981 and retired two years later with a first-class career haul of 991 wickets for Glamorgan. He also played club cricket with Swansea and Llanelli and appeared in Minor County cricket for Shropshire in 1982.

NEEDHAM, Patrick John Easthorpe

LHB; RM.

Born: Cardiff, 6 December 1951.

Education: Harrow.

Career: 1 match v Cambridge University at Swansea in 1975 scoring 4 and returning figures of 1-49 and 1-56.

Ricky Needham was in the Harrow XI from 1966 to 1970 and played for Welsh Schools. He opted for a legal career and became a solicitor in Cardiff. Needham has played for St Fagan's since the early 1970s and has captained the club since 1982, including their victory in the 1991 Village Final at Lord's. He also captained Harrow Wanderers in the Cricketer Cup between 1979 and 1985 and played for Wales between 1975 and 1986. He currently serves on the county committee.

NICHOLL, John Illtyd Dillwyn

Batsman.

Born: Merthyr Mawr, 1 May 1861.

Died: Merthyr Mawr, 20 September 1935.

Education: Eton and Christchurch College, Oxford.

Career: 1 match in 1895 against the South Wales CC at Swansea scoring 16 in his only innings.

He was the son of John Cole Nicholl of Merthyr Mawr House and played for Bridgend and the MCC. He was a barrister by profession and was a High Sheriff for Glamorgan in 1899. Nicholl also served on the committee between 1894 and 1903. John Nicholl also played in the 1893 Trial at the Arms Park for Glamorgan against a Colts XXII, scoring 18 and 4 and taking 6-56.

NICHOLL, Louis Dillwyn

Batsman.
Born: Merthyr Mawr, 25 September 1864.
Died: Shipston-on-Stour, 5 January 1956.
Education: Clifton College and the Royal Agricultural College, Cirencester.
Glamorgan debut: 1891 v Monmouthshire at Newport.
Career: 6 matches 1891-93.
HS for Glamorgan: 91 v Monmouthshire at Newport, 1891.
BB for Glamorgan: 1-6 v MCC at Lord's, 1892.

Nicholl, younger brother of J.I.D.Nicholl, played for Swansea and Bridgend, and worked as a land agent.

NORTH, Philip David

RHB; SLA.
Born: Newport, 16 May 1965.
Education: St Julian's, Newport and Nash College of Further Education.

Glamorgan debut: 1985 v Yorkshire at Swansea.
Career: 22 matches 1985-89.
HS for Glamorgan: 41* v Northamptonshire at Wellingborough, 1988.
BB for Glamorgan: 4-43 v Worcestershire at Neath, 1987.

Phil North had a trial with Worcestershire in 1985 and made his Glamorgan debut later that season. He is the son of Stan North who played for Glamorgan during wartime friendlies. Phil has played club cricket for Swansea and Newport and played for Wales in the Minor County championship from 1990. He is a qualified toolmaker and is currently captain of Newport.

O'BREE, Arthur

RHB; RM.
Born: Poona, India, 31 May 1886.
Died: Baragwanath, South Africa, 27 December, 1943.
Glamorgan debut: 1920 v Monmouthshire at Ebbw Vale.
Career: 9 Minor County matches in 1920, plus 18 first-class appearances between 1921 and 1923.
HS for Glamorgan: 116 v Monmouthshire at Briton Ferry, 1920.

Colonel O'Bree joined Glamorgan after colonial service in India and played for Cardiff and Port Talbot. He served on the committee between 1922 and 1923.

O'DALY, Guy Nolan

RHB; RM.
Born: Bramley, Hants, 4 September 1908.
Career: 1 match in 1938 v Cambridge University at Swansea scoring 9 in his only innings.

O'Daly played club cricket for Abergavenny and appeared for Glamorgan II in their Minor County matches in 1936. He made his first-class debut in 1938, but was injured after bowling only seven overs and did not reappear in any other county games.

ONTONG, Rodney Craig

RHB; RM; OB.
Born: Johannesburg, 9 September 1955.
Education: Selbourne College.
Glamorgan debut: 1975 v Australia at Swansea.
Career: 257 matches 1975-89; Cap 1979; Captain 1984-86; Benefit 1989 — £48,394; Transvaal 1976-77, 1977-78; Northern Transvaal 1978-79, 1981-82; Border 1982-83, 1987-88 ; MCC 1987; Border 1972-73, 1975-76; Northern Transvaal 1988-89; T.N.Pearce's XI 1976.

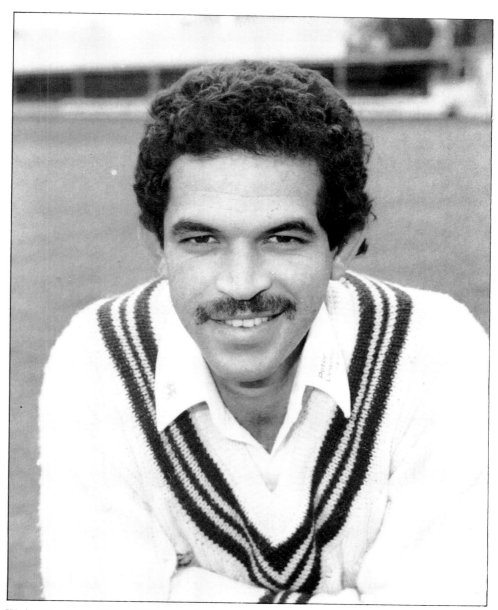

HS for Glamorgan: 204* v Middlesex at Swansea, 1984.
1,000 runs (5); 1,320 (35.67) 1984 best.
BB for Glamorgan: 8-67 v Nottinghamshire at Trent Bridge, 1985.
Full first-class record: 15,071 runs (29.55); 20 centuries; 836 wickets (31.06); 178 catches.

Rodney Ontong came over to the UK to have football trials with Chelsea and during the summer played club cricket in the London area. He was not offered terms by Chelsea, but so impressed the MCC officials with his cricketing skills that he was taken on the Lord's groundstaff from 1971 until 1973. In 1972 he made his first-class debut for Border and during 1973 and 1974 played second team cricket with Middlesex. Ontong was recommended to Glamorgan by Len Muncer and after a trial in 1974 was offered terms. He made his Glamorgan debut in 1975 but did not play regularly until 1977 as he had to qualify as an English player and played regularly for Swansea. Ontong was a hard hitting, but stylish middle-order batsman, who in his early days was also a brisk medium-pace bowler. He soon became an indispensable member of Glamorgan's one-day side and won five Gold Awards in Benson & Hedges matches.

Ontong moved up the order in the early 1980s and proved he had the temperament for the number-three spot by adding 270 for the third wicket with Javed Miandad against Gloucestershire at Bristol in 1981. Later in the season he also took part in a record tenth wicket partnership of 140 with Robin Hobbs against Hampshire at Swansea. Ontong also changed bowling styles in 1983 and converted to off-spin. He was a big spinner of the ball and the change soon produced its rewards as Ontong took 74 wickets in 1984, plus 64 in 1985. During the latter season he scored 130 and returned match figures of 13-106 against Nottinghamshire at Trent Bridge.

In 1983 he became captain of Border and he took over the captaincy of Glamorgan midway through the 1984 season when Mike Selvey retired. His name was also mentioned in the Press as a potential England spinner and he was selected for the MCC against Essex at the start of 1987. His promising career came to an abrupt halt in August 1988 when he badly injured his knee in an horrific car crash *en route* from Essex to a game in Northamptonshire. He had a winter operation and tried to make a comeback during his Benefit season in 1989, but on medical advice he retired as a professional cricketer and returned to South Africa. He has subsequently reappeared as an amateur for Northern Transvaal and also acts as their manager. He is the son-in-law of Jim Pressdee and has worked recently as a cricket commentator for BBC Wales TV.

OSBORNE, Arthur James

Batsman and spin bowler.
Glamorgan debut: 1901 v Surrey II at The Oval.
Career: 47 matches 1901-11.
HS for Glamorgan: 110 v Monmouthshire at Cardiff Arms Park, 1901.
BB for Glamorgan: 6-40 v Philadelphians at Cardiff Arms Park, 1903.

Osborne played for Penarth and Barry and was a solid opening batsman and occasional spin bowler. He served on the county committee from 1909 until 1914.

PARKHOUSE, Richard John

RHB.
Born: Neath, March 1910.
Glamorgan debut: 1939 v Hampshire at Southampton.
Career: 2 matches in 1939, scoring 0 in his only innings against Hampshire.

Parkhouse played club cricket for Clydach and Llanelli and was a schoolmaster by profession. He worked in Egypt shortly before World War Two and appeared for All Egypt against H.M.Martineau's XI in 1939. He returned to the UK after the war and coached in Scotland.

PARKHOUSE, William Gilbert Anthony

RHB; RM.
Born: Swansea, 12 October 1925.
Education: Wycliffe.
Glamorgan debut: 1948 v Essex at Cardiff Arms Park.
Career: 435 matches 1948-64; Cap 1948; Benefit 1957 (£3,750); England 1950-59 (7 Tests); Players 1950-59.
HS for Glamorgan: 201 v Kent at Swansea, 1956.
1,000 runs (15 consecutive seasons 1948-62); 2,071 (49.30) 1959 best.
BB for Glamorgan: 1-4 v Surrey at Llanelli, 1952.
Full first-class record: 23,508 runs (31.68); 32 centuries; 2 wickets; 324 catches.

Gilbert Parkhouse is widely acknowledged to have been the most graceful of Welsh-born batsman and if he had played for a more fashionable county, he would surely have won more than seven caps for England.

He played as a schoolboy with Wycliffe and Swansea and was coached from a young age by Billy Bancroft. He was also a talented young rugby player and appeared for Swansea. Parkhouse made his Glamorgan debut during their wartime friendlies from 1943 and after doing his National Service he joined the staff in 1948. He scored over 1,200 runs in his first season and despite having a slight frame he reeled off a wide range of powerful shots based on immaculate timing. He was also a safe slip fielder and was awarded his cap at the end of the championship winning season.

Parkhouse initially batted at number three but in the 1950s moved up to open the batting, firstly with Emrys Davies and later Bernard Hedges. His running between the wickets with Hedges was a model for the many schoolboys who idolized Parkhouse and he was equally at home against the fastest of bowlers or cunning of spinners.

In 1950 Parkhouse scored 1,742 runs including three consecutive centuries and was selected for the

England side against the West Indies. He played in the Second and Third Tests and made a composed 69 in the second innings at Trent Bridge, which earned him a place on the winter tour to Australia and New Zealand. However, he was plagued by poor health 'down under' and batted only modestly in his three Test appearances. Parkhouse was also competing with Hutton, Washbrook, Edrich and Compton and it highlighted England's rich batting talent that the selectors could omit such a free scoring batsman as Parkhouse, although many felt the England selectors treated the phlegmatic

Parkhouse rather harshly and could have given him an extended run in the side.

Season after season, Parkhouse proved himself the master of county attacks up and down the country and regularly passed 1,000 runs. In 1950 he put on 241 for the first wicket against Somerset at the Arms Park with Emrys Davies, as well as 233 against Surrey at Swansea. In 1954 he scored 182 against Middlesex at Lord's and shared a partnership of 219 with Bernard Hedges for the second wicket against Warwickshire at Llanelli. Parkhouse eventually forced himself back into the England side by sheer weight of runs, making a record 2,071 runs in 1959 at an average of 49.30 and six elegant centuries. He played in the Third and Fourth Tests against India and despite scoring 78 at Headingley, sharing a record opening partnership of 146 and being on the winning side on both occasions, the England selectors dropped Parkhouse in favour of Raman Subba Row and one can only wonder what he might have achieved at Test level had the selectors put more faith in him.

Parkhouse returned to county cricket and continued to be a heavy scorer, with a record of scoring a century against every other county side. He struggled with back injuries in 1962 and 1963 and eventually retired in 1964 with over 23,000 runs to his name. Parkhouse briefly had a spell coaching Worcestershire before acting as cricket coach at Stewarts-Melville College in Edinburgh. He held that post from 1966 until 1987 when he retired and was given a testimonial. To mark his achievements, Glamorgan played a match in his honour against Scotland.

PAULINE, Duncan Brian

RHB; RM.
Born: Aberdeen, 15 December 1960.
Education: Bishop Fox School, East Molesey.
Glamorgan debut: 1986 v Warwickshire at Edgbaston.
Career: 12 matches in 1986; Surrey 1979-85 (49 matches).
HS for Glamorgan: 97 v Worcestershire at Neath, 1986.
BB for Glamorgan: 2-48 v Northamptonshire at Swansea, 1986.
Full first-class record: 2,258 runs (25.08); 1 century; 18 wickets (36.77); 22 catches.

Duncan Pauline played for Young England in 1978 and spent seven years on the Surrey staff. Whilst in the south-east he played for East Molesey and Maldon Wanderers and in 1986 joined Glamorgan, where he also appeared for St Fagan's. Pauline retired from county cricket at the end of the season

and returned to his native Scotland who he represented in one-day competitions in 1987 and 1988. His highest first-class score was 115 for Surrey against Sussex at The Oval in 1983, whilst his best bowling figures were 5-52 against Derbyshire at Derby in 1985.

PEARSON, Dr Cecil Joseph Herbert

RHB; OB.
Born: Poplar, 22 January 1888.
Died: Porthcawl, 14 September 1971.
Glamorgan debut: 1 match in 1922 against Nottinghamshire at Cardiff Arms Park scoring 9 and 0.

Dr Pearson played for Swansea, Porthcawl and the Glamorgan Nomads and also appeared in Minor County matches for Devon.

PEATFIELD, Albert Edward

Batsman.
Born: Retford, June 1874.
Died: Retford, 12 December 1953.
Glamorgan debut: 1903 v Devon at Cardiff Arms Park.

Career: 5 matches in 1903; England XI 1906.
HS for Glamorgan: 44 v Philadelphians at Cardiff Arms Park, 1903.
Full first-class record: 18 runs (18.00).

Peatfield was a schoolmaster and moved from his native Nottinghamshire in the early 1900s to take up a science post at Merthyr County School. He joined the Hill's Plymouth club and after some impressive innings, made his county debut in 1903. Soon afterwards he moved to a post in Lancashire and played League cricket. In 1906 Peatfield appeared for an England XI against the West Indian tourists at Blackpool and can therefore lay claim to being the first Glamorgan player to play for England. Peatfield also appeared for the Lancashire Nomads and went on their South Wales tour in 1905.

PENFOLD, W.H.

Wicketkeeper.
Career: 1 match against Wiltshire at Cardiff Arms Park in 1908, scoring 1 and 9*.

Penfold was a professional attached to the Hills Plymouth club in Merthyr and also appeared for South Wales against Australia at Cardiff Arms Park in 1909, scoring 3 and 6.

PERKINS, Arthur Lionel Bertie

RHB.
Born: Swansea, 19 October 1905.
Education: Bromsgrove School.
Glamorgan debut: 1925 v Leveson-Gower's XI at Swansea.
Career: 2 matches in 1925 and 4 in 1933.
HS for Glamorgan: 26* v Leveson-Gower's XI at Swansea, 1925.

Bertie Perkins went to school in Birmingham but was a native of Swansea and played for the Swansea club during the 1920s. He made his county debut in 1925 before emigrating and going into business in Malaysia. He returned to South Wales on holiday in May and June 1933 and reappeared in four matches for Glamorgan.

PERRY, Neil James

RHB; SLA.
Born: Sutton, Surrey, 27 May 1958.
Glamorgan debut: 1979 v Sri Lanka at Swansea.
Career: 13 matches 1979-81.
HS for Glamorgan: 6 v Warwickshire at Edgbaston, 1980.
BB for Glamorgan: 3-51 v India at Swansea, 1979.

Perry joined Glamorgan after having trials with

Surrey in 1978. Whilst in South Wales, he played for Neath and Gowerton, but the left-arm spinner failed to maintain a regular place in the Glamorgan side and was released at the end of 1981.

PHILLIPS, Martin

RHB; RFM.
Glamorgan debut: 1897 v Wiltshire at Swindon.
Career: 3 matches in 1897.
HS for Glamorgan: 3 v Worcestershire at Kidderminster, 1897.
BB for Glamorgan: 1-15 v Wiltshire at Swindon, 1897.

Phillips played for Cardiff and St Mary's.

PINCH, Francis Brewster

RHB; RM.
Born: Bodmin, 24 Feburary 1891.
Died: Ashford, 8 October, 1961.
Glamorgan debut: 1920 v Wiltshire at Cardiff Arms Park.
Career: 6 Minor County matches in 1920, plus 41 first-class appearances between 1921 and 1926; Wales 1924.
HS for Glamorgan: 138* v Worcestershire at Swansea, 1921.

BB for Glamorgan: 4-9 v Wiltshire at Cardiff Arms Park, 1920.
Full first-class record: 1,082 runs (15.91); 1 century; 39 wickets (32.43); 25 catches.

Pinch was a schoolmaster by profession and played for Barry before World War One. He subsequently joined Cardiff and made his county debut in 1920. He made his first-class debut in 1921 and scored a century on his first appearance. However, he only made sporadic appearances owing to his teaching commitments, but showed that he had the ability to have commanded a regular place in the middle-order.

PITCHFORD, Leonard

RHB; OB.
Born: Wing, Buckinghamshire, 4 December 1900.
Glamorgan debut: 1935 v Yorkshire at Neath.
Career: 2 matches in 1935.
HS for Glamorgan: 14* v Warwickshire at Swansea, 1935.

Len Pitchford played Minor County cricket for Bedfordshire before moving to South Wales and serving as the professional at Ebbw Vale between 1931 and 1935. He later appeared for the Elba Club, but despite a prolific record in club cricket was never called upon by Glamorgan after two brief appearances in 1935.

PLEASS, James Edward

RHB.
Born: Cardiff, 21 May 1923.

Education: Canton High School, Cardiff.
Glamorgan debut: 1947 v Derbyshire at Derby.
Career: 171 matches 1947-56; Cap 1952.
HS for Glamorgan: 102* v Yorkshire at Harrogate, 1955.

Jim Pleass played club cricket for Welsh Secondary Schools and then appeared for Cardiff, before making his Glamorgan debut in 1947 as an amateur. He turned professional in 1948 and became an aggressive middle-order batsman and a fine cover fielder. Even so, he only hit one century during his career, against Yorkshire at Harrogate in 1955 as Glamorgan secured their first ever victory on Yorkshire soil. He left the staff at the end of the 1956 season and went into business in Cardiff. During his career, Pleass also played for Pontardawe, Hills Plymouth and Briton Ferry Town, as well as football for Cardiff Cosmopolitans. He served on the county committee during the 1970s and 1980s and is currently secretary of the Glamorgan Former Players' Association.

POOK, Neil Robert

RHB; RM.
Born: Rainham, 9 February 1967.
Education: Chafford Comprehensive School.
Career: 1 match in 1990 against Oxford University at Oxford scoring 0 and 0*; Essex 1988 (1 match).
Full first-class record: 6 runs (3.00); 3 catches.

Pook was on the MCC groundstaff between 1985 and 1988 and in the latter season made his Essex debut scoring six against Cambridge University at Fenners. He joined Glamorgan in 1990 but was released midway through the season. He played club cricket for Rainham, Ilford and Cardiff.

POOLE, William

All-rounder.
Born: Leicester, 1869.
Died: Cardiff, 16 November 1913.
Career: 1 match in 1903 against Philadelphians at Cardiff Arms Park scoring 2* and 0.

Poole was the professional with the Cardiff club in 1903 and 1904, but was only called up by Glamorgan to play the Philadelphians in 1903.

PORTER, Arthur

RHB; OB.
Born: Clayton-le-Moors, Lancs, 25 March 1914.
Education: Mount Pleasant School, Accrington.
Glamorgan debut: 1936 v Worcestershire at Neath.
Career: 38 matches 1936-49; Cap 1946.
HS for Glamorgan: 105 v Surrey at The Oval, 1946.

BB for Glamorgan: 4-25 v Gloucestershire at Cardiff Arms Park, 1946.

Arthur Porter played Lancashire League cricket for Enfield, before taking up a job with the Newport Borough Police Force. He joined the town's cricket club and made two first-class appearances in 1936. He played in Minor County matches before the war, but not in first-class games owing to his duties as a policeman. Porter appeared regularly in 1946

and 1947 when Glamorgan were short-staffed and proved himself to be a useful middle-order batsman and spin bowler. He made one appearance in both 1948 and 1949, before returning to club cricket with Newport. Porter left the police force in 1948 and became a welfare officer with the British Steel Corporation in Newport.

POWELL, Tyrone Lyndon

RHB; OB.
Born: Bargoed, 17 June 1953.
Education: Hereatunga College, Upper Hutt, New Zealand.
Career: 1 match in 1976 against the West Indies at Swansea scoring 0 in both innings; New Zealand Under-23 1971-72.
Full first-class record: 24 runs (6.00).

Powell was brought up in New Zealand, where he played for their Under-23s in 1971-72. He joined the Glamorgan staff in the mid 1970s, but only made one first-class appearance. Powell subsequently moved to East Anglia and played Minor County cricket for Norfolk between 1982 and 1986. His highest first-class score was 14 for the New Zealand Under-23 XI against Otago at Dunedin in 1971-72.

PREECE, Trevor

RHB; OB.
Born: Bridgend, December 1882.
Died: Whitchurch, 21 September 1965.
Glamorgan debut: 1902 v Monmouthshire at Swansea.
Career: 13 Minor County matches between 1902 and 1920, plus 1 first-class appearance in 1923.
HS for Glamorgan: 73 v Carmarthenshire at Llanelli, 1908.
BB for Glamorgan: 2-21 v Devon at Plymouth, 1920.

Preece played hockey and cricket for Cardiff, Barry and St Fagan's and appeared occasionally before World War One for Glamorgan. He occupied a regular spot in the middle-order in 1908 when he made a career-best 73 against Carmarthenshire. He made one appearance in 1920 during Glamorgan's

West Country tour and reappeared in 1923 when the county found themselves a batsman short against Lancashire at the Arms Park. Preece was a heavy scorer in club cricket and it was surprising that he never made more runs at county level. He retired in 1925 and served as the groundsman at the Arms Park until 1939.

PREEDY

All-rounder.
Glamorgan debut: 1907 v Monmouthshire at Newport.
Career: 23 Minor County matches 1907-09.
HS for Glamorgan: 42* v Cornwall at Penzance, 1907.
BB for Glamorgan: 6-17 v Devon at Swansea, 1908.

Preedy was the professional with Cardiff between 1906 and 1909, before taking an appointment with Gloucester in 1910 and 1911. He also played Minor County cricket for Devon in 1912 and 1913.

PRESSDEE, James Stuart

RHB; SLA.
Born: Mumbles, 19 June 1933.
Education: Oystermouth School, Swansea.
Glamorgan debut: 1949 v Nottinghamshire at Swansea.
Career: 322 matches 1949-65; Cap 1955; Benefit 1964; North-East Transvaal 1965-66, 1969-70; MCC 1964.
HS for Glamorgan: 150* v Cambridge University at Pontypridd, 1965.
1,000 runs (6); 1,911 (34.74) 1962 best.
BB for Glamorgan: 9-43 v Yorkshire at Swansea, 1965.
100 wickets (1); 104 (21.03) 1963 best.
The double: once for Glamorgan and once in all first-class games in 1964.
Full first-class record: 14,267 runs (28.82); 13 centuries; 481 wickets (22.17); 371 catches.

Jim Pressdee was an outstanding schoolboy sportsman and made his debut for Glamorgan in 1949 against the RAF at Maindy Barracks, Cardiff aged 16 years and 23 days old. He showed great promise as a batsman and left-arm spinner, taking 6-55 and earning a championship debut. Pressdee was also an exceptional footballer and won a Welsh Schoolboy cap as a full-back, before appearing for Swansea Town between 1953 and 1955. However, he put cricket first and turned down a chance to play for the England Youth team against Germany at Wembley because he was playing for Glamorgan II.

Pressdee played regularly for Glamorgan from 1954 onwards after doing his National Service and he topped the bowling averages in 1955 with 72

wickets at a cost of 19, besides holding 42 catches in the leg trap to earn his county cap. He formed a useful spin partnership with Don Shepherd and Jim McConnon and developed into a hard hitting middle-order batsman. Pressdee was promoted to the number-three spot in 1959 and responded by hitting his maiden century against India at Cardiff. He followed this with two more hundreds, including a century before lunch at Dartford against Kent. Pressdee had a modest year in 1960, but returned to form in 1961 scoring 1,898 runs and then a career-best 1,911 in 1962 with hundreds against Cambridge University, Essex and Kent. He also proved himself to be a brave and dour batsman prepared to play a match-saving innings if the team needed it and also kept wicket in one game when David Evans was injured.

However, Pressdee lost confidence as a bowler in the late 1950s and took only five wickets between 1959 and 1962. However, he regained belief in himself playing club cricket for Springs in South Africa and returned to the Glamorgan attack in 1963 with remarkable results. He took 104 wickets

and performed the double with 1,435 runs for the Welsh county. He was almost unplayable on turning wickets and returned remarkable figures of 15-12-5-6 against Nottinghamshire at Ebbw Vale, plus a match return of 11-148 against Kent at Dover. The following year he took 97 wickets and played a leading role in the defeat of the 1964 Australians at Swansea, taking 6-58 and 4-65. He took a career-best 9-43 against Yorkshire in 1965, but his career with Glamorgan came to an abrupt halt at the end of the summer when after several disagreements with Wilf Wooller, Pressdee announced that he was emigrating to South Africa.

He played for North-East Transvaal until 1969-70 and returned to Glamorgan in 1986 to lead the Colts side. He is the father-in-law of Rodney Ontong and during his career played club cricket for Swansea, Pontardawe, Llanelli and Maesteg Celtic.

PRICE, Mark Richard

RHB; SLA.
Born: Liverpool, 20 April 1960.
Education: Harper Green Secondary School, Bolton.
Glamorgan debut: 1984 v Gloucestershire at Sophia Gardens, Cardiff.
Career: 17 matches 1984-85.
HS for Glamorgan: 36 v Nottinghamshire at Swansea, 1985.
BB for Glamorgan: 4-97 v Leicestershire at Swansea, 1985.

Mark Price joined Glamorgan in 1984 after trials with Lancashire. He played for Gowerton and Llanelli, but was released at the end of 1985 and returned to Lancashire League cricket with Ramsbottom.

PRICHARD, Hubert Cecil Collins CBE (also COLLINS-PRICHARD)

RHB.
Born: Clifton, 6 February 1865.

Died: Pwllywrach, Cowbridge, 12 November 1942.
Education: Clifton College; Magdalene College, Cambridge and RMC Sandhurst.
Glamorgan debut: 1899 v Surrey at The Oval.
Career: 4 matches 1899-1900; Gloucestershire 1896 (2 matches).
HS for Glamorgan: 50 v MCC at Cardiff Arms Park, 1899.
Full first-class record: 46 runs (11.50) and 1 catch.

Prichard played for Gloucestershire in 1896 before moving back to his native South Wales where his family had their home at Pwllywrach having formerly lived at Llanover Court. He played his club cricket for Bridgend and St Fagan's, but only appeared occasionally due to his military career with the Glamorgan Yeomanry. He commanded PoW camps in Scotland during World War One and was awarded the CBE in 1919.

PRITCHARD, Archie J.

Fast/medium pace bowler.
Career: 1 match in 1920 against Carmarthenshire at Llanelli, scoring 2 in his only innings and taking 3 wickets.

Pritchard played for Swansea for many years and coached at Christ College, Brecon during the 1940s. He was the Swansea professional from 1902 until 1912 when he badly fractured his bowling hand. His subsequent career was as an amateur.

PRUEN, F.H.

Batsman.
Career: 1 match in 1897 against Surrey II at The Oval scoring 21 in his only innings.

Pruen played for Cardiff and Newport.

PULLEN, William Wade Fitzherbert

RHB, occ WK.
Born: Itchington, Gloucestershire, 24 June 1866.
Died: Southampton, 9 August 1937.
Education: Bristol University.
Glamorgan debut: 1895 v Herefordshire at Cardiff Arms Park.
Career: 6 matches in 1895; Somerset 1881 (1 non first-class friendly); Gloucestershire 1882-92 (91 matches).
HS for Glamorgan: 77 v Herefordshire at Hereford, 1895.
Full first-class record: 2,765 runs (17.39); 1 century; 3 wickets; 63 catches and 4 stumpings.

Pullen made his debut for Somerset in a friendly with Hampshire in 1881 when only 15 years and two months old, before playing for Gloucestershire

Tom Reason played cricket for Neath and Skewen and was a leading member of Swansea Bay Golf Club, whom he represented in the Glamorgan Amateur championships.

REED, George Henry
RHB; LFM.
Born: St Fagan's, 8 August 1906.
Died: Cardiff, December 1988.
Glamorgan debut: 1934 v Lancashire at Cardiff Arms Park.
Career: 25 matches 1934-38.
HS for Glamorgan: 11 v Sussex at Eastborune, 1938.
BB for Glamorgan: 5-30 v Worcestershire at Worcester, 1936.

Reed played for St Fagan's in the early 1920s, before joining Cardiff as their professional in 1929, for whom he played until World War Two. He established several club records for wicket-taking with the Cardiff club and his best season was 1934 when he took 74 wickets. He became a policeman after retiring from cricket.

REES, Alan
RHB; RM.
Born: Port Talbot, 17 February 1938.
Education: Port Talbot Comprehensive School.
Glamorgan debut: 1955 v Somerset at Weston-super-Mare.
Career: 216 matches 1955-68; Cap 1963.
HS for Glamorgan: 111* v Lancashire at Cardiff Arms Park, 1964.
1,000 runs (4); 1,206 (30.15) 1964 best.
BB for Glamorgan: 3-68 v Kent at Cardiff Arms Park, 1960.

Alan Rees was one of the finest cover point fielders in county cricket during the 1960s. He was also a talented rugby player, playing for Maesteg, Aberavon and Llanelli and won three Welsh caps in 1962 before turning professional and joining Leeds RLFC. He achieved notoriety for being dismissed 'handled the ball' against Middlesex at Lord's in 1965 and played club cricket for Briton Ferry Town, Dafen, SCOW, Maesteg Town, Port Talbot and Ammanford. Later employed as sports officer for Afan Borough Council.

REES, Edward Lennox
RHB; RFM.
Born: Southampton, March 1868.
Died: St Mellons, 13 October 1911.
Glamorgan debut: 1893 v Monmouthshire at Cardiff Arms Park.
Career: 9 matches 1893-96.
HS for Glamorgan: 17 v MCC at Lord's, 1896.

BB for Glamorgan: 6-42 v Herefordshire at Hereford, 1895.

Eddie Rees was one of the fastest amateur bowlers in the Cardiff area in the 1890s. He played for Cardiff and St Pauls.

REES, Revd Richard Morgan
Batsman, occ WK.
Born: Pontypridd, 22 April 1875.
Died: Porthcawl, 28 June 1932.
Education: St John's School, Leatherhead and Magdalene College, Oxford.
Glamorgan debut: 1896 v Monmouthshire at Cardiff Arms Park.
Career: 4 matches 1896-97, plus 1 in 1904.
HS for Glamorgan: 25 v Wiltshire at Swindon, 1897.

He was the son of the Revd Rees of Treherbert Parsonage, Pontypridd and was in the St John's XI from 1891 until 1893 where he emerged as a sound batsman and smart wicketkeeper, before going up to Oxford to read History. During his summer vacations he played for Cardiff and Treherbert and appeared occasionally for Glamorgan. Morgan opted to follow his father into the clergy and served curacies at Bordesley and St John's in Cardiff, allowing him to reappear for Glamorgan in 1904 in their end of season match with Devon at Exeter. He subsequently became chaplain of Christ Church, Oxford and rector of Semley in Wiltshire.

REES, Stanley H.
Batsman.
Glamorgan debut: 1901 v Monmouthshire at Cardiff Arms Park.
Career: 36 matches 1901-14.
HS for Glamorgan: 82 v Carmarthenshire at Llanelli, 1910.

Stanley Rees played for Swansea.

REID, Dr Edgar W.
All-rounder.
Born: Swansea, 26 June 1865.
Died: Swansea, 19 September 1924.
Education: Swansea Grammar School and Guy's Hospital.
Glamorgan debut: 1890 v Warwickshire at Cardiff Arms Park.
Career: 5 matches 1890-94, plus 1 in 1900.
HS for Glamorgan: 14 v Somerset at Cardiff Arms Park, 1890.
BB for Glamorgan: 5-39 v Warwickshire at Cardiff Arms Park, 1890.

Dr Edgar Reid was a talented sportsman, playing rugby, hockey and cricket for Swansea and Guy's Hospital. He was also a Welsh international hockey player, as well as being one of the top amateur golfers in South Wales at the turn of the century, finishing as runner-up in the 1898 Welsh Amateur championship at Aberdovey. He was a surgeon in both Swansea and London.

REYNOLDS, Graham Edward Arthur
LHB; RM.
Born: Newport, 23 September 1937.
Education: St Julians High School and St Luke's College, Exeter.
Glamorgan debut: 1970 v Jamaica at Swansea.
Career: 1 match in both 1970 and 1971.
HS for Glamorgan: 23* v Northamptonshire at Northampton, 1971.
BB for Glamorgan: 2-24 v Jamaica at Swansea 1970.

Graham Reynolds played cricket for Newport and football for Newport County. He taught for many years in Newport and became the county's schools liason officer and talent scout from 1990.

RHYS, Hubert Ralph John
RHB.
Born: Aberdare, 31 August 1897.
Died: Llandaff, 18 March 1970.
Education: Shrewsbury.
Glamorgan debut: 1929 v Leicestershire at Pontypridd.
Career: 7 matches 1929-30; Wales 1929-30; Free Foresters 1929.
HS for Glamorgan: 35 v Surrey at Swansea, 1930.
Full first-class record: 383 runs (21.27); 5 catches.

Hubert Rhys was in the Shrewsbury XI between 1913 and 1915 and captained the school in his final year. He played club cricket for Cardiff and St Fagan's and also appeared for the Free Foresters, hitting 149 against Cambridge University at Fenners in 1929 on his first-class debut. This performance brought him a place in the Glamorgan side later in the summer. He married the daughter of W.S.R.Sweet-Escott and their son W.E.Rhys has been chairman of Brains Brewery since 1971.

RICHARDS, Gwyn
RHB; OB.
Born: Maesteg, 29 November 1951.
Glamorgan debut: 1971 v Leicestershire at Sophia Gardens, Cardiff.
Career: 107 matches 1971-79; Cap 1976.
HS for Glamorgan: 102* v Yorkshire at Middlesbrough, 1976.

BB for Glamorgan: 5-55 v Somerset at Taunton, 1978.

Gwyn Richards was on the MCC groundstaff in 1971 and 1972 before joining the Glamorgan staff as a middle-order batsman and off-spinner. He won a regular place in the side from 1976, during which he hit his maiden century against Yorkshire and won his county cap. Richards was also a useful performer in one-day matches and his accurate bowling was a key element in Glamorgan's Gillette Cup run in 1977. He played club cricket for Briton Ferry Steel, Gowerton and Maesteg Celtic and he has also appeared for Wales.

RICHARDS, Isaac Vivian Alexander
RHB; RM; OB.
Born: St John's Antigua, 7 March 1952.
Education: Antigua Grammar School.
Glamorgan debut: 1990 v Leicestershire at Sophia Gardens, Cardiff.
Career: 18 matches in 1990; Cap 1990; Leeward Islands 1971-; Somerset 1974-86 (191 Matches, Cap 1974, Benefit 1982); Queensland 1976-1977; West Indies 1974-75 to 1991 (121 Tests, Captain from 1986).
HS for Glamorgan 164* v Hampshire at Southampton, 1990.
1,000 runs (1); 1,425 (61.96) 1990 best.
BB for Glamorgan: 2-27 v Sussex at Hove, 1990.

Full first-class record: 34,255 runs (50.01); 111 centuries; 219 wickets (44.77); 429 catches and 1 stumping.

Viv Richards joined Glamorgan after an illustrious career with Somerset and the West Indies. He had hoped to play for the Welsh county in 1989, but a recurrence of a haemorrhoid problem prevented him from playing and he eventually made his debut the following season. Richards made an immediate impact with seven centuries and signed a futher two-year contract for 1992 and 1993. The presence of the 'Master Blaster' gave confidence to the youngsters in the Glamorgan side and helped them improve their game. His match-winning centuries

Norman Riches, Glamorgan's best batsman during their Minor Counties days and the Welshmen's first captain in the County Championship.

against Hampshire and Northants also saw Glamorgan to their highest championship position since 1970. Richards scored over 14,000 runs whilst with Somerset, including a career-best 322 against Warwickshire in 1985. His best bowling figures of 5-88 came on West Indies' 1981-82 tour of Australia against Queensland. He has played in 116 Tests and over 180 one-day internationals and has captained the West Indies since 1986. In 1988-89 he became the first West Indian to score 100 hundreds.

RICHARDS, John E.

Batsman.
Glamorgan debut: 1 match in 1920 against Carmarthenshire at Llanelli scoring 19 and 3.

Richards played for Briton Ferry Town and Briton Ferry Steel.

RICHES, John Dansey Hurry

RHB; SLA.
Born: Cardiff, 30 December 1920.
Education: Repton.
Career: 1 match in 1947 against Yorkshire at Sheffield scoring 4 and 1.

John Riches was in the Repton XI in 1937 and captained Glamorgan II in their Minor County games between 1946 and 1954. He was the son of N.V.H.Riches and played for Cardiff, MCC, XL Club and the South Wales Hunts. He served on the county committee and was a solicitor in Cardiff.

RICHES, Norman Vaughan Hurry

RHB; RM, occ WK.
Born: Cardiff, 9 June 1883.
Died: Cyncoed, Cardiff, 6 November 1975.
Education: Guy's Hospital.
Glamorgan debut: 1900 v Monmouthshire at Cardiff Arms Park.
Career: 136 Minor County matches 1900-20, plus 82 first-class games 1921-34; Captain 1913-14, 1921, 1929; Wales 1923-30; MCC.
HS for Glamorgan: 217 v Dorset at Blandford Forum, 1907.
1,000 runs (2); 1,103 (91.92) in 1911 and 1,080 (43.20) 1921 best.
BB for Glamorgan: 1-1 v Berkshire at Cardiff Arms Park, 1902.
Full first-class record: 5,750 runs (35.27); 9 centuries; 4 wickets; 49 catches and 6 stumpings.

Norman Riches was Glamorgan's finest batsman during their Minor County days and captained the Welsh side in their inaugural season in the cham-

pionship, leading them to their first success against Sussex at the Arms Park. He was coached as a youngster by his father Carlton Riches, a well-known Cardiff dentist and Gowan Clark, the Cardiff and Glamorgan batsman. He made his county debut aged 17 and in 1904 hit 183 against Monmouthshire at Swansea. An illustrious career was predicted for the young batsman but he opted to follow his father into dentistry and only played for Glamorgan during his holidays from Guy's Hospital.

Riches' finest season was in 1911 when he hit three centuries and became the first Minor County player to score over 1,000 runs in a season. He played regularly for the MCC and the Minor Counties and was even considered for a tour to the West Indies after World War One. A Glamorgan official was contacted to see if Riches was available but nothing came of it, although Riches would have jumped at the chance if he had received an invitation. Had he played regular county cricket, he would undoubtedly have caught the selectors' eye and he showed his class in 1928 by scoring 140 against the powerful Lancashire attack and all at the age of 45!

Riches retired from county cricket in 1934, but continued to play for Cardiff until 1939 before becoming involved with the club's administration, serving as chairman from 1947 until 1954. He later became a trustee and patron of Glamorgan CCC and held these posts until his death in 1975.

RICKERS, G.H.

Career: 1 match in 1920 against Devon at Plymouth scoring 0 in his only innings.

Rickers was a late replacement when Glamorgan had only ten players on the morning of the game at Plymouth.

RIPPON, Thomas John

RHB; WK.
Born: Swansea, 6 July 1918.
Education: Brynmill School, Swansea.
Glamorgan debut: 1947 v Warwickshire at Swansea.
Career: 3 matches 1947-48.
HS for Glamorgan: 30 v Northamptonshire at Kettering, 1947.

John Rippon was Swansea's wicketkeeper and understudy to Haydn Davies after the war. He regularly played for the seconds in their Minor County matches and worked in the National Fire Service. He still acts as scorer for Swansea.

ROBATHAN, George Lionel

RHB.
Born: Brighton, September 1878.
Died: Lower Bourne, Surrey, 3 August 1951.
Education: Epsom College.
Glamorgan debut: 1910 v Worcestershire at Cardiff Arms Park.
Career: 8 matches 1910-11; Gloucestershire 1922 (3 matches).
HS for Glamorgan: 30 v Staffordshire at Stoke, 1911.
Full first-class record: 118 runs (19.66); 1 catch.

Robathan played for Newport and Monmouthshire and was a schoolmaster by profession. He moved to the West Country after World War One and played for Gloucestershire in 1922 where he made a career-best 42.

ROBERTS, John Frederick CBE, OBE

LHB.
Born: Pontardawe, 24 February 1913.

Education: Pontardawe Grammar School.
Glamorgan debut: 1934 v Warwickshire at Swansea.
Career: 4 matches 1934-36; Combined Services 1946-49.
HS for Glamorgan: 47* v Warwickshire at Swansea, 1934.
Full first-class record: 204 runs (20.40); 7 catches.

Roberts played for Glamorgan II in their Minor County games between 1935 and 1937 and played club cricket for Pontardawe. He served with the RAF where he had an illustrious military career, rising to the rank of air vice-marshall and being awarded both the CBE and OBE. He reappeared in first-class cricket for the Combined Services after the war and scored 52 against the South Africans at Portsmouth in 1947. He also played for the MCC, Watford and Cheltenham.

ROBERTS, Martin Leonard

RHB; WK.
Born: Mullion, Cornwall, 12 April 1966.
Education: Helston Comprehensive School.
Glamorgan debut: 1985 v Zimbabwe at Swansea.
Career: 10 matches 1985-91.

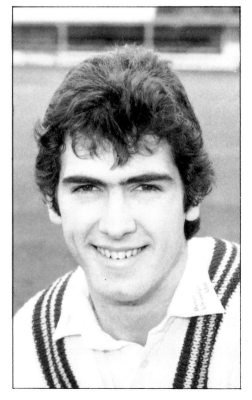

Martin Roberts played for Cornwall in 1983 and 1984 and after moving to South Wales played for Newport. He acted as reserve wicketkeeper for both Terry Davies and Colin Metson and was occasionally included as a specialist batsman after scoring centuries for the second eleven. He was released from the staff at the end of 1991.

ROBINSON, Maurice

RHB; RM.
Born: Lisburn, County Antrim, 16 July 1921.
Glamorgan debut: 1946 v India at Cardiff Arms Park.
Career: 66 matches 1946-50; Cap 1946; Bombay Europeans 1943-44; Warwickshire 1951-52 (8 matches); Europeans 1942-43, 1944-45; Combined Services 1946; Hyderabad 1943-44; Madras 1944-45.

HS for Glamorgan: 190 v Hampshire at Bournemouth, 1949.
BB for Glamorgan: 3-17 v Sussex at Eastbourne, 1949.
Full first-class record: 2,719 runs (22.10); 2 centuries; 34 wickets (25.58); 23 catches.

Maurice Robinson made his first-class debut during World War Two in domestic cricket in India, where he took a career-best 7-51 for the Europeans against the Indians at Madras in 1944-45. After the war he was stationed at RAF St Athan and he made his Glamorgan debut in 1946. He left the county staff in 1950 and joined Warwickshire, where he played club cricket for Moseley in the Birmingham League.

ROBINSON, Theodore

RHB; RM.
Born: Beaminster, Dorset, 16 February 1866.
Died: West Town, Somerset, 4 October 1959.
Glamorgan debut: 1889 v Warwickshire at Cardiff Arms Park.
Career: 13 matches 1889-91; Somerset 1884-94 (10 matches).
HS for Glamorgan: 70 v MCC at Swansea, 1890.
BB for Glamorgan: 6-26 v Monmouthshire at Cardiff Arms Park, 1891.
Full first-class record: 152 runs (8.44); 2 wickets; 3 catches.

Theo Robinson played for Somerset between 1884 and 1888, before moving to South Wales and joining Cardiff. He was an ever present member of Glamorgan's side in 1890, but in 1892 returned to the West Country and joined Clifton. He was the brother of Somerset's C.J.Robinson and was a member of a family who could field their own eleven.

ROEBUCK, Paul Gerard Peter

LHB; RM.
Born: Bath, 13 October 1963.

Education: Millfield School and Emmanuel College, Cambridge.
Glamorgan debut: 1988 v Hampshire at Sophia Gardens, Cardiff.
Career: 2 matches in 1988; Cambridge University 1983-85 (Blue 1984-85); Gloucestershire 1984 (1 match).
HS for Glamorgan: 46 v Hampshire at Sophia Gardens, Cardiff.
Full first-class record: 771 runs (25.70); 6 wickets (44.83); 8 catches.

Paul Roebuck was in the Cambridge side between 1983 and 1985 and won a Blue in his last two years in residence. Whilst up at Cambridge he scored a career-best 82 against Somerset at Taunton in 1985 and took 2-44 against Kent at Cambridge in 1983. He played for Gloucestershire in 1984 and made his Glamorgan debut in 1988 after a trial the previous season. He is the brother of Somerset's P.M.Roebuck and whilst in South Wales played for Cowbridge.

ROGERS, Basil Leonard

RHB.
Born: Bedford, 20 June 1896.
Died: Ripon, December 1975.
Glamorgan debut: 1923 v Northamptonshire at Swansea.
Career: 2 matches in 1923.
HS for Glamorgan: 16* v Northamptonshire at Swansea, 1923.
BB for Glamorgan: 1-22 v Lancashire at Cardiff Arms Park, 1923.

Rogers played Minor County cricket for Bedfordshire and Oxfordshire and whilst with Glamorgan, was attached to the Swansea club.

ROONEY, Edward James

All-rounder.
Born: Shoreditch, Middlesex, December 1868.
Glamorgan debut: 1890 v Monmouthshire at Newport.
Career: 2 matches in 1890.
HS for Glamorgan: 11 v Somerset at Bath, 1890.
BB for Glamorgan: 2-23 v Monmouthshire at Newport, 1890.

Edward Rooney played for Cardiff, St Pauls and Taff Vale and was the brother of Robert and Samuel Rooney. He played as a late substitute for the MCC against Gloucestershire at the Arms Park in 1889.

ROONEY, Robert Alexander

Batsman.
Born: Hornsey, Middlesex, September 1873.
Glamorgan debut: 1893 v Herefordshire at Cardiff Arms Park.
Career: 13 matches 1893-1901.
HS for Glamorgan: 54* v MCC at Cardiff Arms Park, 1900.

Robert Rooney played for Cardiff, St Pauls and St Fagan's and was the brother of Edward and Samuel Rooney.

ROONEY, Samuel

Batsman.
Born: Llandaff, December 1874.
Glamorgan debut: 1893 v MCC at Lord's.
Career: 1 match in both 1893 and 1894.
HS for Glamorgan: 14 v Monmouthshire at Swansea, 1894.

Samuel Rooney played for St Pauls, St Andrews and Penarth and was the younger brother of Edward and Robert Rooney.

ROWE, Charles James Castell

RHB; OB.
Born: Hong Kong, 27 November 1951.
Education: Kings Canterbury.
Glamorgan debut: 1982 v Warwickshire at Edgbaston.
Career: 53 matches 1982-84; Cap 1983; Kent 1974-81 (122 matches, Cap 1977).
HS for Glamorgan: 105 v Somerset at Taunton, 1982.
1,000 runs (1); 1,071 (32.45) 1982 best.
BB for Glamorgan: 4-29 v Nottinghamshire at Ebbw Vale, 1983.
Full first-class record: 6,173 runs (26.38); 6 centuries; 128 wickets (40.05); 63 catches.

Charles Rowe spent eight years on the Kent staff during which time he scored a career-best 147* against Sussex at Canterbury and took 6-46 against Derbyshire at Dover in 1976. He played for Glamorgan for three years before taking a job in the city of London. He has also played for the MCC and the Stragglers of Asia.

Charles Rowe

HS for Glamorgan: 143 v Berkshire at Cardiff Arms Park, 1899.
BB for Glamorgan: 7-43 v Devon at Exeter, 1903.

William Russell played for Middlesex II in 1894 and 1895, before joining Cowbridge as their professional and becoming a regular in the Glamorgan side of the early 1900s. He was an aggressive middle-order batsman and a useful spin bowler to support Harry Creber.

RYAN, Francis Peter

LHB; SLA.
Born: New Jersey, USA, 14 November 1888.
Died: Leicester, 5 January 1954.
Education: Bedford Grammar School.
Glamorgan debut: 1922 v Combined Oxford and Cambridge XI at Cardiff Arms Park.
Career: 215 matches 1922-31; Hampshire 1919-20 (23 matches); Wales 1923-30.

ROWNTREE, R.E.

All-rounder.
Glamorgan debut: 1899 v Surrey at Swansea.
Career: 2 matches in 1899.
HS for Glamorgan: 7 v Surrey at Swansea, 1899.
BB for Glamorgan: 1-22 v Monmouthshire at Cardiff Arms Park, 1899.

Corporal Rowntree served with the Welch Regiment and played for Cardiff and Fairwater.

RUSSELL, William

Batsman and spin bowler.
Born: Norfolk, 1867.
Died: Cowbridge, 8 March 1908.
Glamorgan debut: 1897 v MCC at Cardiff Arms Park.
Career: 102 matches 1897-1906.

HS for Glamorgan: 46 v Northamptonshire at Northampton, 1925.
BB for Glamorgan: 8-41 v Derbyshire at Cardiff Arms Park, 1925.
100 wickets (5); 133 wickets (17.46) 1925 best.
Full first-class record: 1,908 runs (7.98); 1,013 wickets (21.03); 103 catches.

Frank Ryan was one of the most charismatic figures ever to appear in county cricket. Born in America he moved to England at an early age and served with the Royal Flying Corps during World War One. He joined Hampshire in 1919, but after two seasons went into Lancashire League cricket and found much success as a left-arm spinner. He was approached by Glamorgan who were looking to boost their spin attack and the story goes that he arrived in 1922 in a penniless state after hitch-hiking his way to South Wales. Ryan qualified with Cardiff and won a regular place in the Glamorgan side from 1923 and over the next nine seasons became the mainstay of Glamorgan's attack.

He took over 900 wickets, with a high flowing action and considerable powers of spin and established himself as one of the best left-arm spinner's in county cricket. Ryan claimed 106 wickets in his first full season, followed by 120 wickets in 1924, when he returned match figures of 12-65 against Somerset at Taunton and 11-64 against Leicestershire at Swansea. His best season was 1925 when he claimed 133 victims, including 14 wickets against Essex at Swansea and 13 Derbyshire wickets at Cardiff. Ryan claimed a further 106 victims in 1926 and although he took only 71 wickets in 1927, he took 9-95 against Nottinghamshire at Swansea to prevent the visitors from becoming county champions.

Ryan also had a great liking for the more social aspects of a county cricketer's life and there are many stories of his drinking, including one where he was found fast asleep one morning under the covers having forgotten where the team were staying. The most famous of tales about Ryan concerned his late arrival for a match at the Arms Park. He had stayed on after play the previous day in Lancashire, whilst the rest of the team returned to South Wales by train. Apparently, he carried on drinking, until the early hours of the morning with friends, before hiring a local taxi to take him to Cardiff. He eventually arrived with minutes to spare, entering the dressing-room with the phrase 'Ryan never lets you down'! and left the tired and confused driver to sort out the hefty bill with the club's treasurer!

His womanizing and heavy drinking annoyed several members of Glamorgan's hierarchy and Clay wrote 'there were times when he did not spin, nor did he toil. Ryan had his little weaknesses and if it had not been for these, then he would have been an English Test bowler'. In 1931 he was one of several professionals released by the club, ostensibly for reasons of economy, but one wonders if his off-the-field escapades had lost him too many friends in the committee room. It came as a surprise to many who liked the colourful character and Ryan left the area and returned to League cricket in Lancashire and Yorkshire.

SAMUEL, Astley William

All-rounder.
Born: Llanelli, March 1861.
Died: Newport, 15 December 1937.

Education: Dublin University.
Glamorgan debut: 1889 v Warwickshire at Cardiff Arms Park.
Career: 17 matches 1889-96.
HS for Glamorgan: 46* v Monmouthshire at Swansea, 1892.
BB for Glamorgan: 9-26 v Monmouthshire at Cardiff Arms Park, 1890.

Astley Samuel captained Swansea between 1899 and 1905 and also played for Pontardawe and Morriston. He was also a useful golfer, tennis and hockey player and was an estate agent and surveyor in Swansea.

SAMUEL, Glyndwr Ninian Thomas Watkin

RHB.
Born: Swansea, 26 October 1917.

Died: Hastings, April 1985.
Education: Uppingham.
Glamorgan debut: 1936 v Leicestershire at Swansea.
Career: 3 matches in 1936.
HS for Glamorgan: 22 v Leicestershire at Swansea, 1936.

Glyn Samuel was in the Uppingham XI in 1934 and 1935 and played for Glamorgan II in their Minor County games in 1936 and 1937.

SANT, Stuart Arthur
Batsman.
Career: 1 match in 1893 against Herefordshire at Hereford, scoring 0 and 21.
Stuart Sant played for Cardiff, St Mary's and Coleford.

SAULEZ, Edmund Harrison
Batsman.
Born: Overseas, 21 February 1867.
Died: Havant, 19 November, 1948.
Education: Harrow.
Glamorgan debut: 1893 v Herefordshire at Hereford.
Career: 7 matches in 1893.
HS for Glamorgan: 45 v Monmouthshire at Newport, 1893.

Saulez played for Cardiff and Fairwater before joining the Royal Dublin Fusiliers and the Suffolk Regiment. He later became a major in the Indian Army and appeared for the Europeans in Indian domestic cricket. He was a cousin of Hampshire's H.N.Dumbleton.

SCHOFIELD, Thomas David
Wicketkeeper.
Born: 1865.
Died: Bridgend, 2 January 1928.
Glamorgan debut: 1893 v Herefordshire at Cardiff Arms Park.
Career: 4 matches 1893-96.
HS for Glamorgan: 2* v South Wales CC at Swansea, 1895.

Tom Schofield played in club cricket in northern England and America before moving to South Wales and joining Bridgend. He was also a leading figure in rugby circles, acting as secretary of Bridgend RFC as well as being a well-known rugby referee and member of the WRU. He served on the Glamorgan committee between 1903 and 1923 and was the club's chairman during their inaugural first-class season in 1921.

SCOTT, J.M.
Batsman.
Glamorgan debut: 1895 v South Wales CC at Swansea.
Career: 2 matches in 1895.
HS for Glamorgan: 12 v South Wales CC at Swansea, 1895.

Scott was the professional with the Tynemouth club in northern England, before joining Cardiff in 1892. He filled a similar post at Bridgend in 1894 and Swansea in 1895, when he made his only county appearances against the South Wales CC and Herefordshire.

SELVEY, Michael Walter William
RHB: RFM.
Born: Chiswick, 25 April 1948.
Education: Battersea Grammar School, Manchester University and Emmanuel College, Cambridge.
Glamorgan debut: 1983 v Cambridge University at Cambridge.

Career: 39 matches 1983-84; Captain 1983-84; Surrey 1968-71 (6 matches); Cambridge University 1971 (Blue); Middlesex 1972-82 (213 matches, Cap 1973, Benefit 1982); Orange Free State 1973-74; England 1976-77 (3 Tests).

HS for Glamorgan: 63 v Essex at Sophia Gardens, Cardiff, 1983.

BB for Glamorgan: 6-31 v Oxford University at Oxford, 1984.

Full first-class record: 2,405 runs (12.65); 772 wickets (26.67); 79 catches.

After a brief career with Surrey whilst at university, Mike Selvey moved across London to join Middlesex in 1972 and became in the mid-1970s one of the best medium-pace swing bowlers in the country. His height meant that he could generate pace and bounce and he had the knack of being able to swing the ball late in either direction. In 1976 he returned a career-best 7-20 at Gloucester and won a place in the England side. He made a sensational debut taking the wicket of Fredericks, Richards and Kallicharran with his first 20 balls in Test cricket. Selvey toured India in 1976-77 but despite taking 101 wickets in 1978 he never played for England again. In 1981-82 he toured Pakistan with an International XI and in 1980-81 toured Zimbabwe with Middlesex, when he scored a career-best 67 at Bulawayo against Zimbabwe. Selvey joined Glamorgan as their new captain in 1983, but he struggled for form and fitness due to shoulder and knee injuries. Consequently he was forced to retire midway through 1984 and has gone into broadcasting and journalism and is currently cricket correspondent of *The Guardian*.

SEYMOUR, Hon Reginald Guy

Batsman.
Born: Alcester, 15 January 1880.
Died: Woodstock, Oxford, 4 January 1965.
Glamorgan debut: 1905 v Northumberland at Newcastle.
Career: 2 matches in 1905.
HS for Glamorgan: 8 v Durham at Hartlepool, 1905.

The Hon Reginald Seymour was the grandson of the fifth Marquess of Hertford and Lady Emily Murray. He was a captain in the Royal North Devon Yeomanry and served in the Boer War and World War One and was mentioned in dispatches. Whilst stationed in South Wales, Seymour played for St Fagan's and the Glamorgan Gypsies. After leaving the services he acted as the agent for Lord Wharton of Halswell.

SHARPLES J.E.

Batsman.
Born: Lancashire.
Career: 1 match in 1922 against Leicestershire at Cardiff Arms Park, scoring 0 in his only innings.

Sharples played in Lancashire and for the Hythe club in Kent, before moving to South Wales to work at the National Oil Refinery at Skewen. He played for the local club and Briton Ferry Town before emigrating to work in Turkey and Egypt.

SHASTRI, Ravishankar Jayadritha

RHB; SLA.
Born: Bombay, 27 May 1962.
Education: Don Bosco High School, Bombay.
Glamorgan debut: 1987.
Career: 62 matches 1987-91; Cap 1988; Bombay 1979-80- (Captain 1987-88); India 1980-81- (72 Tests); MCC.
HS for Glamorgan: 157 v Somerset at Sophia Gardens, Cardiff, 1988
1000 runs: (1) 1108 (48.17) in 1991.
BB for Glamorgan: 7-49 v Lancashire at Swansea, 1988.
Full first-class record: 11,650 runs (44.13); 29 centuries; 466 wickets (33.67); 127 catches.

Ravi Shastri made his debut in 1979 as a 17 year old batsman and left arm spinner. He was selected for Young India against Sri Lanka in 1980 and England in 1981, before making his Test debut in 1980-81. He has appeared in over 70 Tests and toured England, West Indies, New Zealand, Australia, Pakistan, Sri Lanka and Zimbabwe with India. His highest Test score of 187 came at The Oval against England in 1990, whilst his best Test figures are 5-75 against Pakistan at Nagpur in 1983-84. In 1981-82 he took a career-best 9-101 for Bombay against the Rest of India at Indore, but he hit the headlines in 1984-85 when scoring the fastest ever 200 on record during Bombay's match with Baroda. During this career-best innings, he hit six sixes in an over from Tilak Raj. Shastri joined Glamorgan in 1987 and made an immediate impact in the one-day matches where his aggressive batting and accurate bowling helped secure a number of victories. He was capped in 1988 and in 1989 appeared in the MCC Bicentenary Test at Lord's as well as playing for the Rest of the World at the Jesmond Festival. He has appeared in over 130 one-day Internationals, including the 1983 and 1987 World Cups. He also captained India in 1988, but was fined £1,450 by the Indian Cricket Board after playing in North America after a tour of the West Indies in 1989.

Ravi Shastri, who made an immediate impact with Glamorgan in one-day matches.

George Lavis shows a young G.B.Shaw the grip for an off-break.

SHAW, George Bernard
RHB; OB.
Born: Treharris, 24 October 1931.
Died: Port Pirie, South Australia, August 1984.
Glamorgan debut: 1951 v Combined Services at Pontypridd.
Career: 16 matches 1951-55.
HS for Glamorgan: 11 v Combined Services at Cardiff Arms Park, 1952.
BB for Glamorgan: 5-38 v Combined Services at Cardiff Arms Park, 1952.

Shaw joined the club on a summer contract in the late 1940s and joined the full time staff after completing his National Service. Shaw was an off-spinner with a high slow loop, but he struggled with accuracy at county level and was released at the end of 1955. He returned to play for Ebbw Vale, whom he captained in 1964 and went into the baking trade. In 1978 Shaw emigrated to Australia and was killed in a road accident six years later.

SHEA, Alfred James
RHB; RM.
Born: Briton Ferry, 7 November 1898.

Died: Briton Ferry, May 1969.
Glamorgan debut: 1928 v Gloucestershire at Bristol.
Career: 2 matches in 1928.
HS for Glamorgan: 10 v Nottinghamshire at Trent Bridge, 1928.
BB for Glamorgan: 1-130 v Gloucestershire at Bristol, 1928.

Alf Shea played for Briton Ferry Town and was the uncle of W.D.Shea.

SHEA, William Dennis
RHB; LB.
Born: Briton Ferry, 7 February 1924.
Died: Ormskirk, 22 September 1982.
Education: Neath Grammar School.
Glamorgan debut: 1947 v Warwickshire at Swansea.
Career: 3 matches 1947-48.

HS for Glamorgan: 18* v Combined Services at Pontypridd, 1948.
BB for Glamorgan: 4-68 v Combined Services at Pontypridd, 1948.

Dennis Shea made his Glamorgan debut during wartime friendlies and also appeared after the war for the second XI in Minor County games. He was the nephew of Alf Shea and played for Briton Ferry Steel, Neath and Southport.

SHEPHERD, Donald John
RHB; RFM OB.
Born: Port Eynon, 12 August 1927.
Education: Gowerton County Grammar School.
Glamorgan debut: 1950 v Somerset at Cardiff Arms Park.
Career: 647 matches 1950-72; Cap 1952; Benefit 1960 (£3,200); Testimonial 1968 (£5,000); Players; MCC.
HS for Glamorgan: 73 v Derbyshire at Cardiff Arms Park, 1961.
BB for Glamorgan: 9-47 v Northamptonshire at Cardiff Arms Park, 1954.
100 wickets (12); 168 (14.03) 1956 best.
Full first-class record: 5,696 runs (9.68); 2,218 wickets (21.32); 251 catches.

Don Shepherd holds the claim as having taken more wickets than any other bowler who has not played Test cricket. He appeared at a time when England were well blessed with spinners such as Laker, Appleyard, Titmus and Underwood, but Shepherd's record of 2,174 wickets for Glamorgan at 20.95 speaks for itself.

Like many vintage spinners, Shepherd began his career as a fast/medium bowler and when serving with the Fleet Air Arm at RAF Defford was offered terms by Worcestershire. However, he agreed to join Glamorgan and in 1948 spent the summer on the MCC groundstaff. Shepherd made his Glamorgan debut in the friendly with the RAF in 1949 and won a regular place in the side from 1950. He took 115 wickets in 1952 with his away swing bowling and topped the 50 mark again in 1953 and 1954.

He lost form during 1955 and found it difficult to hit the seam regularly. He sought advice from Wooller and other senior players and spent long hours practising bowling off-cutters in the nets and the Indoor School. He took 10-85 in the final game of the season against Warwickshire at Neath and decided to change styles in 1956.

It was a switch which produced results beyond his, or Wooller's wildest dreams as he took 168 wickets for Glamorgan in 1956, taking more than five wickets in an innings on 15 occasions, including figures of 8-33 against Hampshire and 8-46 against Sussex. Shepherd topped the 100 mark again on a further 11 occasions and throughout his career was well supported by Glamorgan's close fielders, especially Peter Walker and wicketkeepers Davies,

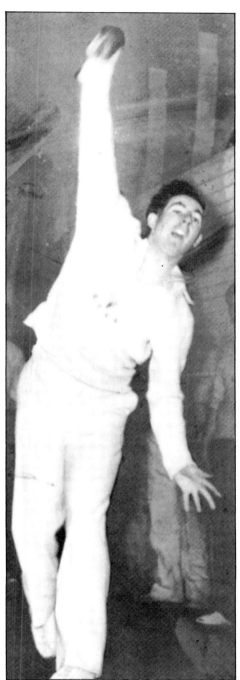

Evans and Jones who 'Shep' preferred standing back rather than up to the stumps. He was not a 'slow' spinner and delivered the ball at almost medium pace with a high action and he had the priceless ability to undercut the ball, as well as making it move in the air to deceive the batsman in misreading its length. He was a match winner on turning wickets as testified by returns of 6-5 against Nottinghamshire at Newport in 1961, 5-2 against Leicestershire at Ebbw Vale in 1965 and 7-7 against Hampshire at the Arms Park in 1966. He had match returns of 11-54 against Warwickshire at Swansea in 1960 and 12-76 against Yorkshire at the Arms Park in 1957, whilst he took a hat-trick at Swansea against Northamptonshire in 1964.

Shepherd was also an aggressive lower-order batsman who frequently launched a series of furious assaults on the bowling. One of his most spectacular innings, which at the time equalled the world record, came against the Australians in 1961 at Swansea when he scored a half century in only 15 minutes with only 11 scoring strokes, six sixes, three fours, a two and a single. The same season he also reached 50 against Derbyshire off 16 balls in only 16 minutes with six sixes. 'Shep' was the senior pro from 1962 and was Lewis' vice-captain during the Championship winning year when his vast knowledge of opposition and grounds proved invaluable. He also led Glamorgan against Australia in 1968 and the Welsh victory was based on 'Shep's' astute thinking and clever tactics.

'Shep' appeared for the Players against the Gentlemen from 1952 until 1957 and was one of Wisden's Cricketers of the Year in 1970. He toured East Africa with Brown's XI in 1961-62, Pakistan with a Commonwealth XI in 1967-68 and 1970-71 and Ceylon and the Far East with the MCC in 1969-70, whilst in 1971-72 he guested for Gloucestershire on their Zambian tour. He retired in 1972 and helped run the family's grocery and post office in the Gower, but he kept a close link with the county through broadcasting with BBC Radio Wales and since 1988 has been the club's bowling coach. In his youth, Shepherd was also a talented footballer and had trials with Swansea City, Cardiff City and Leeds United. His son Mark plays club cricket for Swansea and has also appeared in Minor County matches for Wales.

Don Shepherd (opposite and above), took more wickets than any other bowler not to have played Test cricket.

SHEPHERD, Edwin
Wicketkeeper.
Career: 1 match in 1890 against the MCC at Swansea scoring 0* and 6.
Shepherd kept wicket for Swansea.

SILKIN, Samuel Charles

RHB: LBG
Born: Neath, 6 March 1918.
Died: Oxford, 17 August 1988.
Education: Dulwich and Trinity Hall, Cambridge.
Career: 1 match in 1938 against Cambridge University at Swansea, Cambridge University 1938.
Full first-class record: 4 runs (1.33); 2 wickets; 2 catches.

Silkin won a place in the Dulwich XI between 1934 and 1936 as a leg break and googly bowler. He captained the side in 1936 and also appeared for Surrey Young Amateurs. Silkin was also a good fives player and reached the final of the Public Schools Double Tournament in 1934. In 1936 he went up to Cambridge to read Law and appeared in the University cricket Trials in 1937. But he remained on the fringe of the side and in 1938 eventually made his first-class debut against the Army.

Silkin was a close friend of the Turnbull family and had played for Glamorgan's club and ground team in 1937. The Glamorgan captain knew of Silkin's desire to win a Blue, so he invited his friend to play against the University in the hope of getting Silkin into the side for the Varsity match. But he took only 1-27 and scored 2 and 0 and spent the rest of the summer playing for the Crusaders and the Club and Ground XI.

He opted for a career in Law and Politics and after the war became a barrister in London. Silkin continued to play club cricket for Southgate and occasionally appeared for Middlesex II. In 1964 he became Labour MP for Camberwell, for whom he served until 1974. Between 1968 and 1970 he

led the UK delegation to the Council of Europe and was the Opposition front bench spokesman on Law from 1970 until 1974. In 1974 he was elected MP for Southwark and until 1979 served as Attorney General. He retired as an MP in 1985 and was elevated to the House of Lords.

SILVERLOCK, Arthur John

RHB; RM; LB.
Born: South Hackney, December 1867.
Died: Ardleigh, Colchester, 4 June 1949.
Education: Crouch End School, South Hackney.
Career: 1 match in 1900 against Brownlee's XI at Cardiff Arms Park scoring 0 in his only innings; South Wales 1906-09.

Arthur Silverlock played club cricket initially in London for Ivanhoe and South West Ham, before joining Newport as their professional in 1892. During an association which lastest until World War One, Silverlock created a host of batting and bowling records for both Newport and Monmouth-

shire. He was one of the heaviest scorers in Minor County matches and it was surprising that Glamorgan did not call upon his all-round services more often in their friendlies. In 1895 he scored 120 and took 16 wickets against Herefordshire; 187* against Glamorgan and 142* against Carmarthenshire in 1908; whilst in 1905 he hit a career-best 206* against Berkshire. He also guested for Carmarthenshire in some of their matches. At the end of 1908 he had a disagreement with Newport and returned to his native London to help his brother run a catering business. But he went back as an amateur midway through 1909 and was restored as professional in 1910. Silverlock celebrated his return in 1909 with an unbeaten 246 against Carmarthenshire. He moved back to London after World War One and played for Dedham in East Essex where he ran a smallholding.

SLADE, William Douglas
RHB; RM.
Born: Briton Ferry, 27 September 1941.
Glamorgan debut: 1961 v Hampshire at Swansea.
Career: 67 matches 1961-67.
HS for Glamorgan: 73* v Derbyshire at Swansea, 1963.
BB for Glamorgan: 4-144 v Middlesex at Lord's, 1962.

Billy Slade played for Swansea, Dafen, Pontyberem, Pontardulais and Briton Ferry Town and represented Wales in the ICC Trophy in 1979. He coached at Marlborough School in the late 1960s.

SMART, Cyril Cecil
RHB; LBG.
Born: Lacock, Wilts, 23 July 1898.
Died: Abertillery, 21 May 1975.
Education: Westbury Church of England School.
Glamorgan debut: 1927 v Leicestershire at Cardiff Arms Park.
Career: 190 matches 1927-46; Cap 1934; Benefit 1946 (£556); Warwickshire 1920-22 (45 matches, Cap 1922).
HS for Glamorgan: 151* v Sussex at Hastings, 1935.

1,000 runs: (5); 1,559 (36.25) 1935 best.
BB for Glamorgan: 5-39 v Somerset at Weston-super-Mare, 1939.
Full first-class record: 8,992 runs (26.68); 9 centuries; 180 wickets (41.69); 163 catches.

Cyril Smart moved to South Wales during the mid-1920s after a brief career with Warwickshire. He joined Briton Ferry Town as their professional and qualified for Glamorgan. During the 1930s he became one of the most ferocious middle-order batsman in county cricket, hitting Hampshire's Gerry Hill for 32 in one over (6-6-4-6-6-4) at the Arms Park in 1935. He was the son of T.Smart of Wiltshire and brother of Warwickshire's J.A.Smart.

SMITH, Christopher Lyall
RHB; OB.
Born: Durban, South Africa, 15 October 1958.
Education: Northlands High School, Durban.
Career: 1 match in 1979 against Sri Lanka at Swansea, scoring 67 and 14; Hampshire 1980-91 (222 matches, Cap 1981, Benefit 1990); Natal 1977-83; England 1983-86 (8 Tests).
Full first-class record: 18,028 runs (44.40); 47 centuries; 50 wickets (53.70); 176 catches.

'Kippy' Smith was coached in South Africa by Alan Jones, who invited him to play in the South Wales Leagues and hopefully join Glamorgan. However, Smith was considered an overseas player, having played for Natal since 1977 and he joined Hampshire in 1980. Ironically, he was later classed as English and made his Test debut in 1983. Smith played in eight Tests until 1986 and was awarded a benefit

by Hampshire in 1990. He retired at the end of the 1991 season to become marketing manager of the Western Australian Cricket Association. He is the brother of Robin Smith of Hampshire and England. Chris Smith's career-best score was 217 against Warwickshire at Edgbaston in 1987 during a record first wicket stand of 347 with Paul Terry. He was an occasional off-spinner with career-best figures of 5-69 against Sussex at Southampton in 1988.

SMITH, Douglas James
RHB; OB; occ WK.
Born: Batley, 29 May 1873.
Died: Grahamstown, South Africa, 16 August 1949.
Glamorgan debut: 1898 v Monmouthshire at Newport.
Career: 16 matches 1905-07; Somerset 1896-98 (21 matches); Worcestershire 1901-04 (9 matches).
HS for Glamorgan: 69 v Dorset at Cardiff Arms Park, 1907.
BB for Glamorgan: 2-15 v Northumberland at Newcastle, 1905.
Full first-class record: 558 runs (11.62); 24 catches and 1 stumping.
Douglas Smith joined Glamorgan in 1905 after

spells with Somerset and Worcestershire and played club cricket for St Fagan's and Fairwater. He was the son of John Smith who played in the 1860s for both Yorkshire and Lancashire and the brother of William Smith who played for Somerset and Wiltshire. Douglas Smith coached at East London in South Africa during the winter months when he was on the Glamorgan staff and he emigrated to the Cape after World War One.

SMITH, Ian
RHB; RM.
Born: Chopwell, County Durham, 11 March 1967.
Education: Ryton Comprehensive School.
Glamorgan debut: 1985 v Zimbabwe at Swansea.
Career: 63 matches 1985-91.
HS for Glamorgan: 116 v Kent at Canterbury, 1989.
BB for Glamorgan: 3-48 v Hampshire at Sophia Gardens, Cardiff, 1989.

Ian Smith was a talented schoolboy cricketer and

footballer and had trials with several First Division clubs. He played for Young England against the West Indies in 1984-85 before joining the Glamorgan staff in 1985. He played again for Young England in 1986 against Sri Lanka and developed into a useful all-rounder during 1981. However, he missed all of 1988 due to a hip injury, but he registered his maiden century in 1989. However, Smith continued to struggle for form and fitness in 1990 and he was released from the staff at the end of 1991. He has played club cricket for Cardiff, Llanelli and overseas for Belgrano CC in Argentina and Papatoetoe in New Zealand. He is joining his native Durham for 1992.

SNELL, Henry S.

Batsman.
Career: 1 match in 1920 against Carmarthenshire at Llanelli scoring 0 and 1.

Henry Snell was a Swansea businessman who played for the town club.

SOLANKY, John William

RHB; RM, occ OB.
Born: Dar es Salaam, Tanzania, 30 June 1942.
Glamorgan debut: 1972 v Hampshire at Neath.
Career: 82 matches 1972-76; Cap 1973; East Africa 1963-64, 1964-65.
HS for Glamorgan: 73 v Cambridge University at Swansea, 1975.

BB for Glamorgan: 6-63 v Derbyshire at Buxton, 1975.
Full first-class record: 2,374 runs (20.46); 183 wickets (25.34); 17 catches.

John Solanky made his first-class debut in 1963-64 for East Africa against the touring MCC at Kampala and the following season played for a Coast Invitation XI against PIA at Mombasa. He then moved to play in the UK and played Minor County cricket for Devon between 1967 and 1969, before joining the Glamorgan staff. He proved to be a useful 'bits and pieces' player in one-day cricket and after leaving the staff in 1976, Solanky has been a cricket coach and squash professional in Ireland and South Wales.

SOLOMAN, Harry G.

Batsman.
Born: London.
Died: Canton, Cardiff, 4 October 1938.
Career: 1 match in 1901 against the Public School Nondescripts at Swansea scoring 38 in his only innings.

Soloman was a tailor and draper in Cardiff, who played for the town club.

SOMAIA, Kamal Anilkumar

RHB; SLA.

Born: Brent, London, 22 July 1968.
Education: Victoria College, Melbourne and
Melbourne University.
Glamorgan debut: 1989 v Gloucestershire at Bristol.
Career: 3 matches in 1989.
HS for Glamorgan: 15 v Gloucestershire at Bristol,
1989.
BB for Glamorgan: 5-87 v Leicestershire at Sophia
Gardens, Cardiff, 1989.

Kamal Somaia was born in London and lived in
India until the age of seven, before his East African
parents moved to Australia. He joined Glamorgan
in 1989 after trials with Somerset and a few Minor
County appearances for Staffordshire. He played
club cricket for Heckmondwyke in Yorkshire and
Ringwood in Australia.

SPENCER, Charles Richard

RHB; WK.
Born: Llandough, 21 June 1903.
Died: South Havant, Hants, 29 September 1941.
Education: Clifton and Magdalen College, Oxford.
Career: 1 match in 1925 against Leveson-Gowers
XI at Swansea scoring 0 in his only innings and
making one stumping; Oxford University 1923.
Full first-class record: 46 runs (11.50); 1 catch and
1 stumping.

Charles Spencer was the son of a well-known Cardiff
solicitor and played one match for Glamorgan
whilst up at Oxford. However, he failed to win a
regular place in the Oxford side despite some
impressive performances in the University trials in
1923. After leaving Oxford he taught at Stowe and
served with the Royal Marines before his death in
1941.

SPENCER, Helm

RHB; RFM.
Born: Padiham, Lancashire, 31 December 1891.
Died: Burnley, 7 December 1974.
Glamorgan debut: 1923 v Hampshire at Cardiff
Arms Park.
Career: 39 matches 1923-25; Lancashire 1914 (2
matches); Wales 1923-24.
HS for Glamorgan: 56 v Nottinghamshire at Cardiff
Arms Park, 1924.
BB for Glamorgan: 7-33 v Northamptonshire at
Swansea, 1925.
Full first-class record: 799 runs (11.57); 111 wickets
(22.67); 40 catches.

Helm Spencer was one of the most promising young
fast bowlers in northern England before World War
One. He made two appearances for Lancashire in
1914 and also played for Saltaire and Eccleshill in

the Bradford League. After the war, he joined
Llanelli and qualifed for Glamorgan, although he
was by now only bowling at a brisk medium pace.
In 1926 he returned north and played for Colne
and Lowerhouse in the Lancashire Leagues. He was
thought to have been a relative of Derbyshire's
Harry Spencer.

SPILLER, Cecil Willmington

RHB; RM.
Born: Cardiff, 19 August 1900.
Died: Cardiff, 1974.
Glamorgan debut: 1922 v Sussex at Hove.
Career: 2 matches in 1922.
HS for Glamorgan: 14 v Hampshire at Southampton, 1922.
BB for Glamorgan: 3-50 v Sussex at Hove, 1922.

Cecil Spiller played for Cardiff and was a cousin
of Billy Spiller.

SPILLER, William

RHB.
Born: St Fagan's, 8 July 1886.
Died: Cardiff, 9 June 1970.
Education: Lansdowne School.

for the Welsh county in 1922. He played club cricket for Briton Ferry Steel and Port Talbot and twice toured Jamaica with Tennyson's XI in 1926-27 and 1927-28.

SWAIN, George William

Batsman.
Born: Stepney, Middlesex, June 1872.
Career: 1 match in 1894 against Wiltshire at Swindon scoring 12 in his only innings.
Swain played for the Mackintosh club in Cardiff and was the superintendent of the Mercantile Marine Department at Cardiff Docks.

SWART, Peter Douglas

RHB; RM.
Born: Bulawayo, Rhodesia, 27 April 1946.
Education: Jameson High School, Gatooma, Rhodesia.

Glamorgan debut: 1978 v Worcestershire at Sophia Gardens, Cardiff.
Career: 44 matches 1978-79; Cap 1979; Rhodesia 1965-66; Western Province 1967-68 to 1980-81, 1983-84; Boland 1981-82 to 1982-83.
Hs for Glamorgan: 122 v Worcestershire at Swansea, 1979.
1,000 runs (1); 1,078 (31.70) 1978 best.
BB for Glamorgan: 4-24 v Middlesex at Swansea, 1978.
Full first-class record: 6,093 runs (25.60); 6 centuries; 370 wickets (25.31); 114 catches.

Peter Swart played domestic cricket in South Africa from the mid-1960s and in 1969 toured England with the International Cavaliers. During the 1970s he played League cricket for Accrington, Haslingden and East Lancashire and toured Pakistan with D.H.Robin's XI in 1974. Between 1974 and 1976 he played Minor County cricket with Cambridgeshire, before a two-year spell with Glamorgan, where he proved himself a useful player in the one-day competitons. His career-best bowling figures were 6-85 for Western Province against Natal at Pietermaritzburg, 1971-72.

SWEET-ESCOTT, Edward Rhys

RHB; OB.
Born: Brompton Ralph, Somerset, 27 July 1879.
Died: Penarth, 1 July 1956.
Glamorgan debut: 1902 v Monmouthshire at Newport.
Career: 63 Minor County matches 1902-20, plus 1 first-class game in 1921.
HS for Glamorgan: 129 v Carmarthenshire at Llanelli, 1909.
BB for Glamorgan: 2-12 v Dorset at Cardiff Arms Park, 1907.

Sweet-Escott played cricket and hockey for Cardiff and won two Welsh hockey caps in 1912. He served on the Glamorgan committee in 1910 and 1911.

SWEET-ESCOTT, Henry Herbert

Batsman.
Born: Bridgwater, 13 October 1885.
Died: Spaxton, 27 December 1954.
Education: Dulwich and Merton College, Oxford.
Glamorgan debut: 1909 v Carmarthenshire at Llanelli.
Career: 1 match in both 1909 and 1910.
HS for Glamorgan: 7 v Carmarthenshire at Llanelli, 1909.

Henry Sweet-Escott was the son of Revd E.H.Sweet-Escott, the curate of Camberwell and a housemaster at Dulwich for 30 years. H.H. played cricket and hockey for Penarth and won 13 Welsh hockey caps between 1907 and 1914. He went up to Oxford in 1904 but did not take a degree. During the 1920s he took up golf with the Glamorganshire club and appeared in the Glamorgan Amateur championships. He acted as chairman of Brain's Brewery from 1934 until 1955.

SWEET-ESCOTT, Ralph Bond

Batsman and occasional wicketkeeper.
Born: Penkridge, 11 January 1869.
Died: Germiston, South Africa, 10 November 1907.
Education: King Henry VIII, Coventry and St Peter's College, Cambridge.
Glamorgan debut: 1891 v Monmouthshire at Cardiff Arms Park.
Career: 25 matches 1891-97.
HS for Glamorgan: 57 v Monmouthshire at Cardiff Arms Park, 1895.

Ralph Sweet-Escott was the son of Revd William Sweet-Escott, the rector of St Fagan's. He played cricket and rugby for Cardiff and won three Welsh caps between 1891 and 1895. He also played rugby for Blackheath and Penarth and was a founder member of the Barbarians RFC. Sweet-Escott

worked as an architect in Cardiff until the early 1900s when he emigrated to South Africa to take over the running of a gold mine. Sadly, he failed to make his fortune and died of enteric fever at the age of 38.

SWEET-ESCOTT, William Sidney Rice

All-rounder.
Born: Bedford, 10 October 1867.
Died: Penarth, 29 October 1926.
Education: King Henry VIII, Coventry and Trinity College, Oxford.
Glamorgan debut: 1891 v Gloucestershire at Cardiff Arms Park.
Career: 42 matches 1891-99.
HS for Glamorgan: 82 v Monmouthshire at Swansea, 1894.
BB for Glamorgan: 7-41 v Monmouthshire at Newport, 1892.

He was the elder brother of R.B.Sweet-Escott and played for Cardiff and the Water Rats. Sweet-Escott was a solicitor and a close friend of J.H.Brain and married his niece Ethel Brain. He served as chairman of Brain's Brewery from 1921 until 1926.

SYMONDS, Henry George

LHB; SLA.
Born: Cardiff, 24 June 1889.
Died: Canton, Cardiff, 1 January 1945.
Glamorgan debut: 1908 v Monmouthshire at Newport.
Career: 39 Minor County matches 1908-20, plus 22 first-class appearances 1921-25; South Wales 1912; Wales 1925-29.
HS for Glamorgan: 76 v Worcestershire at Cardiff Arms Park, 1922.
BB for Glamorgan: 2-41 v Surrey at The Oval, 1923.
Full first-class record: 766 runs (16.65); 8 wickets (38.37); 5 catches.

Harry Symonds played for Cardiff and acted as their captain in 1920. He was also the manager of the Cardiff Arms Park Greyhound Racing Company.

TAIT, John Robert

RHB; OB.
Born: Shetland Islands, 20 November 1886.

Died: Clifton, 13 April 1945.
Glamorgan debut: 1911 v Monmouthshire at Swansea.
Career: 30 Minor County games 1911-20, plus 43 first-class matches 1921-26; Wales 1923.
HS for Glamorgan: 100* v Webb's XI at Cardiff Arms Park, 1913.
BB for Glamorgan: 1-5 v Sussex at Hove, 1922.
Full first-class record: 1,477 runs (18.35); 1 wicket; 22 catches.

'Jock' Tait was a multi-talented sportsman playing cricket and rugby for Swansea, football for both Cardiff Corinthians and Newport County and winning a Welsh Amateur Football cap, against England at Llandudno in February, 1913. During World War One, Tait was a lieutenant in the Welch Regiment, but he had to be invalided home and consequently played little rugby or football after the war. He served on the Glamorgan committee between 1921 and 1926 and in 1921 scored 96 in Glamorgan's inaugural championship match, against Sussex at the Arms Park. He managed an insurance company based in Cardiff and Swansea and moved to Bristol shortly before World War Two.

TAMPLIN, Cyril

RHB; WK.
Born: Cardiff, 27 May 1921.
Glamorgan debut: 1947 v South Africa at Cardiff Arms Park.
Career: 3 matches in 1947; Bengal 1942-43.
HS for Glamorgan: 40* v Kent at Newport, 1947.
Full first-class record: 56 runs (18.66); 8 catches and 2 stumpings.

Tamplin played for Cardiff and Cardiff YMCA and made his first-class debut in Indian domestic cricket whilst on National Service. He was Haydn Davies' understudy and appeared for Glamorgan in Minor County matches after the war.

TAYLER, Herbert William

RHB; RM.
Born: Aldsworth, Glos, 6 December 1887.
Died: Dawlish, 17 April 1984.
Education: Wellingborough.
Glamorgan debut: 1920 v Capt J.H.P.Brain's XI at Cardiff Arms Park.
Career: 1 Minor County game in 1920, plus 10 first-class matches 1921-27; Gloucestershire (2 matches, 1914).
HS for Glamorgan: 44 v Nottinghamshire at Swansea, 1926.
Full first-class record: 344 runs (18.10) and 3 catches.

Tayler made two appearances for Gloucestershire

in 1914, before moving to work in South Wales and joining Cardiff. He was the brother of F.E.Tayler of Warwickshire and Gloucestershire.

TAYLOR, Henry Thomas
RHB.
Born: Cardiff, 7 July 1911.
Died: Pontypridd, 20 July 1970.
Glamorgan debut: 1932 v Kent at Swansea.
Career: 3 matches 1932-34.
HS for Glamorgan: 16* v Worcestershire at Cardiff Arms Park, 1934.

Henry Taylor played for St Fagan's and he also appeared in Minor County cricket for Glamorgan II in 1935.

TENNICK, Leslie
All-rounder.
Born: St Fagan's, 18 January 1899.
Died: Fairwater, Cardiff, 9 September 1969.
Career: 1 match in 1920 against Monmouthshire at Ebbw Vale, scoring 26 in his only innings.

Leslie Tennick played cricket and hockey for St Fagan's. He captained the hockey club in 1925-26 and won a Welsh cap against Scotland in 1925. He was the son of Arthur Tennick who was secretary of the St Fagan's hockey club and kept the Plymouth Arms in the village.

THACKERAY, Alec Guy
Batsman.
Born: Cardiff, March 1882.
Died: Cardiff, 25 July 1909.
Education: Uppingham
Glamorgan debut: 1901 v Monmouthshire at Newport.
Career: 11 matches 1901-06.
HS for Glamorgan: 78 v Northumberland at Newcastle, 1906.
BB for Glamorgan: 1 wicket against Wiltshire at Chippenham, 1904.

He was the youngest son of Alex Thackeray, a leading Cardiff stockbroker. After leaving Uppingham, Alec served with the Monmouthshire Militia, but found time to play cricket for Cardiff. He served for a while in India where he also played cricket, before returning to South Wales in 1905. He captained Cardiff and was poised to take over the Glamorgan captaincy from J.H.Brain, but in July 1909 Thackeray was taken seriously ill at the Angel Hotel in Cardiff. He was diagnosed as suffering from acute pneumonia and died shortly afterwards at the premature age of 27.

THISSEN, Daniel Richard
RHB; WK.
Born: Swansea, December 1857.

Died: Landore, 12 November 1928.
Glamorgan debut: 1889 v Warwickshire at Cardiff Arms Park.
Career: 21 matches 1889-1900.
HS for Glamorgan: 44* v Wiltshire at Cardiff Arms Park, 1892.

Thissen played for Morriston and Swansea and was Glamorgan's wicketkeeper in their inaugural match in 1889. He played regularly until 1892 for Glamorgan and then made one appearance in 1893, 1897 and 1900 as William Brain became the county's first-choice 'keeper.

THOMAS, Arthur Emlyn
RHB.
Born: Briton Ferry, 7 May 1895.
Died: Briton Ferry, 11 February 1953.
Glamorgan debut: 1913 v Surrey II at The Oval.
Career: 1 Minor County match in 1913 and 1 first-class match in 1925 against Northants at Swansea.
HS for Glamorgan: 26 v Surrey II at The Oval, 1913.

Arthur Thomas played for Briton Ferry Town.

THOMAS, Arthur W.
Batsman.
Glamorgan debut: 1908 v Devon at Exeter.
Career: 2 matches in 1908.
HS for Glamorgan: 19 v Cornwall at Truro, 1908.

Arthur Emlyn Thomas, the Briton Ferry batsman who made one Minor County appearance and one first-class appearance for Glamorgan.

'Sergeant' Thomas was a policeman in Neath and played and umpired for the Neath Club.

THOMAS, David John

RHB; LM; SLA.
Born: Swansea, 25 November 1911.
Education: University College, Swansea.
Career: 1 match in 1932 against Northamptonshire at Swansea scoring 10* in his only innings and taking 0-63.

Thomas played for Pontardulais and bowled cutters at almost medium pace. He played one match in 1932 whilst still at university when Wilf Jones was rested, but was not called up by the county again despite a fine record in club cricket.

THOMAS, Dillwyn

LHB; RM.
Born: Neath Abbey, 13 February 1905.
Glamorgan debut: 1939 v Essex at Ilford.
Career: 2 matches in 1939.
HS for Glamorgan: 14* v Yorkshire at Bradford, 1939.
BB for Glamorgan: 5-64 v Essex at Ilford, 1939.

Dillwyn Thomas played for Neath and Elba and made two appearances for Glamorgan shortly before World War Two at the age of 33. His fine record in the local leagues made it even more surprising that Glamorgan did not call upon him when he was younger and able to play regularly. He took five wickets on his debut and played again when Clay was unavailable for the Yorkshire match. However, he did not appear again and was past his best when county cricket resumed in 1946.

THOMAS, Harold T.

Batsman.
Glamorgan debut: 1894 v Monmouthshire at Swansea.
Career: 10 matches 1894-1911.
HS for Glamorgan: 62 v Carmarthenshire at Llanelli, 1911.

Harry Thomas played cricket and hockey for Swansea and won two Welsh hockey caps in 1900.

THOMAS, John Gregory

RHB; RF.
Born: Trebanos, 12 August 1960.
Education: Cwmtawe High School and South Glamorgan Institute of Higher Education.
Glamorgan debut: 1979 v Sri Lanka at Swansea.
Career: 106 matches 1979-88; Cap 1986; Northamptonshire 1989-1991 (44 matches, Cap 1991); Border 1983-84, 1986-87; Eastern Province 1987-88; England 1985-86, 1986 (5 Caps).
HS for Glamorgan: 110 v Warwickshire at Edgbaston, 1988.
BB for Glamorgan: 6-68 v Nottinghamshire at Trent Bridge, 1988.
Full first-class record: 3,419 runs (16.44); 2 centuries; 525 wickets (31.05); 74 catches.

Although Greg Thomas made his debut in 1979 he was not a regular in the Glamorgan side until 1984 after training to be a teacher and undergoing surgery to rectify a stress fracture in his back. He earned the tag 'the fastest white man' after some fiery spells in South Africa and despite a series of niggling injuries in 1985 he won a place on England's winter tour to the West Indies. He played in the first four Tests and took eight wickets and played

in the Second Test the following season against New Zealand at Trent Bridge. Thomas was recalled to the England squad for the one-day series with Pakistan in 1987 but was unable to press for a Test place after breaking down with an ankle injury.

Indeed, injury dogged his career with Glamorgan, where he failed to take 50 championship wickets during any of his seasons in the first XI. Whilst he was capable of delivering the ball at blistering pace, he was also erratic and loose at times and gradually became frustrated by the slow Welsh wickets which he felt were hindering his claims of a place in the England side. He asked to be released from the final year of his contract at the end of 1987, but the club insisted he honour his commitment in 1988. Thomas joined Northamptonshire in 1989 and during the season played for an England XI against Holland. However, he was still not called up for the Test team, so with a certain disillusionment at the selectoral policy, he went on the 'rebel' England tour to South Africa in 1989-90. He has continued to play for Eastern Province and in 1990 took a career-best 7-75 against Glamorgan at Northampton. Thomas was dogged by a pelvic injury during 1991 and was forced into retirement at the end of the season.

THOMAS, John Leslie Gwyn

RHB.
Born: Neath, June 1891.
Died: Neath, 10 April 1932.
Education: Neath Grammar School and Edinburgh University.
Glamorgan debut: 1910 v Carmarthenshire at Swansea.
Career: 20 Minor County matches 1910-20, plus 1 first-class game in 1922.
HS for Glamorgan: 44 v Surrey II at The Oval, 1920.

Gwyn Thomas was the elder son of Dr J.W.Thomas, a former mayor of Neath and played rugby and cricket for Edinburgh University. During World War One he served as a captain in the Northumberland Fusiliers and was mentioned in dispatches. He returned to his native Neath after the war and continued his rugby and cricket career with the town club. Thomas captained Neath RFC in 1920-21 and was a reserve for the Welsh side in 1921. He was a bold striker of the ball and was known in local cricket circles as 'Doctor Gwyn' because of his powerful hitting. He also played for Llanelli and the Gentlemen of Carmarthenshire.

THOMAS, Richard James

RHB; RM.
Born: Griffithstown, 18 June 1944.
Education: West Monmouth Grammar, Pontypool.
Career: 1 match in 1974 against Lancashire at Liverpool scoring 8* in his only innings and taking 1-40.

Richie Thomas first played for Glamorgan in the Sunday League game with Derbyshire at Ebbw Vale in 1969, taking 1-13 in seven overs. He continued to be a regular performer for the second eleven in the early 1970s and was called up to the first XI for one game at the start of the 1974 season

when the club were hit by injuries. He works for a steel company and plays club cricket for Panteg.

THOMAS, William Morgan

Batsman and right-arm seam bowler.
Career: 1 match in 1890 against Monmouthshire at Newport scoring 4 and 9 and taking 0-18.

Thomas was a solicitor and played for Bridgend and Llwynypia.

TODD, Paul Adrian

RHB; RM.
Born: Morton, Notts, 12 March 1953.
Education: Edward Cludd School, Southwell.
Glamorgan debut: 1987 v Derbyshire at Chesterfield.

Career: 14 matches in 1987; Nottinghamshire 1972-83 (156 matches, Cap 1977).
HS for Glamorgan: 135 v Worcestershire at Worcester, 1987.

1,000 runs (3); 1,181 (29.52) 1978 best.
Full first-class records: 7,663 runs (26.79); 9
centuries; 119 catches.

Todd was on Nottinghamshire's staff for 11 years
and scored over 7,000 runs for them, including eight
centuries and a career-best 178 against Gloucestershire at Trent Bridge. Sadly, the opener had to give
up cricket at the end of 1982 owing to family reasons
and played only a handful of games for Collingham
in 1983. He returned to regular club cricket in 1984
and the following year played for Staffordshire and
the Minor Counties. Indeed, it was performances
for the latter which led to his reappearance in the
first-class game. In 1987 he scored a match-winning
107 against Glamorgan in a Benson & Hedges Cup
match and he was signed on by the Welsh club
after an injury to Alan Butcher. Whilst in South
Wales, Todd played for Gowerton and he currently
plays for Hull and works for the British Sugar
Corporation.

TOMLINSON, Harry
LHB; OB.
Born: Barwell, Leics, 1886.
Died: Briton Ferry, 29 November 1944.
Glamorgan debut: 1920 v Monmouthshire at Briton
Ferry.
Career: 2 Minor County matches in 1920, plus 8
first-class games 1921-23.
HS for Glamorgan: 73 v Carmarthenshire at
Llanelli, 1920.
BB for Glamorgan: 1-30 v Northamptonshire at
Swansea, 1922.

Harry Tomlinson played for both Briton Ferry
Town and Briton Ferry Steel.

TRICK, William Mervyn Stanley
RHB; LM; SLA.
Born: Briton Ferry, 31 October 1916.
Education: Cwrt Sart School, Neath.
Glamorgan debut: 1946 v Kent at Dover.
Career: 19 matches 1946-50.
HS for Glamorgan: 15 v Leicestershire at Swansea,
1949.
BB for Glamorgan: 6-29 v Somerset at Swansea,
1948.

Stan Trick made his county debut in 1936 playing
for Glamorgan II in their Minor County games.
However, he did not make his first-class debut until
1946 and owing to work commitments he could
not play on a regular basis. However, when he was
available he often proved to be a match winner

and took 12 wickets against Somerset at Swansea
in 1948 as Glamorgan won by 137 runs. He played
club cricket for Neath and Briton Ferry Steel.

TURNBULL, Bertrand
RHB; occ WK.
Born: Cardiff, June 1887.
Died: Southerndown, 17 November 1943.
Glamorgan debut: 1911 v Carmarthenshire at
Swansea.
Career: 4 matches 1911-20; Gloucestershire 1911 (1
match).
HS for Glamorgan: 45 v Carmarthenshire at
Swansea, 1920.
Full first-class record: 35 runs (35.00) and 1
stumping.

Turnbull played for both Gloucestershire and
Glamorgan in 1911, but did not reappear for the

Maurice Turnbull, one of the greatest names in Glamorgan's history.

English county in the following seasons and continued to play in Minor County games for Glamorgan. He was also a talented hockey player with Penarth and Cardiff and won 19 Welsh caps between 1907 and 1914. Turnbull also appeared in the British side which played in the 1908 Olympics in London. Bertrand was the son of Lewis Turnbull, who had created a shipping line at the flourishing Cardiff Docks. Bertrand and his brother Cyril took over the company after World War One, but the depression of the 1930s forced them to dispose of the vessels and they went into business as ship brokers. He served on the Glamorgan committee from 1922 and acted as the county's chairman from 1928 until 1939.

TURNBULL, Maurice Joseph Lawson
RHB; OB.
Born: Cardiff, 16 March 1906.
Died: Montchamp, France, 5 August 1944.

Education: Downside and Trinity College, Cambridge.
Glamorgan debut: 1924 v Lancashire at Swansea.
Career: 314 matches 1924-39; Captain 1930-39; Secretary 1933-39; Cambridge University 1926-29 (Blue 1926, 1928, 1929); England 1929-30, 1936 (9 Tests); MCC, Gentlemen, The Rest.
HS for Glamorgan: 233 v Worcestershire at Swansea, 1937.
1,000 runs (8); 1,665 (32.64) 1930 best.
BB for Glamorgan: 1-4 v Somerset at Bath, 1931.
Full first-class record: 17,544 runs (29.78); 29 centuries; 4 wickets; 280 catches.

Maurice Turnbull was one of the greatest figures in Glamorgan's history and who knows what else he might have achieved both on and off the field had he not been killed by a sniper's bullet during World War Two. He was Glamorgan's top scorer on his first class debut in 1924 and achieved the same feat in his final innings in 1939 with 156 against Leicestershire. In between these dates he scored over 14,000 runs and helped the club survive a troubled financial period.

Turnbull was a member of a Penarth ship owning family and he went to school at Downside in Somerset. He established a fine schoolboy record and made his county debut in 1924 whilst still at school. He scored over 1,000 runs in his final year at Downside and was one of the bright young things of Glamorgan cricket in the 1920s. In 1926 he went up to Cambridge, won a Blue and scored his maiden century against Worcestershire at the Arms Park. However, in 1927 and 1928 he was dogged by an old rugby injury and made little progress in county cricket. He put these disappointments behind him in 1929 when he captained Cambridge and scored over 1,000 runs for the university. At the end of the season he was selected for the MCC tour to Australia and New Zealand and in January 1930 Turnbull made his Test debut at Christchurch. On his return he took over the Glamorgan captaincy and helped transform the side into a successful county outfit. During his first season in charge he amassed 1,665 runs and won a place in the MCC party for the winter tour to South Africa, where he played in all five Tests and scored 139 against Western Province.

During his ten seasons in charge, Turnbull proved himself to be an inspirational leader, always getting the best out of both the professionals and amateurs at his disposal and putting great faith in the young Welsh players. Turnbull led with a cool and debonair authority and always insisted that the professionals made an appointment if they wanted to see him, whilst he ensured that the amateurs always travelled in first-class accomodation. He led by example with the bat and was often at his best

in a race against the clock as the side needed quick runs to declare or chase a target. Turnbull had all the text book strokes and loved to play the unorthodox shot to dishearten the bowlers, but his finest innings was a superb 205 as Larwood and Voce experimented with 'Bodyline' bowling at the Arms Park in 1932.

During that season Turnbull took over the secretary's duties and together with his friend Clay, made stenuous efforts to boost Glamorgan's finances and ensure that the club did not fold. During the winter of 1932-33 he was out almost every night raising money for the club and it was claimed that he danced more miles than he had scored runs the previous summer and he had passed the 1,300 mark! In 1933 Turnbull amassed over 1,500 runs, including 200* against Northants and was recalled to the England side at Lord's and The Oval. He led the Rest in the Test Trial in 1934 and as with Glamorgan displayed an astute cricket brain. Indeed, he has been described as the best of his generation never to captain England. This could have been the result of several brushes with the MCC authorities over what they viewed as

captain, but Walker had not always seen eye to eye with some of the clubs officials and after only being offered a match contract, he announced his retirement at the end of 1972. He subsequently went into broadcasting and journalism and has been part of the BBC TV commentary team at Tests and Sunday matches. He wrote a book called *Cricket Conversations* based on his tea-time chats with leading players and currently writes for *The Mail on Sunday* besides owning a TV and video company in Cardiff.

WALTERS, Cyril Frederick

RHB.
Born: Bedlinog, 28 August 1905.
Education: Neath Grammar School.
Glamorgan debut: 1923 v Lancashire at Cardiff Arms Park.
Career: 75 matches 1923-28; Wales 1927-29; Worcestershire 1928-35 (137 matches); England 1933-34 (11 Tests).
HS for Glamorgan: 116 v Warwickshire at Swansea, 1926.
Full first-class record: 12,145 runs (30.94); 21 centuries; 5 wickets; 101 catches.

Cyril Walters was one of the most talented schoolboy batsmen in South Wales in the 1920s, before starting a career as an architect and surveyor. He was one of the bright young hopes of Glamorgan

cricket, but in 1927 he accepted a business offer and only played in the first six games of the season. Walters reappeared for six games in the middle of the 1928 season, before announcing that he was taking the secretary's post with Worcestershire and joining the Midlands county. The loss of the Neath batsman was not fully appreciated until the 1930s when he opened for England alongside Herbert Sutcliffe. He captained Worcestershire from 1931 until 1935 and toured Jamaica with Tennyson's XI in 1931-32 and India and Ceylon with MCC in 1933-34. He captained England against Australia at Trent Bridge in 1934 when R.E.S.Wyatt fractured his thumb. Walters' career-best score was 226 for Worcestershire against Kent at Gravesend in 1933. He was also a useful rugby player and played for Swansea.

WARD, Donald John

RHB; OB.
Born: Trealaw, 30 August 1934.
Education: Haverstock School, Chalk Farm.
Glamorgan debut: 1954 v Essex at Colchester.
Career: 135 matches 1954-62; Cap 1961.
HS for Glamorgan: 86 v Somerset at Cardiff Arms Park, 1956.

BB for Glamorgan: 7-60 v Lancashire at Blackpool, 1962.

Don Ward was brought up in London and played for the English Schools Cricket Association in 1950 before going on to the MCC groundstaff in 1951. He played club cricket for Briton Ferry Town, Pontardulais, Gorseinon, Maesteg Celtic, Gowerton, Pontardawe, Neath and Maesteg Town. He retired at the end of the 1962 season and took up a post with a transport company, he still plays club cricket for Porthcawl.

WARNER, Claude Charles
RHB; RM.
Born: Cardiff, 31 March 1882.
Died: Llanelli, 29 December 1965.
Career: 1 match in 1923 against Nottinghamshire at Swansea scoring 7 in each innings and taking 0-47; Border 1929-30 (2 matches); Cape Province 1930-31 (1 match).
Full first-class record: 93 runs (11.50) and 2 catches.

Claude Warner was a stockbroker in Llanelli and played for both the town side and Carmarthenshire. He served with the RFC in the Middle East during World War One and worked in South Africa in the late 1920s, where he appeared in domestic cricket.

WATKIN, Steven Llewellyn
RHB; RFM.
Born: Duffryn Rhondda, 15 September 1964.
Education: Cymmer Afan Comprehensive School, Swansea College of Further Education and South Glamorgan Institute of Higher Education.
Glamorgan debut: 1986 v Worcestershire at Worcester.
Career: 83 matches 1986-; Cap 1989; England 1991 (2 Tests); England 'A' and MCC.
HS for Glamorgan: 31 v Leicestershire at Leicester, 1989.
BB for Glamorgan: 8-59 v Warwickshire at Edgbaston, 1988.
Full first-class record: 584 runs (8.71); 301 wickets (30.54); 18 catches.

Steve Watkin was a promising schoolboy cricketer and footballer, having trials with several clubs as a goalkeeper. However, he opted for a career in cricket and after several promising performances for Maesteg Town, Watkin joined the Glamorgan staff in the mid-1980s. His opportunities were restricted by studies at South Glamorgan Institute, but he made his first-class debut at the end of the 1986 season. In 1987 Watkin went on the British Colleges tour to the West Indies and at the end of 1988 made rapid headway as an opening bowler with 46 wickets. He played regularly in 1989 and

Steve Watkin, joint highest wicket-taker in the country in 1989.

took 94 wickets to win his county cap and become joint highest wicket-taker in the country.

Watkin toured Holland with an England XI in 1989 and played for the MCC at the Scarborough Festival, plus an appearance for England at Jesmond. He took 65 wickets in 1990 and won a place on the 'A' tours to Zimbabwe in 1989-90 and Pakistan/Sri Lanka in 1990-91. Despite being injured on the latter tour, Watkin remained in the selectors' minds and appeared for the MCC against the Champion County at the start of 1991, before appearing in the first two Tests against the West Indies in 1991. His sister Lynda has represented Wales and Great Britain at hockey.

WATKINS, Albert John ('Allan')

LHB; LM.
Born: Usk, 21 April 1922.
Glamorgan debut: 1939 v Nottinghamshire at Trent Bridge.

Allan Watkins, played for England more times than any other Glamorgan cricketer.

Career: 407 matches 1939-61; Cap 1947; Benefit 1955 (£4,750); England 1948-52 (15 Caps); MCC; Players.

HS for Glamorgan: 170* v Leicestershire at Swansea, 1954.

1,000 runs (13); 1,557 (36.20) 1951 best.

BB for Glamorgan: 7-28 v Derbyshire at Chesterfield, 1954.

100 wickets: Once for Glamorgan in 1955 and once in all first-class games in 1954.

The double: Once in 1955.

Full first-class record: 20,361 runs (30.57); 32 centuries; 833 wickets (24.48); 461 catches.

Allan Watkins holds the record for the most number of England caps by a Glamorgan player and was the first person from the club to take part in an Ashes series. He gave yeoman service to the Welsh county after joining the staff in the late 1930s. In his early years he mixed cricket with professional football for Plymouth Argyle and Cardiff City. In fact, his maiden century against Surrey at the Arms Park at the end of 1946 only occurred because the Plymouth manager agreed to release the winger from pre-season training.

Watkins retired from football in 1948 and became a valuable member of the championship winning side, hitting two centuries, scoring over 1,100 runs and bowling over 500 overs of brisk left arm seamers. After advice from Wilf Wooller, he also developed the leg-cutter allowing him to bowl at a slower or medium pace to complement the spin attack of Muncer, McConnon and Shepherd. It proved successful and he became invaluable to Glamorgan in the sense that he was two bowlers in one and could change styles depending on conditions and the wicket.

His mix of attractive strokeplay, solid defence and gritty determination in Glamorgan's middle order, plus his alert fielding in their leg trap, attracted the eye of the Test selectors and he was called up for the Fifth Test against Australia at The Oval in 1948. During the winter he went on the MCC tour to South Africa, where he played in all five Tests and in the Fourth Test at Johannesburg became Glamorgan's first centurion in Test cricket by scoring 111.

Watkins was hampered by injury in 1949 and 1950, but he returned to full fitness in 1951 and became the county's leading run scorer with 1,557 runs, plus 61 wickets and 37 catches. He was rewarded by selection as senior professional on the MCC tour to India, Pakistan and Ceylon where he had the unenviable job of being stock bowler in the high temperatures. He typically bowled with great determination and remarkably finished the tour as leading run scorer in the Tests. His finest hour was in the First Test at Delhi where his

unbeaten 137 in a nine-hour innings saved England from defeat.

He appeared in the first three Tests of 1953 against Australia and produced a fine all-round performance against Leicestershire at Neath. Firstly, he took 5-16 with his leg cutters and then hit an aggressive 107 to see Glamorgan to an innings victory. However, his most-successful season for Glamorgan was in 1955 when he performed the double with 1,114 runs and 113 wickets as the ever willing workhorse delivered 950 overs of either seam or slower cutters. During the winter, he served as senior professional once again on the MCC 'A' tour to Pakistan. It was his final tour in England colours and he played in the first two unofficial Tests before losing his place.

Watkins returned to county cricket and continued to be a jovial and energetic all-rounder once again passing 1,000 runs from 1957 until 1960. However, the years of hard work gradually took its toll and in his latter years he was increasingly troubled by injury and asthma. He retired in June 1962 and took a wardens post at Usk Borstal. He later returned to cricket through coaching at Christ College, Brecon, Framlingham and Oundle and in 1991 became a life member of the MCC.

WATKINS, William Martin

RHB; LBG.

Born: Swansea, 18 January 1923.

Education: Dynevor Grammar School, Swansea.

Career: 1 match in 1950 against Hampshire at Swansea scoring 3 in his only innings.

Watkins played for Swansea and had a military career with the RAF.

WATSON, William Hastings

All-rounder.

Died: Ayr, 14 October 1936.

Glamorgan debut: 1889 v MCC at Lord's.

Career: 9 matches 1889-93.

HS for Glamorgan: 58 v Surrey II at The Oval, 1889.

BB for Glamorgan: 3 wickets against Devon at Exeter, 1893.

Hastings Watson was a timber importer at the Cardiff Docks and played for the town club, Fairwater and the Water Rats.

WEBB, Arthur Stuart

Born: Bridge, Kent, 6 August 1868.

Died: Briton Ferry, 3 December 1952.

Career: 1 match in 1912 against Surrey II at The

Oval, scoring 29 and 9; Hampshire 1895-1904 (149 matches); South Wales 1912; Players of South 1904. Full first-class record: 5,515 runs (21.54); 2 centuries; 22 wickets (46.50); 83 catches.

Arthur Webb had a ten-year career with Hampshire where he scored over 5,000 runs with a top score of 162* in his Benefit match with Surrey in 1904. He left Hampshire at the end of that season and coached in Natal and Manchester, before securing a professional appointment with the Hills Plymouth club in Merthyr. In 1912 he joined Briton Ferry Steel and appeared for South Wales against the South African tourists. Webb also played for Llanelli and Panteg before rejoining Briton Ferry Steel as their professional and groundsman. He also coached at Christ College, Brecon during the 1920s and 1930s. His brother Fred was a jockey and rode Doncaster to victory in the 1873 Derby.

Arthur Webb, scored over 5,000 runs for Hampshire before joining Glamorgan.

WENT, Gwilym John Hubert

RHB; LB.
Born: Barry, 25 March 1914.
Education: Barry County School.
Career: 1 match in 1934 against Gloucestershire at Llanelli scoring 14* and 0.

Went played club cricket for Barry and also appeared for Glamorgan II in their Minor County games in 1937.

WHEATLEY, Oswald Stephen

RHB; RFM.
Born: Low Fell, Durham, 28 May 1935.

Education: King Edward's School, Birmingham and Caius College, Cambridge.

Glamorgan debut: 1961 v Essex at Cardiff Arms Park.

Career: 206 matches 1961-69, 1970; Cap 1961; Captain 1961-66; Free Foresters 1956; Cambridge University 1957-58 (Blue both years); Warwickshire 1957-60 (63 matches, Cap 1959); Gentlemen; MCC.

HS for Glamorgan: 30 v Oxford University at Oxford, 1961.

BB for Glamorgan: 9-60 v Sussex at Ebbw Vale, 1968.

100 wickets (3); 133 (18.57) 1962 best.

Full first-class record: 1,251 runs (5.76); 1,099 wickets (20.84); 111 catches.

Ossie Wheatley was brought up in the Birmingham area and made his first-class debut for the Free Foresters in 1956 before winning a Blue at Cambridge, where he took a record 80 wickets at 17.63 in 1958. After coming down, he embarked on a successful, yet brief, career with Warwickshire as a brisk medium pace bowler. He took 237 wickets for the Midland county, including 110 in 1960. During his time at Edgbaston, Ossie Wheatley also went on the MCC tour to Brazil and Argentina in 1958-59 and Swanton's XI to the West Indies in 1960-61.

He moved to South Wales in 1961 to take over the captaincy of Glamorgan and formed an effective opening partnership with Jeff Jones. He took over 100 wickets in his first two seasons with Glamorgan and in 1964 proudly led the county to their historic victory over the 1964 Australians. He also appeared for the Gentlemen against the Players between 1958 and 1962 and in the 1961 match at Scarborough hit a career-best 34.

Wheatley went into semi-retirement in 1967, handing over the captaincy to Tony Lewis, but despite Achilles tendon trouble, he played a key role in Glamorgan's attack in 1968 taking 82 wickets at 12 apiece, a feat which brought him the accolade of being one of Wisden's Cricketers of the Year in 1969. He finally hung up his boots after Glamorgan's West Indian tour in 1969-70 and went into advertising and broadcasting in South Wales and married a well-known Welsh TV presenter. In more recent times, he has also been involved in hotel and leisure management, but has maintained his links with cricket. In 1973 and 1974 he served as a Test Selector and acted as Glamorgan's chairman between 1977 and 1983. Since 1987 he has been a trustee of the county club and has been chairman of the Sports Council of Wales. He has also served for the TCCB and is currently chairman of the TCCB cricket committee.

WHITE, David William

LHB; RFM.

Born: Sutton Coldfied, 14 December 1935.

Career: 1 match in 1972 against Gloucestershire at Swansea scoring 8 and taking 1-32; Hampshire 1957-71 (315 matches, Cap 1960, Benefit 1969 £4,547); England 1962-62 (2 Tests).

Full first-class record: 3,080 runs (10.58); 1,143 wickets (23.54); 106 catches.

'Butch' White joined Glamorgan towards the end of his career to play primarily in one-day games. He played twice for England whilst on tour with the MCC to India and Pakistan. He also toured the West Indies with the International Cavaliers in 1964-65. His career-best score was 58* against Essex at Portsmouth in 1963, whilst he returned figures of 9-44 against Leicestershire at Portsmouth in 1966. He took 100 wickets in a season on four occasions, with a best of 124 at 19 apiece in 1960. White appeared for Glamorgan in the Benson & Hedges matches during 1972 picking up five wickets, as well as a couple of Sunday League games and one championship match. He still plays in charity matches and is a leading member of the Lord's Taverners.

WHITE M.E.

Batsman.

Career: 1 match in 1909 against Carmarthenshire at Swansea scoring 17 in his only innings.

White played for Swansea and appeared for Glamorgan when T.A.L.Whittington had to withdraw on the morning of the game with Carmarthenshire in 1909.

WHITEHILL, William Kenneth

RHB; WK.

Born: Newport, 13 June 1934.

Glamorgan debut: 1960 v Worcestershire at Stourbridge.

Career: 7 matches in 1960.

HS for Glamorgan: 16 v Gloucestershire at Bristol, 1960.

Willie Whitehill kept wicket for Newport and in 1990 and 1991 has played for Wales in the Over-50s tournament.

WHITMAN, Eric Loan Emlyn

RHB; RM.

Born: Barry, 31 July 1909.

Died: Cromer, 5 December 1990.

Education: Barry Boys School and Cardiff University.

Glamorgan debut: 1932 v Leicestershire at Leicester.

Career: 2 matches in 1932.

HS for Glamorgan: 16 v Leicestershire at Leicester, 1932.

BB for Glamorgan: 2-113 v Warwickshire at Edgbaston, 1932.

Eric Whitman had a brief career with Glamorgan and also played Minor County cricket with Cambridgeshire and Bedfordshire. He was a teacher by profession and was master in charge of cricket at Bournemouth School between 1946 and 1955. He later became headmaster of a school at Sutton Coldfield and vice-principal of Bourneville College. Amongst the clubs he played for were Barry and Bournemouth Sports Club.

WHITTINGTON, Thomas Aubrey Leyshon

RHB.

Born: Neath, 29 July 1881.

Died: St Pancras, 19 July 1944.

Above: Willie Whitehill; below: Eric Whitman; opposite: 'Tal' Whittington.

Education: Weymouth School, Merchiston College
and Corpus Christi, Oxford.
Glamorgan debut: 1901 v Public School Nondes-
cripts at Swansea.
Career: 88 Minor County games 1901-20, plus 47
first-class appearances 1921-23; Captain 1908-12,
1919-20, 1922-23; Secretary 1909-22; West of
England 1910.
HS for Glamorgan: 188 v Carmarthenshire at
Llanelli, 1908.
BB for Glamorgan: 3-26 v Surrey II at The Oval,
1904.
Full first-class record: 2,302 runs (19.84); 2
centuries; 23 catches.
'Tal' Whittington was the son of Dr
T.P.Whittington, the Medical Officer to Neath
RDC who played cricket for Glamorganshire in
1869 and won a Scottish rugby cap in 1873. Tal
Whittington won a place in the Glamorgan side
whilst reading Law at Oxford and captained the
county from 1908. He was also selected in the Minor
Counties side and captained the XI from 1912 until
1920. He also took time off from his solicitor's
practice to tour the West Indies with the MCC in
1910-11 and 1912-13. He acted as the county's
secretary from 1909 and it was through his influence
and wholehearted efforts that Glamorgan's campaign for first-class status saw fruition in 1921. He
acted as vice-captain in their inaugural championship season, before taking over the captaincy again
in 1922 and 1923. He retired at the end of the season
to take up a teaching post in Sussex and to honour
his service to the club he became their first Life
Member.

WILKINS, Alan Haydn
RHB; LM.
Born: Cardiff, 22 August 1953.
Education: Whitchurch High School, Cardiff and
Loughborough University.
Glamorgan debut: 1976 v Middlesex at Swansea.
Career: 51 matches between 1976 and 1979 and 14
in 1983; Gloucestershire 1980-82 (40 matches);
Northern Transvaal 1981-82.
HS for Glamorgan: 70 v Nottinghamshire at
Worksop, 1977.
BB for Glamorgan: 6-79 v Hampshire at Southamp-
ton, 1979.
Full first-class record: 902 runs (9.49); 243 wickets
(30.90); 34 catches.

Alan Wilkins made his county debut after leaving
Loughborough University where he trained as a
teacher. However, his first team appearances were
limited owing to the presence of fellow left-arm
seamer Malcolm Nash. He joined Gloucestershire

in 1980, but returned to Glamorgan in 1983, before
emigrating to South Africa to start a career in
broadcasting. He returned to Cardiff in 1989 to
work for BBC Wales. Wilkins played club cricket
for Cardiff and Cowbridge and was also a useful
rugby player, appearing for Cardiff, Bristol and
Glamorgan Wanderers. His career-best bowling
performance was 8-57 for Gloucestershire against
Lancashire in 1981 at Old Trafford.

WILKINSON, William
RHB; RFM.
Born: Kimberley, Notts, 5 July 1859.
Died: Nottingham, 6 October 1940.
Glamorgan debut: 1889 v MCC at Lord's.
Career: 2 matches in 1889; Nottinghamshire 1892-
93 (5 matches).
HS for Glamorgan: 19 v MCC at Lord's, 1889.
BB for Glamorgan: 4-10 v MCC at Lord's, 1889.
Full first-class record: 34 runs (6.80); 5 wickets
(26.60); 4 catches.

Wilkinson was Cardiff's professional in 1889 and
was selected for Glamorgan's London tour that
season. He returned to his native Nottinghamshire
and played for the county in 1892 and 1893.

WILLIAMS, David Lawrence

LHB; RFM.
Born: Tonna, 20 November 1946.
Education: Neath County Grammar School.
Glamorgan debut: 1969 v Yorkshire at Swansea.
Career: 150 matches 1969-76; Cap 1971; England
Under-25 XI v England 1971.

HS for Glamorgan: 37* v Essex at Chelmsford,
1969.
BB for Glamorgan: 7-60 v Lancashire at Blackpool,
1970.
Full first-class record: 403 runs (5.52), 364 wickets
(27.15); 38 catches.

Lawrence Williams graduated from club cricket
with Ynysygerwn and Gorseinon into the Glamorgan side in their Championship winning year in
1969. The 'Tonna Terror' had an immediate impact
with 56 wickets with his fast medium seamers and
won a regular place in the county's seam attack
in the early 1970s. He was capped in 1971 after
regularly taking over 50 wickets and setting a club
record of 33 wickets in a Sunday League season.

He struggled with injury in 1975 and failed to regain
form the following season. Even so, it was still a
shock when he was one of the players to receive
a letter from the committee in 1976 warning him
about his performance. Williams was shocked at
this abrupt treatment and quit county cricket.

WILLIAMS, Dyson Bransby MC, DSO

RHB.
Born: Killay, 13 October 1877.
Died: London, 18 April 1922.
Education: Malvern.
Glamorgan debut: 1901 v Monmouthshire at
Newport.
Career: 16 Minor County games 1901-14, plus 1 first-
class appearance in 1921; Hon Treasurer 1913-21.
HS for Glamorgan: 43 v Kent at Bromley, 1913.

He was a member of the Bransby-Williams family
of Killay, who organized games of country house
cricket in the grounds of Killay House and ran a
wandering eleven called Public School Nondescripts.
Dyson Williams was a well-known figure in the

commercial world of Swansea, where he had a solicitors practice and was drafted on to the committee in 1912 to organize fund-raising, before being elevated to the office of treasurer in 1913. He captained Swansea in 1912 and 1913, before serving in World War One with the Welch Regiment. He was awarded the MC in 1916 and the DSO in 1918, but was mentally scarred by the horrors of war and suffered from depression. He also lost money gambling and in business deals and his solicitors' practice closed. He was a close friend of French boxer Georges Carpentier and went to London to work for a boxing promotor after resigning from the treasurer's post. He hoped for a change of fortune, but he continued to lose money and committed suicide in his London office in April 1922. He had also been a talented musician and under the name 'Florian' and 'Florian Brock' he wrote the scores of several successful songs and poems. He also changed his name by deed poll to Dyson Brock Williams.

WILLIAMS, F.I.

Batsman.
Career: 1 match in 1920 against Carmarthenshire at Llanelli scoring 24 and 0.

WILLIAMS, Ievan

RHB.
Born: Brynamman, 17 March 1909.
Died: Eastbourne, 3 March 1964.
Education: Liverpool University.
Glamorgan debut: 1931 v Gloucestershire at Cheltenham.
Career: 2 matches in 1931.
HS for Glamorgan: 7 v Gloucestershire at Cheltenham, 1931.

Ievan Williams played for Glanamman and made his county debut after some impressive performances in university cricket. He went into dentistry and had practices in Brynamman, Bridgend, Chester, London and Poole.

WILLIAMS, Jestyn

Batsman and medium-pace bowler.
Born: Miskin Manor, 14 April 1867.
Died: Dyffryn, Neath, 16 June 1922.
Education: Charterhouse and Oxford University.
Glamorgan debut: 1890 v Monmouthshire at Newport.
Career: 4 matches 1890-91.
HS for Glamorgan: 16 v Somerset at Bath, 1890.

He was the second son of Judge Gwilym Williams

of Miskin Manor and was in the Charterhouse XI in 1883 and 1884 before winning a football blue at Oxford. He played for Fairwater and married the daughter of J.E.Moore-Gwyn thereby becoming the brother-in-law of H.G. and J.G.Moore-Gwyn. Williams served with the Yorkshire Regiment and was a quartermaster general with the Monmouthshire Regiment. After leaving the Army, he became land and mineral agent on Lord Treowen's Llanover Estate in Monmouthshire and Glamorgan. Williams was also a keen huntsman and a good shot and is reputed to have played amateur football for Wales.

WILLIAMS, Lewis Erskine Wyndham

RHB.
Born: Bonvilstone, 28 November 1900.
Died: St Hilary, 24 April 1974.
Education: Oratory.
Glamorgan debut: 1928 v Oxford University at Oxford.
Career: 4 matches 1928-30.
HS for Glamorgan: 53* v Oxford University at Oxford, 1928.

'Tip' Williams was the founder of the South Wales Hunts CC and served on the Glamorgan committee between 1924 and 1926. He was a leading batsman with the Cowbridge club and was a close friend of J.C.Clay. It was through their joint influence that Glamorgan staged county matches at Cowbridge in the early 1930s.

WILLIAMS, William Henry

All-rounder.
Born: Cardiff, 1855.
Glamorgan debut: 1889 v MCC at Lord's.
Career: 8 matches 1889-91.
HS for Glamorgan: 37 v Somerset at Cardiff Arms Park, 1890.
BB for Glamorgan: 1-16 v Surrey II at The Oval, 1889.

Williams played rugby and cricket for Cardiff. In 1880 he appeared for a Cardiff XXII against the United South of England and he captained the Cardiff club in 1888 and 1889. He also led the county in some of their games in 1890. He was a leading official with the Bute Docks Railway Company and served on the county committee between 1888 and 1892, when he left Cardiff to take up a new business appointment in London.

WINDSOR-CLIVE, Hon Archer

LHB; LM.
Born: Redditch, Worcestershire, 6 November 1890.

Died: Landrecies, France, 25 August 1914.
Education: Eton and Trinity College, Cambridge.
Glamorgan debut: 1908 v Monmouthshire at Cardiff Arms Park.
Career: 5 matches 1908-12; Cambridge University 1910-12.
HS for Glamorgan: 16 v Cornwall at Swansea, 1909.
BB for Glamorgan: 1-7 v Surrey II at Cardiff Arms Park, 1912.
Full first-class record: 108 runs (8.30); 3 wickets; 1 catch.

Archer Windsor-Clive was the third son of Lord Plymouth and was in the Eton XI between 1907 and 1909. He went up to Cambridge and played occasionally for the XI without winning a Blue, but he was also a useful tennis player and won a Blue in 1911 and 1912. When World War One broke out he joined the Coldstream Guards, but tragically was killed in the Battle of Mons only a fortnight after leaving Cardiff. He played for St Fagan's and I Zingari and was tipped as a future captain of the club. His career-best performances of 22 and 3-56 were both achieved when he was up at Cambridge.

WOLFE, Arthur

Batsman.
Career: 1 match in 1895 against the South Wales CC at Swansea, scoring 9 in his only innings.

Arthur Wolfe played for Swansea and was a centre-half with Swansea AFC, captaining the side in 1892-93.

WOOLLER, Wilfred

RHB; RM.
Born: Rhos-on-Sea, 20 November 1912.
Education: Rydal School and Christ's College, Cambridge.
Glamorgan debut: 1938 v Yorkshire at Cardiff Arms Park.
Career: 400 matches 1938-62; Cap 1939; Captain 1947-60; Secretary 1961-78; Cambridge University 1935-36 (Blue both years); Gentlemen; MCC.
HS for Glamorgan: 128 v Warwickshire at Neath, 1955.
1,000 runs (4); 1,138 (36.70) 1953 best.
BB for Glamorgan: 8-45 v Warwickshire at Ebbw Vale, 1953.
100 wickets (2); 120 (24.55) 1949 best. The Double 1955.
Full first-class record: 13,593 runs (22.58); 5 centuries; 958 wickets (26.96); 412 catches.

If Maurice Turnbull was the architect of Glamorgan, Wilf Wooller was the man who laid the post-war foundations and watched the club build on the success of the 1948 championship winning side during the next 50 years. He has fulfilled almost every role with the club from player to captain and secretary to president.

Wooller learnt his cricket in North Wales, playing first for Rydal School and then Minor County cricket for Denbighshire in 1933 and 1934. He went up to Cambridge and won a Blue in 1935 and 1936, establishing himself as a bold all-rounder. During the summers he continued to play in North Wales and was even approached by Lancashire, but he turned down the offer and remained playing for Colwyn Bay.

Wilfred Wooller, the great servant to Glamorgan who has filled almost every role with the club. Wooller was architect of Glamorgan's rise after World War Two.

In the 1930s Wooller hit the headlines more for his prowess on the rugby field. He graduated from the Rydal XV into a place in the centre for Sale, alongside Welsh International Claude Davey who was impressed by the aggressive schoolboy and he persuaded the selectors to include Wooller in the 1932-33 Trial. A fortnight later the sixth former had a place in the Welsh side against England and helped Wales to their first ever win at Twickenham. Wooller won a total of 18 caps between 1932-33 and 1938-39, impressing everyone with his strong running and powerful kicking. He also played in the Cambridge XV and following a move to work in South Wales he played for Cardiff from 1936 onwards and captained them in 1938-39 and 1939-40.

Whilst playing for Cardiff he built up a friendship with Turnbull and it was the Glamorgan captain who persuaded Wooller to turn out for Glamorgan in 1938 when their seam attack was hit by injury. He had an immediate impact taking 5-90 on his debut and he played whenever he could get time off during the next two seasons. He had a wonderful game against the West Indies in 1939 when he hit his maiden century. He came in at 156-6, but counter-attacked the bowling hitting 111 in two hours, before taking 5-69 to see Glamorgan to a remarkable 73-run victory.

Wooller served in the Far East during World War Two, but was taken prisoner and for a while there were fears about his safety. However, he turned up in a PoW camp and remained in captivity for the rest of the war. When hostilities were over he returned to Cardiff determined to carry on with his sporting career and he became Clay's right-hand man as the veteran spinner got Glamorgan back on their feet in 1946. Wooller took over the captaincy in 1947 and fostered a marvellous team spirit, moulding a successful team based on home-grown talent and shrewd signings from other counties. He typically led from the front in 1947, taking 79 wickets, passing 1,000 runs for the first time and sharing in a record seventh wicket partnership of 195 with Willie Jones against Lancashire at Liverpool.

In 1948 Wooller skilfully led Glamorgan to their first-ever championship title, displaying great leadership skills and an ability to get the best out of his team. Wilf put great faith in his spinners Muncer and Clay, bowling to a cluster of fielders close in on the legside, including the fearless Wooller standing at short-leg. Wooller was a ruthless captain, always leading from the front and was never afraid to ask anyone to do a thing which he himself would not think twice about. He was ready to do anything in the sides best interest and during the 1950s opened both the bowling and

batting. By sheer application and hardwork, he made himself into a first-class all-rounder and achieved the double in 1954 scoring 1,059 runs and taking 107 wickets and all at the age of 41. Even more remarkably, he often assumed the mantle of stock bowler and despite being well into his forties and with heavy strapping on his legs and various ailments, Wooller would bowl for hour after hour. He also made an impact off the field and took steps in the 1950s to strengthen the club's finances by creating the Glamorgan Supporters' Club to run fund raising activities.

Wooller was a forthright individual who had occasional brushes with authority and opposing players but never left anyone in doubt what he thought of them. There are a host of stories about Wooller, many no doubt apocryphal, but the best concerns an innings by Bob Gale which frustrated the Glamorgan bowlers. As the Middlesex batsman was making his way back to the pavilion after scoring 200, Wooller bellowed at him: "That's the worst bloody 200 I've ever seen!" But whilst Wooller played hard on the field, he was always willing to have a drink and a chat with opponents after play was over.

He had a few disagreements with Glamorgan's committee, in the late 1950s and was so disgusted at the way he was being treated that he tendered his resignation. The sorry dispute was resolved and Wooller continued as captain until 1960 when he retired, although he did reappear in one game in 1962. Despite having an insurance business, Wooller took over the secretary's duties in 1961 and continued to be a Test selector, a post he held from 1955 to 1962 during which time he helped mould a successful England side.

Wooller also became a leading sports journalist, writing on cricket and rugby for the *Sunday Telegraph* and commentating on cricket broadcasts for BBC Wales. Indeed, Wooller was at the microphone when Sobers hit six sixes in 1968. His forthright views on the air or in print showed that he still lived and breathed Glamorgan cricket and although some people took exception to what was said or written, Wooller had a great desire to see Glamorgan become successful once again. He retired from the secretary's post in 1978, but has remained closely linked with the club and in 1991 was elected Glamorgan's president.

WORSLEY, Francis Frederick

RHB.
Born: Kensington, 2 June 1902.
Died: Stepney, 15 September 1949.
Education: Brighton College and Balliol College, Oxford.

Glamorgan debut: 1922 v Northamptonshire at Northampton.
Career: 2 matches 1922-23.
HS for Glamorgan: 21 v Northamptonshire at Northampton, 1922.

Worsley had a fine record with Brighton College and had a trial with Glamorgan whilst on vacation from Oxford. He played briefly for Cardiff, but on coming down moved into broadcasting and after the war produced the popular ITMA programme on BBC Radio.

YORATH, Herbert William Friend

Batsman.
Career: 1 match in 1895 against Monmouthshire at Usk, scoring 10 in his only innings.

Yorath was a businessman in Cardiff and played for the town club.

YORATH, Dr Tom Howel Bruce

Right handed batsman and bowler.
Born: Cardiff, 9 September 1868.
Died: Conwyl Elvet, Carmarthen, 16 October 1943.
Education: Guy's Hospital.
Glamorgan debut: 1891 v MCC at Lord's.
Career: 6 matches 1891-95.
HS for Glamorgan: 29 v Devon at Exeter, 1892.

Dr Bruce Yorath played for Llanelli and was the Medical Officer and Public Vaccination Officer for Conwyl District, operating from a surgery in Pontyberem. He also appeared for the MCC as a late substitute against Glamorgan in 1889.

YORATH, William Lougher

Batsman.
Born: Cardiff, 2 December 1862.
Died: Cardiff, 3 April 1924.
Education: Bedford School.
Glamorgan debut: 1889 v MCC at Lord's.
Career: 4 matches 1889-90.
HS for Glamorgan: 21 v MCC at Lord's 1889.

William Yorath played rugby and cricket for Cardiff. He was Cardiff secretary from 1886 until 1889 and then carried out the same duties for Glamorgan until 1892. He was also a useful golfer and captained Radyr Golf Club. Yorath had a distinguished career in local politics, serving as a city councillor and was deputy mayor of Cardiff in 1905-06. He was a solicitor by profession and acted as coroner to Cardiff City Corporation.

YOUNG, George Avery

Batsman.

W. L. Yorath (above), G. A. Young (below).

Born: Tynemouth, June 1866.
Died: Penarth, 21 January 1900.
Education: Malvern College.
Glamorgan debut: 1892 v Devon at Exeter.
Career: 3 matches 1892-93.
HS for Glamorgan: 61 v MCC at Lord's, 1892.

George Young played cricket for Bridgend and rugby for Cardiff. He captained their XV in 1887-88 and won two Welsh Caps in 1886.

YOUNIS AHMED, Mohammed

LHB; LM; SLA.
Born: Jullunder, India, 20 October 1947.
Education: Moslem High School, Lahore and Government College, Lahore.
Glamorgan debut: 1984 v Oxford University at Oxford.

Career: 58 matches 1984-86; Cap 1985; Lahore 1963-64, 1964-65; Surrey 1965-78 (262 matches, Cap 1969); Karachi 1967-68; PIA 1969-70; South

Australia 1972-73; Worcestershire 1979-83 (85 matches, Cap 1979); Pakistan 1969-70, 1986-87 (4 Tests).
HS for Glamorgan: 177 v Middlesex at Sophia Gardens, Cardiff, 1985.
1,000 runs (2); 1,421 (64.59) 1985 best.
BB for Glamorgan: 1-38 v Kent at Swansea, 1985.
Full first-class record: 26,073 runs (40.48); 46 centuries; 49 wickets (42.76); 244 catches.

The much travelled Younis Ahmed joined Glamorgan after a long career with Surrey and a much briefer one with Worcestershire where he was released for disciplinary reasons. He made his Test debut in 1969-70, but was banned from Tests by the Pakistani authorities after visiting South Africa with D.H.Robin's XI in 1973-74. He also toured Jamaica with the International Cavaliers in 1969-70 and went on three other tours to South Africa during the 1970s. He was released by Glamorgan at the end of 1986 and remarkably reappeared in Tests the following winter. He is the half-brother of Pakistan's Saeed Ahmed and is currently coaching the Universals CC in Zimbabwe. His career-best score was 221* for Worcestershire against Nottinghamshire at Trent Bridge in 1979 and his best bowling performance was 4-10 for Surrey against Cambridge University at Fenners in 1975.

The following have only appeared in limited-overs games.

FRANCIS, Kenneth McKoy Valentine

RHB; RM.
Born: St Kitts, 14 March 1950.
Career: Played in the Sunday League match against Surrey at Sophia Gardens, Cardiff in 1973 scoring 0* and taking 1-25 in 8 overs.

Kenny Francis appeared in one Sunday League fixture in 1973, but did not play in any first-class matches whilst on the Glamorgan staff. He plays club cricket for the Progressive side in Cardiff.

KIRNON, Samuel

RHB; RM.
Born: Preston, 25 December 1962.
Education: Monserrat Secondary School, West Indies.
Glamorgan debut: 1991 v Surrey at The Oval.
Career: Played in the Sunday League match against Surrey at The Oval in 1991 scoring 0 and taking 1-36.

Sam Kirnon was born in Lancashire, but brought up in the West Indies. After leaving school he joined the British Army and was posted to West Germany as a Physical Training Instructor. He played for Dortmund and in 1990 had a trial with Glamorgan, which led to him taking a six month sabbatical to play county cricket, during which time he was attached to Cardiff.

NORKETT, Kim Thomas

RHB; RFM.
Born: British Military Hospital, Malta, 24 December 1955.
Education: Monmouth School.
Career: Played in the 1974 Sunday League game with Hampshire at Basingstoke scoring 0 and taking 1-34 in 8 overs.

Kim Norkett was a talented schoolboy sportsman and made his Glamorgan debut whilst still at Monmouth. He was also an outstanding rugby player and appeared for Newport and Ebbw Vale. He played in second eleven and under-25 games but did not play any first-class cricket and went into teaching. He captained Ebbw Vale in 1985.

The following played in trial games during the 1890s and 1900s.

ARDASEER, J.G.

Batsman.
He appeared in the Trial game against a Colts XVIII at Cardiff Arms Park in 1906. Ardaseer was a batsman with Swansea and also played for the Gentlemen of Glamorgan.

BIGGS, Norman Witchell

Batsman.
Born: Cardiff, 3 November 1870.
Died: Sakaba, Nigeria, 27 February 1908.
Education: Cardiff College and Cambridge University.

Biggs played in the 1893 Trial against a Cardiff and District XI, scoring 6 and 5. He played cricket for St Andrews and the Water Rats and was a Welsh rugby international. He won eight caps between 1888 and 1894 and appeared for Cardiff, Bath, London Welsh, Somerset, Richmond and the Barbarians. He was the brother of Cecil and Selwyn Biggs and in the early 1900s left Britain to join the Nigerian Police. He met a decidedly sticky fate in 1908 when he was killed by a poisoned arrow during native unrest.

BIRCHAM, Humphrey Francis William DSO

Batsman.
Born: Monmouth, 1875.
Died: Pozieres, France, 23 July 1916.
Education: Eton and Sandhurst.

Humphrey Bircham was in the Eton XI in 1892 and 1893 and played in the 1893 Trial against Cardiff and District scoring 17 and 2. He played club cricket for Cardiff and Newport and also represented Monmouthshire, United Services, Green Jackets, MCC and I Zingari. He had a distinguished military career with the King's Royal Rifle Corps and was mentioned in dispatches during the Boer War. He was awarded the DSO in June 1915, but died 13 months later after being hit by a shell during an attack on German trenches.

CASBOURNE, F.

All-rounder.
Casbourne was a professional from Buckinghamshire who played in the 1893 Trial against Cardiff and District, scoring 0 and 3 and returning figures of 23-11-44-3.

COPE, William (later Lord Cope of St Mellons)

All-rounder.
Born: Roath, Cardiff, 18 August 1870.
Died: St Mellons, 15 July 1946.
Education: Repton and Clare College, Cambridge.

Cope played for Repton and Cardiff and appeared in the 1893 Trial against Cardiff and District scoring 2 and 16 and taking 1-13. He read Law at Cambridge, where he won a football Blue and played rugby for the university XV, but failed to win a Blue. He also played for Cardiff and Blackheath and won one Welsh cap in 1896. Cope was called to the Bar in 1893 and practiced in London until 1902, when he returned to South Wales. He entered local politics and became Conservative MP for Barry in 1918 and was elevated to the peerage in 1946. Cope was also a keen huntsman and rode and owned several horses in point-to-points in Wales and was a Junior Lord of the Treasury. He was also a director of a colliery and electric power station.

COURTIS, Sir John Wesley

Batsman.
Born: Williamstown, Australia, 19 February 1859.
Died: Llandaff, 19 December 1939.

Courtis was a rags-to-riches Australian who owned a brickworks in Cardiff and made his fortune out of the building boom in the Welsh capital in the late nineteenth century. He played for Cardiff and appeared in the 1893 Trial against Cardiff and District scoring 12 and 4. He became Lord Mayor of Cardiff in 1911 after a successful career in local politics and stockbroking.

GABE, Rhys Thomas (born Rees Thomas Gape)

Batsman.
Born: Llangennech, 22 June 1880.
Died: Cardiff, 15 September 1967.
Education: Llanelli Intermediate School and Borough Road College.

Rhys Gabe appeared in the 1906 Trial against a Colts XVIII at the Arms Park scoring none in his only innings and taking two catches. He played rugby and cricket for both Cardiff and Llanelli and won 24 Welsh rugby caps between 1901 and 1908. He also played rugby for Llangennech, London Welsh and Middlesex. He was also a talented cyclist and billiards player, and represented Borough Road College at water polo.

LEWIN, H.

Lewin was a professional who appeared in the 1893 Trial against Cardiff and District, scoring 3* and 0 and taking 2-30 and 2-12.

MOSS, Samuel

RHB; RFM.
Born: 1867.
Died: Featherstone, 7 August 1923.

Sam Moss was the professional with Merthyr and appeared in the 1892 Trial match at Swansea against a Colts XXI. He scored 2 in his only innings and despite returning figures of 11-5-8-11 and 7.2-5-2-4 he was not called upon again. Moss was reputed to have been one of the fastest bowlers in England and was once on the Old Trafford groundstaff. He also played for Staffordshire and had engagements with Bacup, Padiham, Haslingden, Barnsley and Batley. He was the father of Ernest Moss and was killed in August 1923 when walking along the railway line to watch a match at Featherstone.

ROFFEY, Sir George Walter

All-rounder.
Born: Brentford, 21 May 1870.
Died: Templecombe, 13 March 1940.
Education: Harrow.
Career: 1 match in 1893 against a Cardiff and District XI at Cardiff Arms Park scoring 0 and 0* and taking 2-39 and 2-51.

Sir George Roffey was in the Harrow XI in 1888 and appeared in a trial game at the end of the 1893 season. He was a merchant by trade and became chairman of the Home Cereals committee. He was a member of the MCC between 1889 and 1936 and was knighted in 1918.

WALDRON, Arthur

Batsman.
Born: Llandaff, 7 July 1861.
Died: Cardiff, 8 January 1947.
Education: Magdalen College, Oxford.

Waldron was a solicitor in Cardiff and appeared in the 1891 Trial against a Colts XI at Cardiff Arms Park, scoring 6 and 7. He played for Fairwater and the Water Rats.

WATSON, Revd Arthur Hawtrey

RHB; RM.
Born: Derbyshire, 18 June 1865.
Died: Norwich, 7 September 1952.
Education: Derby School and Keble College, Oxford.

Watson appeared in the 1891 Trial at the Arms Park against a Colts XX, scoring 1 and 6* and taking 1-20 in ten overs. He also played for Lincolnshire in 1889 and 1892, Suffolk in 1904 and the Gentlemen of Warwickshire between 1910 and 1912. He entered the clergy after leaving Oxford and held curacies in Worcestershire, Warwickshire and Buckinghamshire. He was also a useful footballer having captained Derby School in 1886 and 1887 and whist studying at Wells Theological College played soccer for Somerset in 1887 and 1888.

WILLIAMS, Llewellyn J.

Williams played for Cardiff and appeared in the 1893 Trial against Cardiff and District at the Arms Park scoring 1 and 2.

Career Records in all Glamorgan Matches 1889-1991

N.B. The games between 1889 and 1920 were minor county fixtures and friendlies, whilst those from 1921 onwards were first-class matches. It has not been possible to obtain a full set of bowling figures for some of the minor county games owing to missing scorebooks or incomplete details in newspapers. The wickets taken in those matches are given in brackets.

Name	Career	Mchs	Inns	NO	Runs	Ave	100s	Overs	Mds	Runs	Wkts	Ave	Ct/St
Abel T.E.	1922-1925	32	55	1	821	15.20	1	76.5	14	258	8	32.25	16
Alexander H.G.	1898	4	7	2	42	8.40	-	-	-	-	-	-	2
Allin A.W.	1976	13	16	8	108	13.50	-	333.3	96	1,011	44	22.97	3
Anderson R.M.B.	1946	1	1	0	0	-	-	18	4	60	0	-	-
Anthony H.A.G.	1990	6	8	0	127	15.88	-	142.4	32	466	12	38.83	-
Arkell T.M.	1898	2	3	0	15	5.00	-	-	-	-	-	-	1
Armstrong G.D.	1974-1976	30	42	11	426	13.74	-	655.3	122	2,423	72	33.65	10
Arnott T.	1921-1930	188	321	25	4,726	15.96	3	3,697.3	642	11,435	361	31.68	87
Arundale H.	1914-1920	2	2	0	8	4.00	-	37	9	90	1	90.00	-
Bainton H.	1911	1	2	1	89	89.00	-	2	0	22	0	-	-
Bancroft J.	1908-1910	11	14	4	153	15.30	-	-	-	-	-	-	9/5
	1922	9	18	3	36	2.40	-	-	-	-	-	-	4/3
Bancroft W. Jnr	1891	1	-	-	-	-	-	-	-	-	-	-	-
Bancroft W.J.	1889-1914	230	357	19	8,250	24.41	7	47	12	170	10(1)	17.10	185/2
Barlow T.M.	1894-1897	11	18	0	233	12.94	-	4	2	9	0	-	7
Barry J.	1900	1	1	1	24	-	-	-	-	-	-	-	1
Barwick S.R.	1981-	150	145	56	711	7.99	-	3,866	967	10,861	333	32.62	31
Base S.J.	1986-1987	20	25	8	180	10.58	-	426	77	1,434	49	29.26	4
Bastien S.	1988-	36	23	10	131	10.08	-	770.5	206	2,761	77	35.86	3
Bates W.E.	1914-1920	6	10	0	202	20.20	-	82.1	14	299	15	19.93	-
	1921-1931	283	500	15	12,600	25.97	10	2,101.4	202	8,408	224	37.53	182
Batty A.M.	1891	1	2	1	9	9.00	-	-	-	-	-	-	-
Baxter H.W.	1920	1	2	1	61	61.00	-	-	-	-	-	-	-
	1921	1	2	0	11	5.50	-	-	-	-	-	-	-
Beasley H.O.C.	1899	3	6	1	26	5.20	-	-	-	-	-	-	3
Bell J.T.	1924-1931	166	281	18	7,324	27.84	10	43.2	3	205	2	102.50	61
Bennett F.	1914	2	3	1	21	10.50	-	4	0	15	0	-	1
Bestwick W.	1914-1920	4	6	3	6	2.00	-	132.1	32	233	21	11.10	5
Bevan J.M.	1920	1	1	0	3	3.00	-	-	-	-	-	-	1
Biggs C.F.	1906	2	2	0	14	7.00	-	7	3	14	0	-	2
Biggs S.H.	1891-1900	30	48	12	483	13.41	-	723	169	1,943	104(11)	18.68	22
Billings E.A.	1911-1914	17	23	2	290	13.81	-	-	-	-	-	-	17/21
Binch D.	1894-1900	3	3	0	16	5.33	-	20	2	77	2	38.50	1
Blackmore D.	1934	1	1	0	34	34.00	-	-	-	-	-	-	1
Boon R.W.	1931-1932	11	19	2	229	13.47	-	10	0	40	0	-	4
Bowen E.	1928-1933	3	5	1	40	10.00	-	5	2	14	0	-	-
Bowen G.E.	1891-1892	3	4	0	41	10.25	-	8	0	17	0	-	-
Brain J.H.	1891-1908	145	225	17	5,236	25.17	5	99.4	20	317	20(1)	15.85	111/50
Brain J.H.P.	1920	4	6	0	67	11.17	-	-	-	-	-	-	1/2
	1921-1928	6	11	2	86	9.55	-	-	-	-	-	-	4/1
Brain M.B.	1930	1	2	0	9	4.50	-	-	-	-	-	-	-
Brain W.H.	1891-1908	105	155	17	2,257	16.36	2	-	-	-	-	-	122/118
Brierley T.L.	1931-1939	181	292	25	4,760	17.82	3	5	0	33	0	-	153/72

Name	Career	Mchs	Inns	NO	Runs	Ave	100s	Overs	Mds	Runs	Wkts	Ave	Ct/St
Burnett A.C.	1958	8	11	0	71	6.45	-	-	-	-	-	-	1
Burton	1891	3	6	2	17	4.25	-	100	27	210	8	26.25	2
Bush P.F.	1900-1903	4	6	0	12	2.00	-	3	0	16	1	16.00	2
Butcher A.R.	1987-	108	189	16	7,809	45.14	17	150.4	20	625	15	41.67	52
Byass G.R.S.	1920	1	1	0	21	21.00	-	18	5	38	1	38.00	1
Cadogan J.P.	1897-1900	4	7	1	86	14.83	-	-	-	-	-	-	2
Cameron A.W.C.	1900-1913	18	25	3	284	12.91	-	118.5	8	451	24	18.79	11
Cann M.J.	1986-1991	36	55	6	1,248	25.47	1	155.5	22	669	13	51.46	15
Carless E.F.	1934	3	3	0	35	11.67	-	-	-	-	-	-	1
Carr H.L.	1934	1	1	0	6	6.00	-	-	-	-	-	-	-
Carrington W.G.	1896	1	1	0	10	10.00	-	-	-	-	-	-	1
Cartwright T.W.	1977	7	11	2	76	8.44	-	131.2	52	258	10	25.80	2
Chandless J.	1911-1920	9	9	2	77	11.00	-	60.3	20	183	7	26.14	3
	1927	1	1	0	2	2.00	-	43	10	61	3	20.33	-
Clark J.G.	1889-1903	37	58	5	783	14.77	-	60.3	8	244	12	20.33	24
Clarke F.	1956-1960	31	41	15	98	3.76	-	648	143	1,868	50	37.36	10
Clay J.C.	1921-1949	358	536	88	6,868	15.33	2	9,911.1	2,326	25,181	1,292	19.49	171
Clift P.B.	1937-1955	183	306	21	6,055	21.24	7	216.2	38	675	11	61.36	169
Clough	1909	1	1	0	15	15.00	-	3	0	22	0	-	-
Colley R.H.	1899	1	1	0	0	-	-	16	9	30	0	-	-
Cooper E.	1912-1920	3	4	1	26	8.67	-	61	19	139	7	19.86	1
	1921	4	8	0	46	5.75	-	124	17	406	10	40.60	3
Cope J.J.	1935	3	5	1	27	6.75	-	-	-	-	-	-	1
Cording G.E.	1900-1914	19	27	1	314	12.08	-	-	-	-	-	-	13/7
	1921-1923	19	34	4	498	16.60	1	-	-	-	-	-	16/2
Cordle A.E.	1963-1980	312	433	76	5,239	14.67	-	7,013.5	1,615	19,281	701	27.50	141
Cottey P.A.	1986-	63	101	17	2,253	26.82	3	19	0	122	1	122.00	31
Cowley N.G.	1990	14	17	4	536	41.23	-	316.3	64	900	12	75.00	9
Creber A.B.	1929	1	2	0	7	3.50	-	-	-	-	-	-	-
Creber H.	1898-1920	192	240	80	1,665	10.41	-	6,271.5	1,499	16,907	1,161(47)	14.56	62
	1921-1922	33	58	28	155	5.16	-	903.5	177	2,550	95	26.84	6
Croft R.D.B.	1989-	47	63	17	1,213	26.37	-	1,242.3	279	3,796	70	54.23	18
Crowther P.G.	1977-1978	9	14	0	185	13.21	-	7	1	22	1	22.00	3
Cullen J.S.	1893	1	2	0	21	10.50	-	-	-	-	-	-	-
Dale A.	1989-	31	50	7	1,350	31.40	2	249.1	47	903	18	50.17	16
Daniels S.A.B.	1981-1982	16	23	10	227	17.46	-	312.2	55	1,162	28	41.50	7
Dauncey J.G.	1957	2	4	0	54	13.50	-	-	-	-	-	-	1
David A.C.G.	1913	1	2	0	3	1.50	-	-	-	-	-	-	1/1
David A.C.R.	1911-1913	3	2	0	19	9.50	-	10	0	63	1	63.00	4
David E.U.	1889-1900	32	49	3	581	12.63	-	87	20	268	10	26.80	19
David R.F.A.	1925-1929	3	5	0	20	4.00	-	-	-	-	-	-	-
Davies C.B.	1913	1	1	0	1	1.00	-	-	-	-	-	-	1
Davies D.	1923-1939	411	681	61	15,008	24.20	16	3,661.4	774	9,404	271	34.70	193
Davies D.A.	1934-1938	46	64	16	600	12.50	-	185.5	15	760	14	54.28	28
Davies D.E.	1892	1	1	0	6	6.00	-	-	-	-	-	-	-
Davies D.E.	1924-1954	612	1,016	79	26,102	27.85	31	10,263.4	2,359	26,030	885	29.41	211
Davies D.R.	1950	1	1	0	7	7.00	-	-	-	-	-	-	-
Davies G.	1947-1948	2	2	0	9	4.50	-	-	-	-	-	-	1
Davies G.	1932	7	9	1	77	9.62	-	52	15	134	3	44.67	2
Davies H.D.	1955-1960	52	70	26	247	5.61	-	1,103.1	214	3,659	115	31.81	17

Name	Career	Mchs	Inns	NO	Runs	Ave	100s	Overs	Mds	Runs	Wkts	Ave	Ct/St
Davies H.G.	1935-1958	423	596	95	6,515	13.00	-	3	0	20	1	20.00	580/202
Davies J.A.	1952	1	2	0	11	5.50	-	-	-	-	-	-	-
Davies M.	1990	1	1	1	5	-	-	8	1	16	0	-	1
Davies M.K.	1975-1976	2	2	1	14	14.00	-	-	-	-	-	-	2/2
Davies M.N.	1982	2	1	0	0	-	-	-	-	-	-	-	1
Davies T.	1979-1986	100	121	36	1,775	20.88	-	-	-	-	-	-	165/27
Davies T.C.	1971-1972	7	6	4	9	4.50	-	211.1	41	625	18	34.72	-
Davies W.A.	1893	2	3	0	0	-	-	17	6	30	7	4.29	3
Davies W.D.E.	1932-1935	7	12	1	122	11.09	-	13	1	60	0	-	2
Davies W.G.	1954-1960	32	58	0	674	11.62	-	218.4	50	646	16	40.37	14
Davies W.H.	1922-1927	5	10	2	33	4.12	-	58.3	16	130	3	43.33	-
Davis B.A.	1968-1970	60	103	8	2,848	29.97	1	74	17	229	4	57.25	67
Davis F.J.	1959-1967	14	24	7	189	11.11	-	233.3	82	674	18	37.44	7
Davis J.D.D.	1909-1911	3	1	0	27	27.00	-	-	-	-	-	-	2
Davis R.C.	1964-1976	213	369	30	7,363	21.71	5	2,868	700	7,793	241	32.33	208
Davis W.W.	1982-1984	45	51	21	471	15.70	-	1,315.2	285	4,211	142	29.65	14
Dennis S.J.	1989-1991	32	29	2	213	7.89	-	777	180	2,365	60	39.42	6
Derrick J.	1983-1991	95	124	38	1,995	23.20	-	1,675.5	374	5,213	137	38.05	41
Deveraux L.N.	1956-1960	106	187	25	3,292	20.32	1	725.4	224	1,768	72	24.55	60
Dickinson H.J.	1934-1935	7	13	6	37	5.28	-	102	16	335	6	55.83	3
Donnelly C.W.	1890	1	2	1	0	-	-	4.3	1	13	1	13.00	-
Donovan J.	1892-1895	9	15	2	236	18.15	-	3	0	17	0	-	2
Donovan M.	1891	4	6	0	4	1.50	-	-	-	-	-	-	1
Downey J.E.	1891	1	-	-	-	-	-	-	-	-	-	-	-
Duckfield R.G.	1930-1938	191	301	39	6,894	26.31	9	53	1	255	0	-	26
Dudley-Jones R.D.L.	1972-1973	5	7	2	15	3.00	-	88.5	9	351	13	27.00	1
Duncan A.A.	1934	2	3	1	16	8.00	-	-	-	-	-	-	-
Dunford W.B.	1895	1	1	1	0	-	-	-	-	-	-	-	-
Dunn F.W.M.	1911	2	2	0	1	0.50	-	-	-	-	-	-	1
Dyson A.H.	1926-1948	412	696	37	17,920	27.19	24	34	2	160	1	160.00	243/1
Eaglestone J.T.	1948-1949	50	78	7	1,064	14.98	-	-	-	-	-	-	20
Edrich B.R.	1954-1956	52	80	8	1,246	17.30	-	8	3	12	0	-	34
Edwards A.M.E.	1947	1	1	0	0	-	-	21	4	74	3	23.67	-
Edwards J.P.	1895	3	2	0	5	2.50	-	50	11	142	5	28.40	2
Edwards W.A.	1913	2	3	0	38	12.67	-	-	-	-	-	-	1/2
Eldridge A.G.	1891-1896	21	32	8	183	7.63	-	624.3	208	1,462	104(11)	14.06	3
Elers C.G.C.	1910-1911	7	12	5	309	44.14	1	-	-	-	-	-	10/7
Ellis G.P.	1970-1976	75	139	10	2,673	20.72	1	470.4	107	1,418	24	59.08	24
Ellis H.A.	1904-1906	4	6	1	112	22.40	-	3	0	10	0	-	2
Emery W.	1922	2	4	0	5	1.25	-	34	6	111	2	55.50	-
Evans D.G.L.	1956-1969	270	364	91	2,875	10.53	-	4	0	12	0	-	503/55
Evans D.W.	1891	1	1	0	2	2.00	-	-	-	-	-	-	-
Evans G.	1939	7	14	1	164	12.61	-	74	3	331	5	66.20	5
Evans H.P.	1920	3	6	1	76	15.20	-	-	-	-	-	-	-
	1922	1	2	0	9	4.50	-	-	-	-	-	-	-
Evans J.B.	1958-1963	87	129	19	1,515	13.77	-	2,332	505	6,670	246	27.11	45
Evans T.	1934	1	2	1	0	-	-	5.2	0	25	0	-	-
Evans W.H.	1891	1	2	0	2	1.00	-	-	-	-	-	-	-
Evans-Bevan D.M.	1920	1	1	0	4	4.00	-	-	-	-	-	-	1
Every T.	1929-1934	128	198	44	2,518	18.35	1	8	0	49	0	-	108/70

Name	Career	Mchs	Inns	NO	Runs	Ave	100s	Overs	Mds	Runs	Wkts	Ave	Ct/St
Farr C.	1892	1	1	0	2	2.00	-	-	-	-	-	-	-
Featherstone N.G.	1980-1981	45	73	11	2,120	34.19	3	170	47	525	12	43.75	38
Fletcher E.V.	1906	1	2	0	5	2.50	-	-	-	-	-	-	0/1
Foster D.J.	1991-	9	9	3	35	5.83	-	223.5	35	814	25	32.56	3
Francis D.A.	1973-1984	138	237	36	4,938	24.56	3	5	0	31	0	-	62
Fredericks R.C.	1971-1973	45	80	8	2,991	41.54	12	207.1	45	667	20	33.35	21
Freethy A.E.	1908-1920	11	15	2	158	12.15	-	3	0	16	0	-	4
	1921	3	4	1	79	26.33	-	-	-	-	-	-	1
Frost M.	1990-	41	30	13	61	3.59	-	1,111.3	170	3,987	124	32.15	3
Gabe-Jones A.R.	1922	1	1	1	6	-	-	-	-	-	-	-	-
Gage H.F.	1892-1893	2	4	1	52	17.33	-	9	2	26	2	13.00	1
Gatehouse P.W.	1957-1962	19	23	8	85	5.66	-	475.4	84	1,551	53	29.26	3
Geary F.W.	1923	2	4	0	3	0.75	-	13	3	24	0	-	2
Gemmill W.N.	1920	4	6	2	44	11.00	-	12	2	34	2	17.00	7
	1921-1926	47	88	2	1,169	13.59	-	25	4	104	0	-	31
Geoghegan J.P.A.	1891-1901	13	20	5	236	15.73	-	34	11	82	6	13.67	5
Gibbs R.A.	1902-1914	33	54	6	957	19.94	-	-	-	-	-	-	12
Gibson A.	1900-1909	57	85	9	1,140	15.00	-	33	11	130	4	32.50	32
Gibson W.D.	1904-1914	2	1	1	7	-	-	13.3	0	71	2	35.50	-
Glover E.R.K.	1932-1938	47	73	23	406	8.12	-	1,207.5	175	4,284	118	36.30	18
Good D.C	1947	3	5	2	47	15.67	-	60	11	225	7	32.14	1
Green R.C.	1984	2	1	1	3	-	-	31.5	9	92	2	46.00	1
Griffiths W.H.	1946-1948	8	11	2	34	3.77	-	173.3	30	538	17	31.64	-
Gwynn W.H.	1890	2	5	0	72	14.40	-	33	15	70	3	23.33	-
Gwynne D.G.P.	1922-1923	3	6	0	20	3.33	-	-	-	-	-	-	1
Hacker W.S.	1908-1920	61	78	20	622	10.72	-	1,169.2	294	3,295	273(29)	12.07	33
	1921-1923	21	34	10	210	8.75	-	590.5	141	1,689	80	21.11	6
Hadley R.J.	1971	2	3	2	4	4.00	-	32.5	7	93	7	13.28	-
Haines C.V.G.	1933-1934	12	20	2	350	19.44	-	10	2	33	1	33.00	3
Hansford G.	1920	2	3	0	24	8.00	-	-	-	-	-	-	1
Harris A.	1960-1964	49	91	3	1,698	19.29	2	1	1	0	0	-	19
Harris G.J.	1932	1	1	0	0	-	-	-	-	-	-	-	1
Harris K.H.	1913	2	3	0	77	25.67	-	2	0	24	0	-	2
Harris L.J.	1947	3	4	2	7	3.50	-	51	7	183	5	36.60	1
Harris W.E.	1938-1947	5	8	0	59	7.37	-	8	1	43	0	-	1
Harrison G.B.	1924-1925	9	17	0	109	6.41	-	2.3	0	10	0	-	2
Harrison S.C.	1971-1977	5	6	0	32	5.33	-	93	15	314	7	44.85	1
Hedges B.	1950-1967	422	744	41	17,733	25.22	21	94	24	260	3	86.67	200
Hemp D.L.	1991-	1	2	1	12	12.00	-	-	-	-	-	-	-
Henderson S.P	1982-1985	27	45	7	1,204	31.68	3	16	2	96	2	48.00	13
Hever N.G.	1948-1953	133	166	74	869	9.44	-	3,138	629	7,400	318	23.27	60
Hickey D.J.	1986	13	9	5	19	4.75	-	281.5	39	1,102	24	45.91	3
Hickley V.A.	1894-1898	8	14	1	254	19.54	-	-	-	-	-	-	4
Hildyard L.D.	1891	1	2	0	4	2.00	-	-	-	-	-	-	1
Hill E.E.	1911	1	1	1	18	-	-	-	-	-	-	-	1
Hill L.W.	1964-1976	76	130	20	2,690	24.45	-	8.4	1	44	0	-	40/1
Hill M.L.	1923	3	6	1	110	22.00	-	-	-	-	-	-	2/2
Hill P.M.T.	1894-1898	2	3	0	14	4.67	-	1	0	8	0	-	-
Hill R.K.	1975	1	-	-	-	-	-	29	8	58	1	58.00	-
Hill V.T.	1903-1905	5	9	0	46	5.11	-	18	4	43	0	-	4

Name	Career	Mchs	Inns	NO	Runs	Ave	100s	Overs	Mds	Runs	Wkts	Ave	Ct/St
Hills J.J.	1926-1931	104	165	7	3,252	20.58	6	-	-	-	-	-	92/3
Hinwood J.W.J.	1920	3	5	0	18	3.60	-	61	11	255	6	42.50	-
	1923	1	2	0	0	-	-	8	1	25	0	-	-
Hirst J.O.	1907	6	9	0	85	9.44	-	-	-	-	-	-	2
Hoare W.R.	1901	1	2	0	14	7.00	-	-	-	-	-	-	-
Hobbs R.N.S.	1979-1981	41	44	19	246	9.84	-	773.3	204	2,370	65	36.46	20
Hodges A.E.	1936	1	2	0	3	1.50	-	-	-	-	-	-	-
Holmes G.C.	1978-1991	203	325	50	7,529	27.38	9	1,155.2	223	3,963	88	45.03	82
Holmes T.	1894	1	2	0	4	2.00	-	-	-	-	-	-	-
Hopkins J.A.	1970-1988	299	524	32	13,610	27.66	18	26.1	3	148	0	-	210/1
Hordley T.J.	1892-1894	10	12	3	25	2.78	-	176.2	53	399	26	15.35	3
Horsfall R.	1956	5	9	0	76	8.44	-	-	-	-	-	-	2
Horspool J.J.	1905-1913	6	7	2	44	8.80	-	-	-	-	-	-	5/4
Howard A.R.	1928-1933	59	97	2	1,153	12.13	-	18	2	70	0	-	35
Howells P.	1900	1	2	0	6	3.00	-	-	-	-	-	-	-
Hughes D.W.	1935-1938	22	33	8	274	10.96	-	478.5	68	1,692	52	32.53	6
Hughes F.E.	1893	1	1	0	0	-	-	-	-	-	-	-	-
Hughes G.	1962-1964	17	22	4	228	12.67	-	218	75	560	12	46.67	17
Ingledew H.M.	1891	5	8	0	114	14.25	-	21	2	73	2	36.50	-
Jacob N.E.	1920	1	2	0	8	4.00	-	-	-	-	0(3)	-	-
	1922	7	13	0	79	6.07	-	7	0	42	0	-	2
James D.H.	1948	1	1	0	17	17.00	-	24	4	59	1	59.00	1
James E.H.	1920	4	6	1	78	15.60	-	82.2	12	210	24	8.75	1
	1922	3	6	0	13	2.16	-	58.5	5	209	7	29.85	1
James E.L.	1946-1947	9	12	4	232	29.00	-	14	1	45	1	45.00	10
James S.P.	1985-	33	56	4	1,195	22.98	1	-	-	-	-	-	26
Jarrett H.H.	1938	1	1	0	0	-	-	9	1	45	4	11.25	1
Jarrett K.S.	1967	2	3	1	27	13.50	-	12	2	76	0	-	-
Javed Miandad, Khan	1980-1985	83	135	22	6,531	57.79	17	254.3	57	851	21	40.52	50
Jenkins H.	1970	1	2	1	81	81.00	-	-	-	-	-	-	1
Jenkins L.	1889	1	2	0	7	3.50	-	-	-	-	-	-	-
Jenkins V.G.J.	1931-1937	44	69	9	1,072	17.87	-	10.1	0	54	2	27.00	10/7
Jenkins W.L.T.	1921	10	20	1	155	8.15	-	-	-	-	-	-	8/2
Johns J.	1920	2	3	0	0	-	-	32	3	118	11	10.73	-
	1922	1	2	1	4	4.00	-	18	3	63	2	31.50	-
Johns T.S.	1920	1	2	2	14	-	-	-	-	47	6(3)	7.83	1
Johnson R.H.	1902-1908	5	8	1	53	7.57	-	3	0	18	0	-	1
Johnston R.H.	1896	5	9	2	117	16.71	-	37	8	141	2	70.50	3
Jones A.	1957-1983	610	1,102	71	34,056	33.03	52	58.5	15	249	1	249.00	276
Jones A.A.	1980-1981	19	17	5	64	5.33	-	514	90	1,841	49	37.57	5
Jones A.L.	1973-1986	160	278	24	6,548	25.77	5	15.5	0	152	1	152.00	104
Jones D.A.	1938	1	1	0	6	6.00	-	14	3	43	2	21.50	-
Jones D.E.	1889-1890	5	9	0	78	8.67	-	6	0	21	1	21.00	2/2
Jones E.C.	1934-1946	100	142	30	2,016	18.00	2	1,036.1	165	3,299	102	32.34	42
Jones E.C.	1926	1	-	-	-	-	-	-	-	-	-	-	1
Jones E.W.	1890-1911	68	107	5	2,507	24.58	2	15	5	52	0	-	35
Jones E.W.	1961-1983	405	591	119	8,341	17.67	3	0.3	0	5	0	-	840/93
Jones F.N.	1890-1893	6	11	2	69	7.67	-	-	-	-	-	-	5/1
Jones H.B.T.	1920	1	2	0	3	1.50	-	-	-	-	-	-	1

Name	Career	Mchs	Inns	NO	Runs	Ave	100s	Overs	Mds	Runs	Wkts	Ave	Ct/St
Jones H.O.	1946	2	3	3	10	-	-	10	1	53	0	-	-
Jones I.J.	1960-1968	157	180	69	395	3.55	-	3,904.4	979	9,583	408	23.48	36
Jones J.M.	1928-1929	8	13	1	326	27.16	-	-	-	-	-	-	12/8
Jones J.W.	1910-1920	17	26	4	491	22.32	1	56.2	7	230	10(1)	23.00	7
Jones O.	1891-1897	17	28	1	418	15.48	-	213	43	647	26(7)	24.88	7
Jones R.G.	1891-1893	4	5	2	21	7.00	-	72.5	29	137	17(1)	8.06	1
Jones T.C.	1925-1928	3	6	0	36	6.00	-	-	-	-	-	-	-
Jones W.E.	1946-1947	5	1	0	0	-	-	94	9	342	13	26.30	1
Jones W.E.	1929-1933	50	73	30	300	6.97	-	1,020.2	202	2,754	77	35.76	21
Jones W.E.	1937-1958	340	555	63	13,270	26.97	11	1,926.2	438	5,620	189	29.73	117
Jones W.M.	1933-1938	11	15	3	116	9.67	-	58.5	9	214	6	35.67	1
Joseph A.F.	1946	1	2	0	8	4.00	-	-	-	-	-	-	1
Judge P.F.	1939-1947	54	67	24	332	7.72	-	1,175.3	221	3,475	138	25.18	29
Kindersley C.E.	1891	1	2	0	0	-	-	-	-	-	-	-	-
King C.L.	1977	16	27	1	811	31.19	-	259.1	58	730	20	36.50	13
Kingston G.C.	1967-1971	9	15	2	161	12.38	-	60	12	210	4	52.50	4
Lambert W.	1897-1898	12	19	9	38	3.80	-	312	63	845	60	14.8	5
Landers E.	1890	1	2	0	7	3.50	-	-	-	-	-	-	1
Lavis G.	1928-1949	206	312	43	4,957	18.42	3	2,741	515	7,768	156	49.79	71
Lawlor P.J.	1981	1	2	0	8	8.00	-	13	2	50	1	50.00	1
Letcher H.B.	1890-1908	108	167	17	2,357	15.71	1	745.4	189	2,148	96(9)	22.38	63
Lewis A.R.	1955-1974	315	546	52	15,003	30.37	21	55.1	3	306	4	76.50	155
Lewis B.	1965-1968	37	45	5	333	8.32	-	670.1	160	2,001	82	24.40	29
Lewis D.W.	1960-1969	12	17	6	107	9.72	-	286	58	901	21	42.90	3
Lewis E.J.	1961-1966	95	150	10	2,169	15.49	-	1,297.3	363	3,821	151	25.30	53
Lewis H.T.	1903	1	2	0	20	10.00	-	3	0	16	0	-	-
Lewis K.H.	1950-1956	36	48	14	312	9.17	-	695	126	2,044	55	37.16	15
Lewis R.A.	1890-1892	9	15	2	172	13.23	-	39	11	108	6	18.00	1
Lewis S.A.	1906	1	1	0	4	4.00	-	-	-	-	-	-	-
Lewis W.E.	1889-1890	3	5	1	24	6.00	-	-	-	-	-	-	-
Lewis W.L.	1903	1	-	-	-	-	-	-	-	-	-	-	-
Lindley J.V.	1889-1890	5	8	1	58	8.28	-	142.4	51	256	19(8)	13.47	2
Ling A.J.P.	1934-1936	9	13	3	192	19.20	-	2	0	12	0	-	1
Linton J.E.F.	1932	2	4	0	3	0.75	-	25	4	82	1	82.00	-
Llewellyn J.G.	1896	1	2	1	5	5.00	-	-	-	-	-	-	-
Llewellyn M.J.	1970-1982	136	215	30	4,288	23.17	3	227.1	62	615	23	26.73	87
Llewelyn W.D.	1889-1893	14	25	0	418	16.72	-	58.5	11	174	6(8)	29.00	10
Lloyd B.J.	1972-1983	147	184	47	1,631	11.90	-	3,418.3	779	10,133	247	41.02	87
Long J.P.	1891-1893	6	8	0	57	7.13	-	9	0	36	0	-	-
Lowe R.	1896-1901	59	84	7	1,493	19.39	-	499.2	137	1,250	86	14.53	56
Lowe S.	1895-1902	76	99	29	650	9.29	-	1,964.4	532	5,069	333(3)	15.22	43
Lyons K.J.	1967-1977	62	99	14	1,673	19.68	-	81.1	13	252	2	126.00	27
McConnon J.E.	1950-1961	243	350	38	4,514	14.46	-	5,913.2	1,593	15,656	799	19.59	144
McFarlane L.L.	1985	13	6	2	12	3.00	-	259	42	1,008	16	63.00	4
Mack A.J.	1978-1980	21	23	10	60	4.61	-	352	70	1,129	37	30.51	4
McKay J.F.	1895	1	1	0	2	2.00	-	10	3	16	1	16.00	1
Madden-Gaskell J.C.P.	1922	1	2	0	39	19.50	-	-	-	-	-	-	-
Majid Jahangir, Khan	1968-1976	154	270	17	9,610	37.98	21	723.3	216	1,674	51	32.82	155
Malone S.J.	1985	9	6	1	4	0.80	-	174.1	23	654	13	50.30	2

Name	Career	Mchs	Inns	NO	Runs	Ave	100s	Overs	Mds	Runs	Wkts	Ave	Ct/St
Mann A.H.	1896	4	7	0	116	16.57	-	-	-	-	-	-	2
Marley K.R.	1894	1	2	0	82	41.00	-	-	-	-	-	-	-
Marsh W.E.	1947	4	6	1	39	7.80	-	64.1	6	290	8	36.25	2
Martin E.G.	1913	1	2	0	9	4.50	-	-	-	-	0(5)	-	-
	1921	1	2	0	2	1.00	-	22	4	77	1	77.00	1
Martyn O.B.	1891	1	2	0	15	7.50	-	-	-	-	-	-	-
Mathias F.W.	1922-1930	28	46	5	457	11.14	-	16	0	84	1	84.00	7
Matthews A.D.G.	1937-1947	51	71	24	691	14.70	-	1,473.1	353	3,607	277	15.88	12
Maxwell J.	1909-1914	56	78	11	1,616	24.12	3	641.5	125	2,291	173(7)	13.24	43
Maynard M.P.	1985-	153	237	31	8,604	41.77	18	96	13	409	4	102.25	121
Meggitt F.C.	1923	1	2	0	4	2.00	-	-	-	-	-	-	-
Mendelson W.	1896	2	4	0	33	8.25	-	-	-	-	-	-	1
Mercer J.	1922-1939	412	578	100	5,730	11.98	-	13,813.5	3,242	34,058	1,460	23.32	124
Metson C.P.	1987-	119	153	31	2,138	17.52	-	-	-	-	-	-	287/23
Miller H.D.S.	1963-1966	27	40	3	433	11.70	-	514.2	126	1,350	48	28.12	15
Mir P.J.	1979	1	2	0	16	8.00	-	4	0	21	0	-	-
Mizen C.A.	1891	2	4	0	33	8.25	-	5	1	15	0	-	-
Monkhouse S.	1987-1988	9	9	4	23	4.60	-	149	24	481	16	30.06	2
Montgomery S.W.	1949-1953	29	43	2	763	18.60	1	37	10	99	6	16.50	9
Moore-Gwyn H.G.	1903-1912	8	16	1	229	15.27	-	-	-	-	-	-	5/1
Moore-Gwyn J.G.	1906	1	1	0	4	4.00	-	-	-	-	-	-	1
Morgan A.N.	1928-1929	5	9	0	83	9.22	-	64	8	263	3	87.67	1
Morgan E.	1903-1913	3	6	1	10	2.00	-	6	2	18	3	6.00	2
Morgan E.N.	1934	1	1	0	1	1.00	-	-	-	-	-	-	-
Morgan F.W.	1896	1	1	0	3	3.00	-	12	3	33	1	33.00	-
Morgan H.E.	1889-1905	92	151	6	2,831	19.52	4	40	8	129	7	18.43	67
Morgan H.W.	1958	2	3	1	11	5.50	-	22	4	58	2	29.00	-
Morgan J.T.	1925-1934	39	52	3	792	16.16	1	168.5	32	535	11	48.63	9/2
Morgan T.R.	1913-1920	18	25	5	316	15.80	-	20	4	52	2	26.00	8
	1921-1925	39	73	5	1,044	15.35	-	2.5	0	10	0	-	5
Morgan W.	1889-1901	24	37	1	642	17.83	-	547.3	116	1,368	77(5)	17.77	14
Morgan W.G.	1925-1938	45	66	11	976	17.75	-	59.3	4	257	3	85.67	6
Morgan W.P.	1925	1	2	0	4	2.00	-	1	1	0	0	-	-
Morris A.W.	1889-1897	13	23	1	333	15.14	-	3	0	14	2	7.00	7
Morris F.H.	1893-1896	3	6	1	51	10.20	-	-	-	-	-	-	2/1
Morris H.	1981-	179	306	35	10,256	37.85	24	53.1	6	323	2	161.50	97
Morris I.	1966-1968	14	25	2	253	11.00	-	28	4	141	4	35.25	15
Morris V.L.	1920	2	2	0	56	28.00	-	-	-	-	-	-	1
	1921-1929	18	33	1	407	12.71	-	-	-	-	-	-	-
Morris W.P.	1906-1920	46	75	3	1,084	15.06	-	116.5	23	412	26(1)	15.85	28
	1921-1925	8	16	1	157	10.46	-	34	9	99	2	49.50	6
Moseley E.A.	1980-1986	35	43	10	655	19.84	-	910.1	195	2,729	114	23.93	7
Moss E.	1923	1	2	0	15	7.50	-	25	4	70	2	35.00	1
Moynan W.A.	1898	1	1	0	4	4.00	-	-	-	-	-	-	-
Mullens D.	1896-1900	2	4	1	11	3.67	-	19	1	77	3	25.67	1
Mullins A.E.	1890	1	2	0	11	5.50	-	27	2	64	2	32.00	1
Muncer B.L.	1947-1954	224	333	46	6,460	22.50	4	6,642.2	1,807	14,462	708	20.42	111
Murray T.	1911	1	2	1	101	101.00	-	-	-	-	-	-	1
Nash A.	1900-1920	123	158	35	985	8.01	-	3,620	1,172	8,607	604(40)	14.25	104
	1921-1922	36	65	9	315	5.62	-	1,218	360	2,901	133	21.81	6

Name	Career	Mchs	Inns	NO	Runs	Ave	100s	Overs	Mds	Runs	Wkts	Ave	Ct/St
Nash M.A.	1966-1983	335	467	67	7,120	17.80	2	9,193.3	2,426	25,601	991	25.83	148
Needham P.J.E.	1975	1	1	0	4	4.00	-	41.5	11	105	2	52.50	1
Nicholl J.I.D.	1895	1	1	0	16	16.00	-	-	-	-	-	-	-
Nicholl L.D.	1891-1893	6	8	1	217	31.00	-	1	0	6	1	6.00	3
North P.D.	1985-1989	22	25	7	200	11.11	-	412.3	112	1,009	24	42.04	7
O'Bree A.	1920	9	14	2	370	30.83	1	-	-	-	-	-	5
	1921-1923	18	34	1	431	13.06	-	-	-	-	-	-	9
O'Daly G.N.	1938	1	1	0	9	9.00	-	7	1	17	0	-	-
Ontong R.C.	1975-1989	257	413	65	10,825	31.11	18	5,709	1,277	17,279	531	32.54	116
Osborne A.J.	1901-1911	47	69	6	965	15.32	2	306.4	80	952	55(9)	17.31	22
Parkhouse R.J.	1939	2	1	0	0	-	-	-	-	-	-	-	-
Parkhouse W.G.A.	1948-1964	435	759	48	22,619	31.81	32	37.1	8	125	2	62.50	312
Pauline D.B.	1986	12	20	0	455	22.75	-	14	0	67	2	33.50	4
Pearson C.J.H.	1922	1	2	0	9	4.50	-	-	-	-	-	-	-
Peatfield A.E.	1903	5	9	0	120	13.33	-	-	-	-	-	-	4
Penfold W.H.	1908	1	2	1	10	10.00	-	-	-	-	-	-	1/1
Perkins A.L.B.	1925-1933	6	10	3	102	14.57	-	-	-	-	-	-	4
Perry N.J.	1979-1981	13	12	4	19	2.37	-	282.3	73	920	21	43.50	9
Phillips M.	1897	3	4	1	5	1.67	-	17	7	39	2	19.50	1
Pinch F.B.	1920	6	7	0	184	26.69	1	144.2	47	360	30	12.00	3
	1921-1926	41	72	5	1,068	15.94	1	402	84	1,233	37	43.32	24
Pitchford L.	1935	2	3	1	24	12.00	-	3	1	4	0	-	-
Pleass J.E.	1947-1956	171	253	31	4,293	19.33	1	4	0	15	0	-	77
Pook N.R.	1990	1	2	1	0	-	-	8	3	19	0	-	-
Poole W.	1903	1	2	1	2	2.00	-	10	3	23	0	-	-
Porter A.	1936-1949	38	64	7	1,292	22.67	2	161	24	480	16	30.00	16
Powell T.L.	1976	1	2	0	0	-	-	-	-	-	-	-	-
Preece T.	1902-1920	13	21	2	329	17.32	-	10	1	36	2	18.00	3
	1923	1	2	0	8	4.00	-	-	-	-	-	-	1
Preedy	1907-1909	23	30	7	340	14.78	-	256.1	56	766	52	14.73	11
Pressdee J.S.	1949-1965	322	543	83	13,411	29.16	12	3,666.2	1,095	8,988	405	22.18	344
Price M.R.	1984-1985	17	13	4	144	16.00	-	289.4	66	806	19	42.42	2
Prichard H.C.C.	1899-1900	4	7	1	106	17.67	-	-	-	-	-	-	1
Pritchard A.J.	1920	1	1	0	2	2.00	-	-	-	-	0(3)	-	-
Pruen F.H.	1897	1	1	0	21	21.00	-	-	-	-	-	-	-
Pullen W.W.F.	1895	6	7	0	190	27.14	-	-	-	-	-	-	2
Rattenbury G.L.	1905-1912	25	35	6	412	14.21	-	399	85	1,119	50	22.38	12
Reason D.J.	1920	8	12	3	119	13.22	-	5	0	30	1	30.00	2
	1921-1922	2	3	0	3	1.00	-	-	-	-	-	-	3/1
Reason L.	1920	1	1	0	0	-	-	2	1	7	1	7.00	-
Reason T.F.	1914-1920	9	12	1	117	10.64	-	13	1	45	1	45.00	5
	1923	1	2	0	13	6.50	-	-	-	-	-	-	-
Reed G.H.	1934-1938	25	25	12	65	5.00	-	704.4	133	1,941	62	31.30	6
Rees A.	1955-1968	216	372	53	7,681	24.07	2	94.3	11	398	6	66.33	113
Rees E.L.	1893-1896	9	15	5	47	4.70	-	154.3	47	346	20(5)	17.30	6
Rees R.M.	1896-1904	5	9	0	75	8.33	-	1	0	8	0	-	5
Rees S.H.	1901-1914	36	60	1	768	13.02	-	3	0	24	0	-	21
Reid E.W.	1890-1900	6	8	1	74	10.57	-	50	13	109	7	15.57	1
Reynolds G.E.A.	1970-1971	2	3	2	37	37.00	-	32	14	75	2	37.50	-
Rhys H.R.J.	1929-1930	7	13	1	147	12.25	-	-	-	-	-	-	5

Name	Career	Mchs	Inns	NO	Runs	Ave	100s	Overs	Mds	Runs	Wkts	Ave	Ct/St
Richards G.	1971-1979	107	174	26	3,370	22.77	1	691.3	135	2,257	48	47.02	36
Richards I.V.A.	1990-		18	28	5	1,425	61.95	7	137	26	426	5	85.20	8
Richards J.E.	1920	1	2	0	22	11.00	-	-	-	-	-	-	1
Riches J.D.H.	1947	1	2	0	5	2.50	-	-	-	-	-	-	-
Riches N.V.H.	1900-1920	136	212	28	7,228	39.28	16	37.5	9	143	3	47.67	129/27
	1921-1934	82	138	8	4,419	32.99	6	21.3	1	79	0	-	39/6
Rickers G.H.	1920	1	1	0	0	-	-	-	-	-	-	-	--
Rippon T.J.	1947-1948	3	4	2	45	22.50	-	-	-	-	-	-	0/3
Robathan G.L.	1910-1911	8	13	1	94	7.83	-	-	-	-	-	-	3
Roberts J.F.	1934-1936	5	6	1	86	17.20	-	-	-	-	-	-	3
Roberts M.L.	1985-1991	10	10	2	100	12.50	-	-	-	-	-	-	16/4
Robinson M.	1946-1950	66	106	7	2,139	21.60	2	128	18	432	13	33.23	17
Robinson T.	1889-1891	13	24	1	392	17.04	-	363.5	87	768	52	14.77	8
Roebuck P.G.P.	1988	2	4	0	60	15.00	-	-	-	-	-	-	1
Rogers B.L.	1923	2	4	1	46	15.33	-	10	0	33	1	33.00	-
Rooney E.J.	1890	2	4	0	19	4.75	-	18	3	44	3	14.67	1
Rooney R.A.	1893-1901	13	17	3	274	19.57	-	4	0	19	0	-	5
Rooney S.	1893-1894	2	4	0	21	5.25	-	-	-	-	-	-	1
Rowe C.J.C.	1982-1984	53	83	10	1,947	26.67	1	874	189	2,826	69	40.95	20
Rowntree R.E.	1899	2	3	0	8	2.67	-	37	6	128	4	32.00	3
Russell W.	1897-1906	102	153	13	2,665	19.04	1	1,911.3	781	3,733	268(2)	13.93	73
Ryan F.P.	1922-1931	215	312	100	1,699	8.01	-	6,589.2	1,317	19,053	913	20.86	78
Samuel A.W.	1889-1896	17	26	9	181	10.65	-	379.3	97	985	51	19.31	6
Samuel G.N.T.W.	1936	3	4	0	41	10.25	-	-	-	-	-	-	-
Sant S.A.	1893	1	2	0	21	10.50	-	-	-	-	-	-	-
Saulez E.H.	1893	7	12	1	209	19.00	-	-	-	-	-	-	4
Schofield T.D.	1893-1896	4	5	1	3	0.75	-	-	-	-	-	-	3/1
Scott J.M.	1895	2	3	1	26	8.67	-	-	-	-	-	-	-
Selvey M.W.W.	1983-1984	39	42	11	361	11.64	-	941.1	207	3,000	87	34.48	14
Seymour R.G.	1905	2	4	0	14	3.50	-	-	-	-	-	-	1
Sharples J.E.	1922	1	1	0	0	-	-	1	0	1	0	-	-
Shastri R.J.	1987-1991	62	98	18	3,402	42.53	6	1,307.4	340	3,228	95	33.98	32
Shaw G.B.	1951-1955	16	20	13	30	4.28	-	229.2	36	706	26	27.15	4
Shea A.J.	1928	2	3	0	22	7.33	-	41	7	171	1	171.00	-
Shea W.D.	1947-1948	3	3	1	27	13.50	-	51	5	180	5	36.00	-
Shepherd D.J.	1950-1972	647	816	241	5,610	9.75	-	21,514.2	7,334	45,571	2,174	20.96	241
Shepherd E.	1890	1	2	1	6	6.00	-	-	-	-	-	-	-
Silkin S.C.	1938	1	2	0	2	1.00	-	9	0	60	1	60.00	1
Silverlock A.J.	1900	1	1	0	0	-	-	9	0	42	0	-	-
Slade W.D.	1961-1967	67	116	11	1,482	14.11	-	504.3	146	1,493	32	46.65	100
Smart C.C.	1927-1946	190	301	35	8,069	30.34	9	2,097.4	302	6,943	169	41.08	123
Smith C.L.	1979	1	2	1	81	81.00	-	-	-	-	-	-	1
Smith D.J.	1898-1910	16	25	2	365	15.87	-	31	10	91	4	22.75	5/1
Smith I.	1985-1991	63	83	13	1,723	24.61	3	618.4	93	2,450	52	47.16	25
Snell H.S.	1920	1	2	0	1	0.50	-	-	-	-	-	-	-
Solanky J.W.	1972-1976	82	134	22	2,263	20.20	-	1,617.5	397	4,514	176	25.64	17
Soloman H.G.	1901	1	1	0	38	38.00	-	-	-	-	-	-	-
Somaia K.A.	1989	3	6	0	50	8.33	-	78.4	19	245	8	30.63	1
Spencer C.R.	1925	1	1	0	0	-	-	-	-	-	-	-	0/1
Spencer H.	1923-1925	39	68	2	743	11.25	-	844.5	170	2,270	101	22.47	29

Name	Career	Mchs	Inns	NO	Runs	Ave	100s	Overs	Mds	Runs	Wkts	Ave	Ct/St
Spiller C.W.	1922	2	4	0	20	5.00	-	43	8	144	4	36.00	-
Spiller W.	1905-1908	4	6	1	46	9.20	-	-	-	-	-	-	1
	1921-1923	13	22	0	411	18.68	1	4	0	31	0	-	7
Stapleton E.	1908-1909	2	3	0	11	3.67	-	-	-	-	-	-	3
Steele J.F.	1984-1986	48	70	20	1,385	27.70	1	1,044.1	262	3,031	88	34.44	53
Stewart T.L.	1923	1	2	0	4	2.00	-	-	-	-	-	-	-
Stone J.	1922-1923	27	48	2	1,047	22.76	1	-	-	-	-	-	26/12
Storer G.	1891	1	1	0	0	-	-	26	11	41	1	41.00	-
Storrie J.H.	1920	1	1	0	9	9.00	-	13.3	1	65	4	16.25	1
Sullivan D.	1922-1928	115	166	55	811	7.30	-	-	-	-	-	-	128/84
Swain G.W.	1894	1	1	0	12	12.00	-	-	-	-	-	-	1
Swart P.D.	1978-1979	44	73	8	1,996	30.70	4	512.3	123	1,785	64	27.89	34
Sweet-Escott E.R.	1902-1920	63	104	13	2,013	22.12	2	32.5	3	135	6	22.50	34
	1921	1	2	0	13	6.50	-	-	-	-	-	-	-
Sweet-Escott H.H.	1909-1910	2	3	0	10	3.33	-	-	-	-	-	-	1
Sweet-Escott R.B.	1891-1897	25	40	3	574	15.51	-	19	4	45	0	-	11
Sweet-Escott W.S.R.	1891-1899	42	58	12	627	13.63	-	576.2	147	1,599	74(1)	21.61	20
Symonds H.G.	1908-1920	39	55	6	850	17.35	-	35	3	113	3	37.67	9
	1921-1925	22	40	1	547	14.02	-	46	0	201	4	50.25	4
Tait J.R.	1911-1920	30	49	4	1,195	26.56	1	36	6	134	3	44.67	11
	1921-1926	43	81	1	1,475	18.43	-	21	4	87	1	87.00	20
Tamplin C.	1947	3	4	2	56	28.00	-	-	-	-	-	-	6
Tayler H.W.	1920	1	2	0	19	9.50	-	-	-	-	-	-	-
	1921-1927	10	19	3	260	16.25	-	-	-	-	-	-	3
Taylor H.T.	1932-1934	3	4	1	17	5.67	-	2	0	11	0	-	1
Tennick L.	1920	1	1	0	26	26.00	-	4	0	24	0	-	2
Thackeray A.G.	1901-1906	11	16	1	330	22.00	-	19	3	77	0(1)	-	6
Thissen D.R.	1889-1900	21	29	3	316	12.15	-	-	-	-	-	-	34/14
Thomas A.E.	1913	1	2	0	27	13.50	-	-	-	-	-	-	-
	1925	1	2	0	15	7.50	-	-	-	-	-	-	-
Thomas A.W.	1908	2	3	1	24	12.00	-	-	-	-	-	-	2/1
Thomas D.	1939	2	2	1	14	14.00	-	27	4	99	5	19.80	1
Thomas D.J.	1932	1	1	1	10	-	-	17	1	63	0	-	-
Thomas H.T.	1894-1911	10	16	1	180	12.00	-	-	-	-	-	-	7
Thomas J.G.	1979-1988	106	139	24	2,137	18.58	2	2,239.5	386	8,230	256	32.25	38
Thomas J.L.G.	1910-1920	20	22	2	387	19.35	-	-	-	-	-	-	5
	1922	1	2	0	27	13.50	-	-	-	-	-	-	-
Thomas R.J.	1974	1	1	1	8	-	-	10.2	2	40	1	40.00	-
Thomas W.M.	1890	1	2	0	13	6.50	-	4	0	18	0	-	-
Todd P.A.	1987	14	24	0	470	19.58	1	-	-	-	-	-	13
Tomlinson H.	1920	2	3	0	143	47.67	-	-	-	-	-	-	-
	1921-1923	8	16	0	244	15.25	-	48	10	163	1	163.00	2
Trick W.M.S.	1946-1950	19	22	11	52	4.72	-	515.3	196	1,087	56	19.41	9
Turnbull B.	1911-1920	4	4	0	64	16.00	-	-	-	-	-	-	1
Turnbull M.J.L.	1924-1939	314	504	25	14,431	30.12	22	46.4	2	266	2	133.00	253
Tyson C.T.	1926	2	4	0	88	22.00	-	15	1	32	0	-	-
Van Zyl C.J.P.G.	1987-1988	12	10	1	115	12.78	-	286.1	67	850	17	50.00	1
Vaughan-Thomas H.W.	1933	1	1	0	3	3.00	-	-	-	-	-	-	1
Veal C.L.	1910	2	3	0	32	10.67	-					-	1

Name	Career	Mchs	Inns	NO	Runs	Ave	100s	Overs	Mds	Runs	Wkts	Ave	Ct/St
Waite A.	1904	1	2	1	34	34.00	-	12	4	30	1	30.00	1
Walker P.M.	1956-1972	437	738	106	16,510	26.12	12	8,879	2,749	21,652	771	28.08	656
Walters C.F.	1923-1928	75	133	9	2,146	17.31	2	5.2	0	37	0	-	23
Ward D.J.	1954-1962	135	206	33	2,496	14.42	-	1,796.2	448	4,987	187	26.67	65
Warner C.C.	1923	1	2	1	14	14.00	-	15	2	47	0	-	
Watkin S.L.	1986-	83	86	28	547	9.43	-	2,762.1	576	8,404	276	30.45	16
Watkins A.J.	1939-1961	407	649	76	17,419	30.30	29	7,497.5	2,027	17,683	774	22.84	390
Watkins W.M.	1950	1	1	0	3	3.00	-	-	-	-	-	-	-
Watson W.H.	1889-1893	9	15	1	191	13.64	-	4	1	20	0(3)	-	1
Webb A.S.	1912	1	2	0	38	19.00	-	-	-	-	-	-	-
Went G.J.H.	1934	1	2	1	14	14.00	-	5	1	14	0	-	1
Wheatley O.S.	1961-1970	206	227	87	799	5.70	-	6,262.2	1,988	13,356	715	18.67	75
White D.W.	1972	1	1	0	8	8.00	-	17.4	2	32	1	32.00	-
White M.E.	1909	1	1	0	17	17.00	-	-	-	-	-	-	-
Whitehill W.K.	1960	7	11	3	60	7.50	-	-	-	-	-	-	8
Whitman E.I.E.	1932	2	3	0	27	9.00	-	53	8	172	3	57.33	-
Whittington T.A.L.	1901-1920	88	133	5	3,363	26.27	4	13.3	3	54	3	18.00	31/1
	1921-1923	47	85	6	1,152	14.58	-	0.5	0	12	0	-	10
Wilkins A.H.	1976-1983	65	73	22	502	9.84	-	1,252.2	234	4,204	135	31.14	19
Wilkinson W.	1889	2	3	0	29	9.67	-	104.5	40	149	12	12.42	1
Williams D.B.	1901-1914	16	26	2	333	13.88	-	-	-	-	-	-	11
	1921	1	2	0	14	7.00	-	-	-	-	-	-	-
Williams D.L.	1969-1976	150	144	72	399	5.54	-	3,535.4	816	9,839	363	27.10	38
Williams F.I.	1920	1	2	0	24	12.00	-	-	-	-	-	-	-
Williams I.	1931	2	4	0	10	2.50	-	-	-	-	-	-	-
Williams J.	1890-1891	4	6	0	24	4.00	-	3	0	11	0	-	-
Williams L.E.W.	1928-1930	4	8	2	145	24.16	-	7	1	42	0	-	1
Williams W.H.	1889-1891	8	11	3	108	13.50	-	27	5	66	1	66.00	3
Windsor-Clive A.	1908-1912	5	6	0	28	4.67	-	3	0	7	1	7.00	1
Wolfe A.	1895	1	1	0	9	9.00	-	-	-	-	-	-	-
Wooller W.	1938-1962	400	630	72	12,692	22.74	5	9,118.5	2,332	23,513	887	26.50	392
Worsley F.F.	1922-1923	2	3	0	34	11.33	-	-	-	-	-	-	1
Yorath H.W.F.	1895	1	1	0	10	10.00	-	-	-	-	-	-	1
Yorath T.H.B.	1891-1895	6	10	3	106	15.14	-	4	0	21	0	-	3
Yorath W.L.	1889-1890	4	6	0	45	7.50	-	-	-	-	-	-	3
Young G.A.	1892-1893	3	5	1	101	25.25	-	-	-	-	-	-	1
Younis Ahmed, Mohammed	1984-1986	58	88	14	3,635	49.12	8	106.4	29	294	2	147.00	20

Averages

The averages below are the leading performances for Glamorgan in one-day cricket:

Sunday League (40 over competition)

	Inns	NO	Runs	Ave	HS		Runs	Wkts	Ave	BB
A.Jones	195	18	4,702	26.26	110*	M.A.Nash	4,782	215	22.24	6/29
J.A.Hopkins	181	15	3,990	24.04	130*	A.E.Cordle	4,061	164	24.76	5/24
R.C.Ontong	142	20	2,898	23.75	100	D.L.Williams	2,832	142	19.94	5/31
H.Morris	97	8	2,582	29.01	100	R.C.Ontong	4,837	136	32.26	4/28
G.C.Holmes	118	22	2,438	25.40	73	S.R.Barwick	3,064	99	30.95	4/23
Javed Miandad	56	8	2,238	46.63	107*	G.C.Holmes	2,519	97	25.97	5/2
M.P.Maynard	86	5	2,099	25.91	101	J.G.Thomas	2,266	87	26.05	5/38
Majid Khan	82	5	1,958	25.43	93	J.W.Solanky	1,589	73	21.77	4/23
A.L.Jones	78	3	1,642	21.89	82	D.J.Shepherd	1,321	66	20.02	5/31
M.J.Llewellyn	93	19	1,613	21.80	79*	A.H.Wilkins	1,270	64	19.84	5/23
E.W.Jones	162	54	1,572	14.56	48	J.Derrick	2,074	62	33.45	5/32
M.A.Nash	158	24	1,513	11.29	68	S.L.Watkin	1,485	54	27.50	5/23

Benson and Hedges Cup (55 over competition)

	Inns	NO	Runs	Ave	HS		Runs	Wkts	Ave	BB
A.Jones	49	1	1,282	26.70	89	M.A.Nash	1,130	64	17.66	4/12
J.A.Hopkins	49	2	1,251	26.62	103*	R.C.Ontong	1,273	48	26.52	5/30
R.C.Ontong	40	6	938	27.59	81	S.R.Barwick	1,242	44	28.23	4/11
M.P.Maynard	24	3	840	40.00	115	A.E.Cordle	894	34	26.29	4/41
A.R.Butcher	23	0	779	33.87	127	D.L.Williams	463	30	15.43	5/30
G.C.Holmes	32	8	744	31.00	70	G.C.Holmes	650	25	26.00	3/26
H.Morris	27	2	685	27.40	143*	J.G.Thomas	761	25	30.44	4/38
Javed Miandad	15	0	629	41.93	95	J.Derrick	428	19	22.53	4/53
M.J.Llewellyn	30	5	590	23.60	63	A.H.Wilkins	338	15	22.53	5/17
M.A.Nash	41	11	472	15.75	103*	J.W.Solanky	511	13	39.31	3/18
Majid Khan	17	1	365	22.81	97*	J.F.Steele	308	13	23.69	3/32
R.J.Shastri	14	3	362	32.91	138*	M.W.W.Selvey	135	11	12.27	4/10

NatWest Bank Trophy/Gillette Cup (60 over competition)

	Inns	NO	Runs	Ave	HS		Runs	Wkts	Ave	BB
A.Jones	36	0	1,077	31.68	124*	M.A.Nash	855	41	20.85	5/31
H.Morris	17	3	887	63.36	154	D.J.Shepherd	491	23	21.34	3/12
R.C.Ontong	18	3	528	35.20	64	S.R.Barwick	430	23	18.69	4/14
M.P.Maynard	15	2	510	39.23	151*	I.J.Jones	319	22	14.50	4/12
A.R.Butcher	11	1	468	46.80	104	A.E.Cordle	798	19	42.00	4/42
A.R.Lewis	19	0	442	23.26	96	D.L.Williams	341	18	18.94	3/15
P.M.Walker	15	3	426	35.50	79	P.M.Walker	300	16	18.75	5/21
J.A.Hopkins	22	0	409	18.59	63	R.C.Ontong	648	15	43.20	4/49
E.W.Jones	29	5	358	14.92	67*	O.S.Wheatley	367	15	24.46	2/29
G.C.Holmes	14	0	280	20.00	57	R.J.Shastri	224	14	16.00	5/13
M.J.Llewellyn	10	1	270	30.00	62*	J.Derrick	237	13	18.23	4/14
M.A.Nash	24	6	259	14.39	51	Majid Khan	127	12	10.58	5/24